CLEOPATRA

Cleopatra Press
11041 Santa Monica Blvd. #703 Los Angeles, CA 90025
ISBN:
978-0-9972056-8-8
Printed in Hong Kong

Creative Direction: Jeff Anderson
Art Direction & Design: Donny Phillips for KIHL Studio
Project Coordination and Photo Editing: Kaylee Carrington
Production layout: Fendi Nugroho

# BAUHAUS

# UNDEAD

## EXPANDED EDITION

### THE VISUAL HISTORY AND LEGACY OF BAUHAUS
#### BY KEVIN HASKINS

Photo: Graham Trott

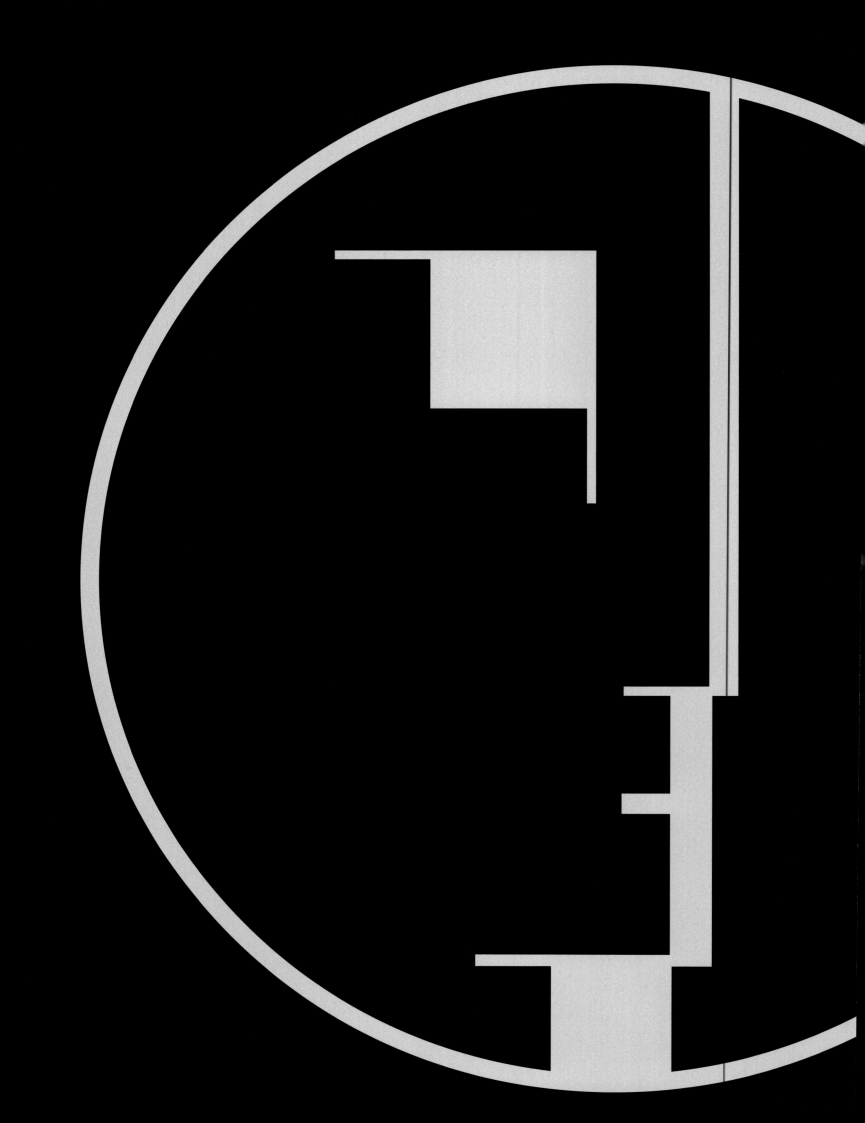

# FOREWORD

**MAYNARD – TOOL, PUSCIFER**

As contradictory as this may seem, Bauhaus being, in my opinion, the Godfathers of Goth, they were a bright artistic light in a vast wasteland of 80's crappy pop darkness. They showed me the way.


**MOBY**

I first heard Bauhaus on WNYU, a college radio station in Manhattan, in 1980 or 1981. Every day, without fail, as I didn't really have friends or a girlfriend, I would come home from school and sit with my finger on the 'record' button of my mom's cassette deck and tape songs off of the radio. I always missed the first 5 or 10 seconds of the song, as I would sit and think about whether I liked the song I was listening to enough to spend precious cassette tape on it.

I heard the first 5 seconds of 'In The Flat Field' one afternoon, and decided it was worthy of 3 minutes of cassette tape. That night I went back and listened to it a few times and realized that it didn't make sense to me, but that I loved it. It wasn't clean like The Clash, or despairing like Joy Division. It didn't sound futuristic like Cabaret Voltaire or Depeche Mode, and it wasn't angry and brutal like Black Flag or Discharge. It was, if I tried to put my finger on it, urgent and desperate, and as I was an urgent and desperate adolescent, it made me uncomfortable and seduced.

Time passed and I heard more Bauhaus, 'Third Uncle', 'Kick In The Eye', and then the song that cemented my love for them, 'All We Ever Wanted Was Everything'.

Bauhaus were complicated, at times earnest, at times distant and ironic, at times delicate, at times vicious. I could never put my finger on them, or what they did, which made me love them even more. My black fingernail'ed Goth friends claimed them as their own, sepulchral and dark and gothic, but I felt like that was selling the band a bit short. They were dark and sepulchral, but also celebratory and bright at times. Every Bauhaus song and album felt like a filmy window into a world that was foreign and seductive, especially for a 15 year old in suburban Connecticut. Pop radio was manufactured and anodyne, pop culture was a barren, anemic place, and Bauhaus were bloody and scary and intimate and complicated. For that I'll always love them.


**PETER HOOK – JOY DIVISION, NEW ORDER**

FROM and TO – OF and THEN

There is one in every group. The one who slavishly collects all the scraps and ephemeral bits that make up this wonderful crazy business of ours.

From the scraps of paper sello-taped on the door of a manky club in the seventies, to the 7 colour poster advertising your 'Sell-Out' gig at The Royal Albert Hall, years later.

From the stuck on generic passes, To the highly collectible Individual laminates.
From the broken pieces of equipment, To the battle scarred cases.
All seeming to bestow on you, those wonderful extra privileges you lusted after as a member of the audience.

Every one of them, telling it's own story.

Of money squandered, then chances missed.
Of dreams crushed, then success.
Of riches, then praise beyond your wildest dreams.
Of heartache, then recriminations and bitterness.

All aimed at the people you started with, you loved, were closest too.
Then in an instant the furthest from, and it's over.
This is all that's left....Enjoy!


**ERIC AVERY – JANES ADDICTION**

When you sit down to write about a band like Bauhaus you are handcuffed by the fact that all the perfect descriptions for Bauhaus have been overused to describe lesser bands. They were a dark, sexual, theatrical band that made music that is timeless. Music that didn't sound like 1983, back then, any more than it sounds like 2016 now. It's the flicker of a film projector. It's the shout down the cone of a carnival barker. It's the slither of a leather constraint. It is music that stands outside of time. It is as beautiful, surprising and singular as it ever was (and will continue to be for the same reason). There has truly, to me, quite literally, never been a band like Bauhaus.

## BILLY CORGAN – THE SMASHING PUMPKINS

There's a particular kind of kismet that rings around Bauhaus' key covers, being the cracked and near ruinous descendants of their twin Bowie-Marc-God. For the lads both inherited the dregs of glam and the haunted foreshadowing of goth; and paid in many ways for their prescience. And as I imagined it they were the Spiders if Ziggy had failed but hung on, or the Rex if he'd never aged. Humour, too, became them, and that too has been lost with time and computer-born aggregators that tell us what to listen to and when to doze. Bauhaus tried to wake us up and somewhat failed, and in the mist are preserved in my own heart as being above it all. For hair metal and grunge and etc etc only proved what they figured out fast: which was, Davy Jones and that other kid with the warbled voice were the nazz, and fuck the rest. Oh, and guitars don't stay in tune so well on the dark side of the moon...

## SAM FOGARINO – INTERPOL

Like a thing of fiction as brilliant a construct as the subject matter and conditions that seemed to fuel & inspire their unique take on sound and vision.

## ROMAN DIRGE – COMIC BOOK ARTIST

Trying to write about one of your all time favorite bands without sounding "all gushy", is surprisingly difficult, especially when you know they'll read it. It doesn't help when you see that some musical heavyweights will also be writing about them, in what I'm sure will be insightful and poignant musings on music that I just don't posses. Given that, I thought I'd just go with an anecdote.

When I think of Bauhaus, I think of the ugliest car in the world and it makes me smile. Please let me explain before you stab me, probably with like a leather stiletto or something.

When I was a teenager and my parents gifted me my first car, it was a hideous bright yellow Ford Fiesta with a luggage rack and wood paneling across the doors. It looked like the 70's threw up on the 80's. However, the minute it became mine, I plastered the windows with Bauhaus stickers, elevating it from a vehicular bee monster, to a cool goth sled that I was happy to be seen in and happier to cart around my fellow little spooky friends. Even after a can of bright pink spray paint rolled in to the sharp rails holding the driver's seat, punctured, and then spun around the interior, coating everything in pink (Or as I called it at the time, Hello Kitty Blood), I was still cool with it. The tape player worked and I countered the pink carnage with more Bauhaus stickers. I drove that poor old car until it died, A Bauhaus tape forever stuck in the tape player.

When asked about Bauhaus, veering anecdotal about an ugly old car might seem like an odd choice, and it is, but I have a semblance of reasoning. I still use the "Bauhaus stickers on a car" methodology to get through life to this day as a 44 year old man. When things are going less then stellar, or hopelessness wants to wrap its claws around me, I put on headphones and blast my eardrums with Bauhaus and the ugly things in my life fade away. The hideous yellow car becomes cool to drive in again.

Their music has always taken me to a magical place where imagination is limitless. The mood and feeling that they create, while intentionally dark in nature, can be audio euphoria given you are in the right mind set. I've created some of my strongest art while guided by the imagery I see in my head when following along to Bela Lugosi is Dead or She's in Parties. Art begets art in that sense. I don't know who inspired them, but I know they inspired me and will be forever grateful that they unwrapped their unique brand of talent for the world to enjoy.

## JEORDIE WHITE a.k.a. TWIGGY – MARILYN MANSON

My first introduction to Bauhaus was through a local professional  juggler in South Florida. I was 18 years old and in order to get into 21 + alternative night clubs, I would dress in a ridiculous frog costume and be his juggling assistant, which basically required me to drop acid and dance to the music provided by the DJ while he juggled fire. This was at the dawn of the 90's and alternative music was about to explode. Being a metalhead at the time, the closest to anything "goth" or "progressive" I listened to was force fed to me through MTV.

I remember hearing the first bass note of "Double Dare" blast through the nightclub's sound system. It was the heaviest note I'd ever heard (and still is). The oddest drum beat came in and I was completely dumbfounded. The guitar speckled with reverb put me in a trance. The words "I dare you, to be real" in the scariest voice I'd ever heard challenged me and I fell in love instantly. I couldn't tell if this was Black Sabbath or David Bowie.It was as if I was Alice entering wonderland , an old world I never knew existed ( it could have been the acid). The subject matter of their songs described exactly how I felt. Their music metaphorically lifted up a rock and exposed all the existential bugs eating at my subconscious and opened my mind to a new genre of music.

I immediately bought everything Bauhaus put out as well as Love and Rockets, Peter Murphy, Tones On Tail, The Jazz Butcher and Dali's Car. I wanted to BE Daniel Ash. (I still do.) No 4 individuals have inspired and changed my artistic life more than the members of Bauhaus.I wanted to write songs that felt the way theirs made me feel.I wore my Bela logsi's Dead shirt religiously on stage with my thrash metal band at the time, which alienated my audience, but got the attention of a person that went by the name Marilyn Manson. We quickly became fast friends and the rest is history.  Yes, a Bauhaus t-shirt altered my life and connected me with someone that I would contribute to the world with.

When I was playing for Nine Inch Nails I had the pleasure and privilege to tour with Bauhaus. To be able to work and become friends with my idols was and is a validating highlight of my life. I had finally arrived where it all started. I was always disappointed that I never was able to see Bauhaus in their "prime" but on that tour, they were in their prime. I watched them every single night and they were unbelievable and unpredictable. To be accepted by these guys as peers blew my mind. The four distinct personalities that make up Bauhaus do not disappoint. The myth is real.

## MAT MITCHELL – PUSCIFER

There was a period of my life where I listened to Bauhaus on repeat. I loved their songwriting and choices of sounds. From the unorthodox guitar parts to the fretless bass riffs to the perfectly sculpted drum patterns and electronic sounds, I still reference Bauhaus for inspiration regularly.

## DANNY CANON – EXECUTIVE PRODUCER, DIRECTOR

It was a t-shirt that first caught my attention. Peter, a kid in my sister's year at a Luton High School, had screen printed the 'Dark Entries' single cover on to a sleeveless shirt. It was striking. There was no internet to check back in 1981 so I went to Sister Ray, a record shop in London's SoHo and asked the nice man who worked there to put on a track. He did, I was impressed. There was a danger, an aggression. Not violent but rebellious. I couldn't compare them to anyone, they were, their own genre. Transporting me to a darker, dangerous, more interesting world, one a 14 year old kid from Luton doesn't get invited to normally. Unlike the punk, new wave and ska records I was buying, Bauhaus painted a more theatrical, cinematic, timeless canvas. It was therefore not surprising to see them in Tony Scott's debut vampire movie, 'The Hunger'. A modern, gothic masterpiece. He had obviously heard and seen in them the cinematic presence I had. The environment he shot them in and the way he cut them, visually articulated the way their music made me feel.

When I met Kevin Haskins in LA much later he told me Pete from Luton had ended up working for the band. A true fan had found his calling. Beautiful. He'd also escaped Luton.

I saw the band play Friars Aylesbury the next year. The crowd dressed to the nines for the evening. Made me think of Bowie's fans, how he gave every freak and wierdo permission to get out of the closet, show their true colors and be their true selves. It wasn't just a gig but a happening. Murphy channeled Bowie's theatrical flair, the band channeled 'Joy Division's' tight, fast paced, heartbeat but added a mood and danger that reminded me of 'The Velvet Underground'. These weren't leather clad punks, petulant school boys pretending to be tough. These guys seemed like sophisticated artists, with a plan and a confident sense of style.

## CHRIS SALESWICZ – JOURNALIST, AUTHOR

The four-piece from Northampton, England are venerated as the highly influential band that spearheaded the post-punk alternative-music scene of the early 80s, with a string of innovative albums and a powerfully dramatic live presentation; their brooding yet electrifying and dynamic sound influenced the likes of Nirvana, Pulp and Nine Inch Nails.

Cemented into celluloid as performers in the opening sequence of the 1983 vampire film The Hunger, which starred David Bowie, Susan Sarandon and Catherine Deneuve, Bauhaus was clearly a unique set-up: charismatic singer Peter Murphy with his perfectly chiseled cheek-bones and idiosyncratic singing style; Daniel Ash, an anti-guitar hero on account of his distaste for conventional guitarist histrionics; iconoclastic bass-player David J [Haskins]; and subtle and intelligent drummer Kevin Haskins.

The historical reputation that Bauhaus now owns stands in stark contrast to the manner in which much of the UK music press at first utterly dismissed the group – although the Radio One disc jockey John Peel was a firm early champion of Bauhaus. Their debut single was Bela Lugosi's Dead, with a running time over 9 minutes, a full-on slab of brooding imagination that Peel regularly played - Bela Lugosi's Dead was recorded after the line-up had only been together for six weeks. Bauhaus scored their biggest hit, with a cover of David Bowie's Ziggy Stardust in the second half of 1982.

A seminal influence on the Goth movement, Bauhaus was part of the punky-reggae party, which their audience – if not the media – immediately picked up on: the four members adoring Lee 'Scratch" Perry, influenced by the likes of The Sex Pistols, The Clash and PIL, but also taking on the mantle of such glam-rock icons as David Bowie and Roxy Music, filtered through funk and the inscrutable Kraut-rock sounds of the likes of Can. Bauhaus pulled these disparate but logical parts into a unique whole.

Time has admirably served the unique, enigmatic Bauhaus; with each passing year the group's reputation only increases, until they are now one of the most revered of all post-punk acts, the influence of their moody music increasingly felt on a global scale.

Much to David's amusement, Daniel had just bumped his knee whilst climbing over the motorway safety rail.
We had just pulled over to allow the radiator of the ill fated hearse to cool down. / Photo: Kevin Haskins

## THE HEARSE

We were recording our third LP, *The Sky's Gone Out*, at the legendary Rockfield Studios in Monmouthshire, Wales and employed the engineer from "Bela Lugosi's Dead", Derek Tompkins, to assist on the session. One day, venturing into the nearby village of Monmouth to stock up on supplies, Daniel and Peter happened upon a hearse that was for sale! This would make a very fine means of convenience for touring, they both thought and after consulting with David and I, the next day the sale was made. Following the deal, we drove it with great excitement back to the studio and showed it off to Derek and the studio owners teenage daughters, who immediately asked us to take them for a spin. Derek was exasperated because we were "supposed to be recording an album, and not driving a bloody hearse around all day!"

After assuring Derek that we would be back in fifteen minutes, the girls took up their positions in the back, where normally the coffin would be placed. With Peter at the wheel we all set off with gusto around the narrow country lanes of Wales. Peter decided to test the capacity of the engine for speed and endurance, and as our lives flashed before our eyes, we went careering around the narrow bends and curves, over humpbacked bridges, and on several occasions, ironically, almost meeting our maker! The poor ladies were being thrown from side to side of the rear compartment, screaming with both fear and delight! Fortunately, we eventually made it back in one piece.

Once the LP was finished we drove the old hearse back to our home town of Northampton and a fine fellow by the name of "Reasonable" Ray Kinsey, set about converting it into a more suitable conveyance for the undead. Ray installed seating and curtains, all in crushed velvet of a beautiful deep blue. A sumptuous carpet finished off the interior with gothic splendor. We could not wait to take it on our next tour, although our long suffering Tour Manager, Harry Isles, was not of a similar persuasion! Unfortunately, his worst fears came to fruition. The bloody thing would constantly overheat and breakdown. Much to the amusement and horror of families taking a leisurely spin, we all too often could be seen pushing the bloody thing along the B roads and streets of Great Britain.

Unfortunately over time, the negatives greatly outweighed the positives, and so on March 14th 1984, the poor beleaguered hearse was finally laid to rest.

# Motor Cover Note

Policy Number _____

Agent TRENTSIDE _____

Proposers' Name and Address:

· MR. H. ISLES ·

~~[redacted]~~ ·

NEWNHAM ·

N. HANTS ·

·                    ·

Number   AA 228244 _____

Date of Issue 31 - 7      19 82 _____

Office Address:

·                    ·

Branch Office: MOORLANDS HOUSE,
24, TRINITY STREET,
STOKE-ON-TRENT. ST1 5LD

·                    ·

The above named having proposed for insurance in respect of the Motor Vehicle(s) described in the schedule below, the risk is hereby covered in the terms of the Company's usual form of Policy applicable thereto and to the Special Conditions or Restrictions (if any) indicated below for the period and time stated,

unless the cover is terminated by written notice to the Proposer at the above address in which case the insurance will thereupon cease and a proportionate part of the annual premium will be charged for the time this insurance has been in force.

**Period of Cover**
30 days from 11·45 AM a.m./p.m. on the 31 · 7      19 82 to the same time on the thirtieth day thereafter.

| **Schedule** Make, Model & Type of Body | Year of Make | Cubic Capacity | Plated Weight | Carrying Capacity | Number of Seats | Value Vehicle | Trailer | Registration Mark or Engine/Chassis/Body Number |
|---|---|---|---|---|---|---|---|---|
| FORD ZEPHYR HEARSE | 1970 | 3000 | | | 4 | £1000 | | NVM 5H · |

| **Cover** COMP £50+5 Insert Comprehensive or Third Party Fire & Theft or Third Party as the case may be | **Use** As defined in USE CLAUSE A overleaf. | If USE CLAUSES overleaf not applicable, state 'use' in this box |
|---|---|---|

**Special Conditions and Restrictions**

The person driving must (a) hold a licence to drive such vehicle or have held and not be disqualified for holding or obtaining such a licence, and, (b) be driving on the Proposer's/Policyholder's order or with his permission.

Additional Special Conditions or Restrictions ANY DRIVER _____

**Certificate of Motor Insurance**

I hereby certify that this Covering Note satisfies the requirements of the relevant law applicable in Great Britain, Northern Ireland, the Isle of Man, the Island of Guernsey, the Island of Jersey and the Island of Alderney.

## Commercial Union Assurance
A MEMBER OF THE BRITISH INSURANCE ASSOCIATION
REGISTERED IN ENGLAND NUMBER 21487 REGISTERED OFFICE: ST. HELEN'S, 1 UNDERSHAFT, LONDON EC3P 3DQ

ON BEHALF OF THE COMPANY

Signed _____

COMMERCIAL UNION ASSURANCE COMPANY LIMITED
Authorised Insurers

J. E. THOMSON

**C U**
**ASSURANCE**

Insurance contract for the hearse

* AUCTIONS TUESDAY 6 P.M., THURSDAY 1 P.M. *

# NORTHAMPTON CAR AUCTIONS
A Member of the Arlington Group

The Auction Hall · Salthouse Road · Brackmills Industrial Estate · Northampton NN4 0BD
Tel: (0604) 64041

Daniel Ash Esq.,

Northampton.

**REMITTANCE ADVICE**

99321

14.3.84

Date ............................................... V.A.T. No. 220 4176 10

| | | £ | p. |
|---|---|---|---|
| Lot No. 36X8 Vehicle Ford Hearse NVM 5H | | | |
| | | 375 | 00 |
| | | | |
| | | | |
| | | | |
| Commission | 25.00 | | |
| Collection | | | |
| Valeting | | | |
| Entry Fees | | | |
| VAT | 3.75 | | |
| | 28.75 | 28 | 75 |
| Cheque Enclosed | | 346 | 25 |

*We have pleasure in enclosing herewith our cheque in respect of the sale of your Vehicle*
*for which we thank you and look forward to being of service to you in the future.*
AG 22

---

*Henry Spencer*

Monmouth 2750
STD 0600

Funeral Service

10 GLENDOWER STREET, MONMOUTH, NP5 3DG.

VAT Reg. No. 135 0076 82

M r. Harry Isles.                                July        1982.

| | | | |
|---|---|---|---|
| Ford Zephyr Six – Coleman Milne Conversion – hearse registered number NVM 5 H.  Sold as seen and agreed | | 850 | 00 |
| M.o.t. test. | | 7 | 50 |
| | | £857 | 50. |

Received the sum stated.
Henry Spencer.

Received the vehicle as described above}

P. Murphy

for Mr. H. Isles.
Newnham,
Daventry.  Northants.

Sales receipts for the Bauhaus hearse

out now.

BELA LUGOSI'S DEAD

# 12" SINGLE ON SMALL WONDER RECORDS

# bauhaus

Original promotional poster for Bela Lugosi's Dead screen printed by Daniel and his father Arthur Ash who was a sign writer. I remember driving around in my Morris Minor in the dead of the night, sticking up the posters with a large brush and a mixture of flour and water.

## BELA LUGOSI'S DEAD

"Bela Lugosi's Dead" was actually the first song that we all wrote together once David was in the band. Previously, Daniel had not wanted David in because he feared that he would be too controlling. After several appeals, I finally persuaded Daniel to let him join because instinctively, I knew that he was the missing piece of the puzzle.

We were rehearsing in a sterile mobile classroom with fluorescent lighting. Hardly the fitting climate to write something so dark, brooding and atmospheric. Daniel knew someone at the Northampton Teacher Training College who allowed us to rehearse in this classroom after school hours. We would load up my Morris Minor and Daniel's Ford Cortina with all our equipment and the passengers would have to lie on top of the gear, sandwiched between it and the roof of the car. The previous night to our first rehearsal with David, Daniel called him to tell him that he had just come up with this beautifully dark and haunting melody. David responded by telling Daniel that he had just written some lyrics about an actor called Bela Lugosi, famous for his portrayal of a vampire. They both acknowledged this intriguing incidence of synchronicity and couldn't wait for the rehearsal the next day.  After setting up the equipment, we began. Peter with lyrics in hand, Daniel playing the beautiful haunting chords and David adding a simple descending and ascending bass line, I recall thinking to myself, what does this need drum wise? And then I remembered one of the three beats that I learnt from my first drum teacher....The Bossa Nova. As soon as I started playing it, it instantly worked! The really special songs reveal themselves so fast, and this was no exception. The very first time we played it is exactly how it sounds on the record. It was done and dusted within 20 minutes! We couldn't wait to record it and I think we imposed a rule not to play it too much so that it would be still fresh by the time we hit the studio.

On January 26th, 1979 we arrived at Beck Studios in Gisburne Road in Peter's home town of Wellingborough for our three hour session. It was all we could afford, and as it turned out, amazing value for money. It wasn't just the homely humble vibe of the studio, but the owner Derek Tompkins was a very important part of the chemistry. A tall middle aged man of slender frame, whose daily diet consisted of four aspirin washed down with several cups of coffee and at least twenty cigarettes for good measure. We would marvel that the mixing desk was still working as his cigarette ash would constantly fall inside between the faders. Derek was a very interesting and intelligent man, very open minded, quite outspoken and something of a rebel in his youth. He also had a natural handle on psychology, something very valuable when producing bands. He was twice our age, and as such, was not clued in to the fads and fashions of the time, which I feel was to his and our advantage. He didn't impose any production ideas unless they were warranted. Rather, he knew exactly how to mix the particular piece of music we were creating. I learned so much from Derek over the years that we recorded with him, and he was such a warm and lovely man. I often thought in retrospect that he was to Bauhaus what George Martin was to The Beatles. On one particular occasion, when mixing one of our songs, I wanted to hear the snare drum louder (This was classic error commonly made when one is not yet experienced with mixing). I kept nagging Derek about it, and with his charming stutter he said, "H-h-h-h hold on K-k-k-kevin" and disappeared out of the room to soon return with a 1/4 inch tape. He placed the tape on the playback machine and hit play. Out of the speakers came Stevie Wonder's classic hit "Superstition". Derek continued, "L-l-l-l-listen to the the s-s-s-snare drum, wu wu what does it s-s-s-s-sound like to you?" I listened with interest and was surprised. I replied, "It sounds awful! Really muddy, and quiet, as if it's being played in the room next door." Derek responded with, "Yes, Kevin, exactly, but d-d-d-does it wu wu work, w-w-w-w-within the song?" First lesson of many learned! The acclaimed producer Trevor Horn was another person who benefitted from Derek's talents, as he would book studio time to learn how to produce and multi track.

A great example of his creativity was a suggestion he offered when we booked a pre-album recording session at Beck. I was looking for a metallic industrial snare drum sound for a song entitled, "Swing The Heartache." So I went outside the studio

and dragged in Derek's metal dustbin. When struck with a stick, it sounded pretty good, but it wasn't the sound I could hear in my head. Then Derek suggested I go and open what I thought was a broom cupboard door in the control room. It revealed a large piece of thick metal about seven feet by four feet, suspended from the closet ceiling. Behind the plate of metal was a speaker and a microphone. Considering this set up to be far too extravagant on the occasion that someone might ask for a metallic snare sound, I asked Derek what it was really for. He explained that it's used for adding plate reverb to a vocal, guitar, etc., hence the metal plate. Whatever sound that one wants reverb added to, you solo that sound and feed it to the speaker. When it leaves the speaker, the sound hits the metal plate, and reverb is created! It's then picked up by the microphone and fed back to the control room speakers. Fascinating! Derek played back the song and instructed me to gently flick the plate using my thumb and finger on every snare drum beat and the effect was perfect. Every flick sounded like a meteorite hitting the Titanic!

Incidentally, this track ("Swing The Heartache") was actually born from an entirely different idea. We had initially gone in to attempt to record a cover of The Walker Brothers "The Electrician" but out of that failed attempt came "Swing The Heartache". "The

Derek Tompkins photo by Mavis Tompkins

Electrician" did in fact make an appearance when we used the original Walker Brothers classic to introduce the shows during the Burning From The Inside tour.  But I digress. It didn't take very long for Derek to set up the levels and it was time to lay down "Bela Lugosi's Dead". We all played together and actually captured it in the first take! I was rather relieved as, although it might sound easy, playing the Bossa nova for over ten minutes, is a bit of a task. As we had captured it so quickly Derek suggested running through a few songs, just for the hell of it. We recorded "Harry", "Boys" (not to be confused with the B side to the "Bela" single, this was an earlier version), "Bite My Hip" and "Some Faces". Now it was time to mix "Bela" and once Derek had a rough mix, Daniel set up his Wem Copycat delay unit in the control room and asked Derek to feed the snare drum and guitar tracks into it. Derek hit the playback button and, inspired by our collective love of Dub Reggae, Daniel manipulated the speed, feedback and tape, giving it the dubbed out, Lee "Scratch" Perry treatment. The delays were recorded on a separate track, and I felt shivers run up my spine when we played back the results. We knew without doubt, that we had created something really, really special! There was however one universal concern. Clocking in at about 13 minutes, it was way too long. Derek told us that this was not a problem and that he could edit out a few minutes. Not knowing how this was done, we casually agreed, but collectively recoiled in horror as he pulled out a razor blade with a view to slicing through the tape! "Stop! Stop! No! No! What are you doing?" We all yelled! I look back with amusement now at our naïveté, but we were naturally very precious about our new creation that he was about to hack to death! Chuckling away, Derek reassured us that he had done this many times before, and that it was a mere formality. Derek did a marvelous job, however, because of all the delays, one can hear where the edit is if one is listening carefully for it.

In September of 1979 "Bela Lugosi's Dead" was released. It quickly climbed to the top of the independent chart where it remained for a very impressive two years.

Photo: Jean Ramsey

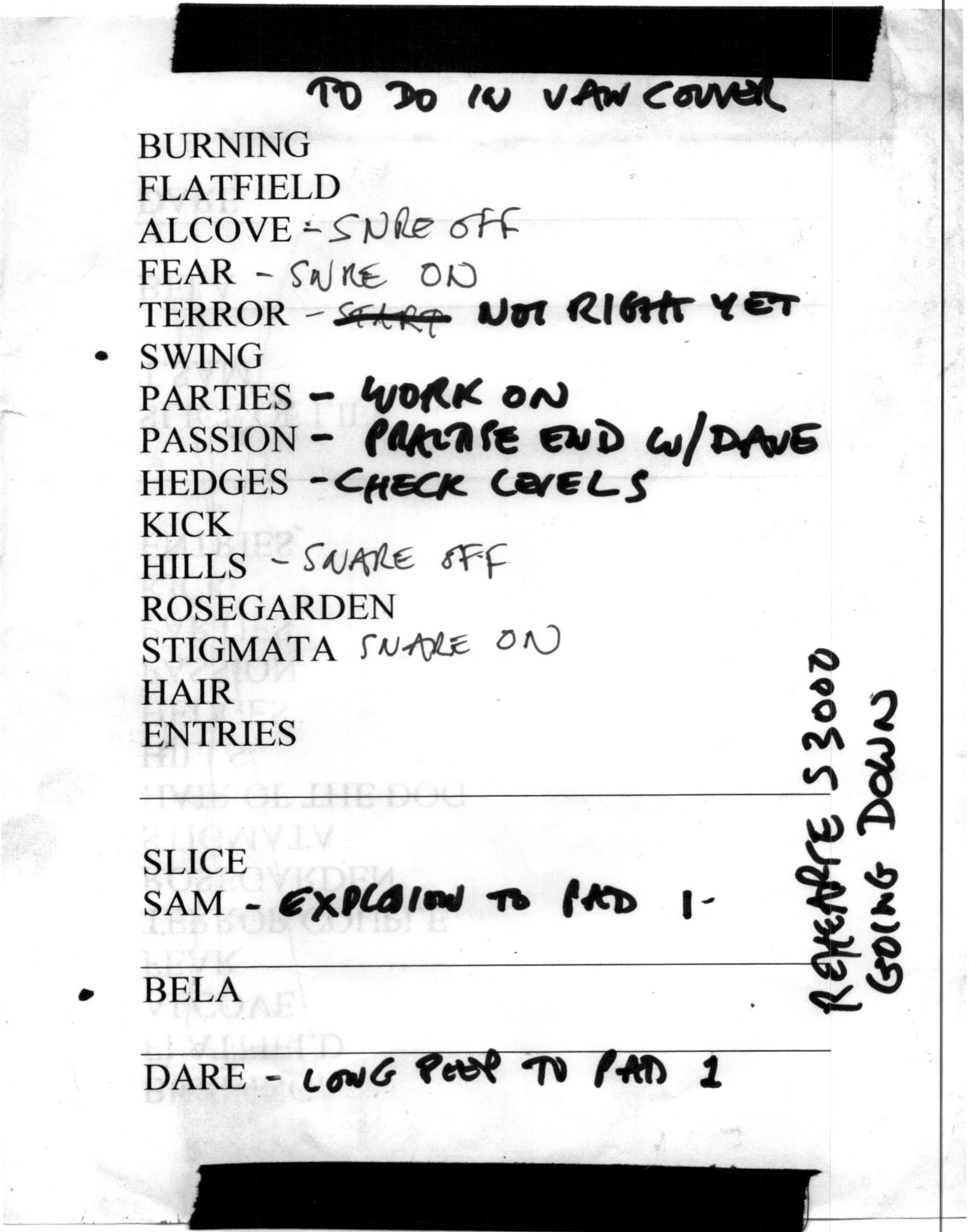

TO DO IN VANCOUVER

BURNING
FLATFIELD
ALCOVE = SNRE OFF
FEAR - SNRE ON
TERROR - ~~SNARE~~ NOT RIGHT YET
• SWING
PARTIES - WORK ON
PASSION - PRACTISE END W/ DAVE
HEDGES - CHECK LEVELS
KICK
HILLS - SNARE OFF
ROSEGARDEN
STIGMATA SNARE ON
HAIR
ENTRIES

SLICE
SAM - EXPLAIN TO PAD 1-

• BELA

DARE - LONG PEEP TO PAD 1

REHEARSE S3000 GOING DOWN

Notes that I made to myself during the Resurrection Tour following the show at the Paramount Theater in Seattle. Although we were several dates in to the tour, there was still some fine tuning to be done, and I would make notes after each performance to implement before the next gig. I also made a note to rehearse switching over to my back up AKAI S3000 sampler in case the main one died on me during a show.

Photo: Jean Ramsey

23

Photo: Suezan Skelton

## DO YOU WANT TO BE IN A BAND?

Exactly five years to the day after Daniel Ash and Peter Murphy had fled the stifling confines of St. Mary's Catholic School, Daniel was sitting in his clapped out Ford Cortina outside Peter Murphy's parents council house in Wellingborough. Having just completed the ten mile journey from Northampton, he was waiting in anticipation for Peter to return home from his job at a printing company. On nothing more than a whim, Daniel had come to ask Peter to be the lead vocalist for his new group. Amazingly, Daniel had absolutely no idea if Peter could sing. He just recalled their mutual appreciation of Roxy Music and David Bowie in high school and that Peter looked really good! Eventually, through the grey drizzle, a lone figure atop a Honda moped with learner plates came trundling down the street.

The last time that Daniel had seen Peter was several months earlier, when he had invited him to see The Craze at an Art School Party promoted by Glenn Campling (Glenn would later become roadie to Bauhaus and along with Daniel, formed the band Tones On Tail). The Craze consisted of Dave Exton, David Haskins, Daniel Ash and myself. With the exclusion of Dave Exton, the remaining three musicians would become the nucleus of Bauhaus and all three members of Love And Rockets.

Just before the show, David had come across some orange fluorescent workmen's vests lying around and, against Daniel's better judgment, persuaded us all to wear them on stage. After the show Peter told Daniel that he was extremely impressed with the music but that he thought the vests looked awful!

As Peter dismounted from his moped, Daniel called over to him to come and listen to some music. Sitting on the passenger seat of the car was a mobile Phillips cassette player, containing a few recordings from the same band that Peter had seen play live. Peter listened intently to the songs "In Praise Of Clark Kent Not Superman" and "You Can't Hold a Candle To A Kiss", and was even more impressed than before. At this point Daniel blurted out, "Do you want to be in a band?" Peter responded emphatically in the affirmative and at that moment, in Daniels clapped out old banger, the formative Bauhaus was born! During subsequent visits to Peter's house they chatted excitedly about their new venture. Daniel, having had previous experiences in bands, would give Peter advice as to what to expect. He informed him that he would have to dedicate all his spare time to the band, and that he would have to give up all hobbies, such as the Medieval Battle Reenactment Society that he belonged to. Daniel went on to explain that once they started playing, everything else in his life would pale in comparison. Daniel asked Peter to consider this very carefully, as there would be no going back!

## THE WASP SPECIAL

Produced by Electric Dream Plant, the Wasp was a very unique little synthesizer made in Britain. Although we had great admiration for Kraftwerk and early synthesizer pioneers, to begin with we consciously avoided bringing them into our helm. By January of 1981, we had fully toured our first LP, *In The Flat Field*, and were about to embark on a more expansive musical horizon. The introduction of a synthesizer at this time seemed to follow our natural evolution. The Wasp Special was the perfect choice for Bauhaus. It was small and mobile so Peter could easily use it on stage and it's sound was very unique. None of us had any idea of how a synthesizer worked and I think in some ways this was to our advantage. It's first of many sessions was at Jam Studios in London, recording "Kick In The Eye", "Satori", "In Fear Of Fear", "In Fear Of Dub" and "Of Lilies And Remains". Now after acquiring a new piece of equipment, most bands tend to plaster it over everything....we were no exception! You can hear it on every track of this session, and it really stamps it's ethereal, other worldly character on each song.

BAUHAUS IN LONDON

KINGSTON POLY KNIGHTS PARK 24

QUEEN ELIZABETH COLLEGE 25

JAN

# IN THE SHATTERLIGHT
## NUMBER FIVE

# BAVHAVS
## OMNI'S -- FEBRVARY 25

CONTRIBVTORS: JASON KEEHN
MATT HOWARTH
MICHAEL McGRATH
STEVE FRITZ
HELEN SCHWARTZ
JULIAN KERNES
FRONT COVER BY HELEN SCHWARTZ AND
JULIAN KERNES

IN THE SHATTERLIGHT is published by Jason Keehn, 40 Netherlands Studios, 4318 Chestnut St., Apt. 310, Phila. PA 19104 USA. All contents © 1981 JASON KEEHN. This special comic issue was a joint Netherlands/Howski/Terminal! production. Special thanks to Lee Paris and the rest of Omni's and of course to Bavhavs. Copies of SHATTERLIGHT #4 (Bunny drums) are available for 25¢ each; subscription price is $2.00 (will get you (2 bucks worth of) the next four or five issues to come out.)

**Past, Present & Future Wear**
2047 Walnut (864-0655)

BAVHAVS: PETE MURPHY
(VOCALS)
KEVIN HASKINS (DRUMS)
DANIEL ASH (GVITAR)
DAVID JAY (BASS)
(ALL LYRICS REPRODUCED W/
THE PERMISSION OF BAVHAVS)

## BAVHAVS DISCOGRAPHY

"BELA LUGOSI'S DEAD" (12" 45)
TEENY 2 (SMALL WONDER RECORDS)
"DARK ENTRIES" AXIS 3
"TERROR COUPLE KILL COLONEL" AD7
"TELEGRAM SAM" (12" AND 7"; 12" HAS COVER OF CALE'S "ROSEGARDEN FUNERAL OF SORES") AD 17

**IN THE FLAT FIELD** (ALBUM) CAD 13 A

NOTES: BAVHAVS WAS JUST IN THE STUDIO WORKING ON A NEW SINGLE; BAVHAVS WILL ALSO BE AT CITY GARDENS (IN TRENTON, NJ) MAR. 13

PHOTO · HELEN SCHWARTZ

# DARK ENTRANCE

*Shatterlight* was a minicomic published in the States to promote our In The Flat Field Tour. It was conceived by Jason Keehn and Matt Howarth (who created *Raising Venom*) collaborated on the art work with him.

Schizophrenic grimace of blasted city towards the sky
flickering shapes, random click and scratch
a massive rumbling - dust swirls into the air
metal chords struggle out of a sea of distortion

OW, MY EARS!
WHO IN THE WORLD
WOULD HAVE THE
NERVE TO PUT ON
A CONCERT THE
DAY AFTER??

WE'RE GOING DOWN TO THE KAMIKAZI
DIVE LIKE MANIC MOTHS IN CHINESE
LANTERNS NOW WE'RE FEELING SO
ALIVE WHAT'S SHOWING?

YOW WHAT'S THAT
ON THE HORIZON?

...LOOKS LIKE
MORE TROUBLE!

AFTERMATH?

HEY, DO YOU
HEAR MUSIC
COMING FROM
SOMEWHERE?

A gut pull drag, the music pulls with deafening haste
the guttural throb crawls and
crashes across the city

THE END!

# OMNI'S

Live pop music

FEB. 26 - FREE ROCK NITE W/REGGAE DJ
27 - PRETTY POISON
28 - CHANDRA AND THE DANCE

MAR. 5 - DOOMED ON THE PLANET EARTH
6 - HUMAN SWITCHBOARD
7 - STRAIN
12 - THE STICKMEN
13 - MISSION OF BURMA (BOSTON)
(FROM BOSTON)
14 - NONA HENDRYX AND ZERO COOL
19 - HINTERBAND
20 - SPECIAL BUNNYDRUMS
BIRTHDAY PARTY
21 - FRED FRITH, BILL LASWELL
AND FRED MAHER ("MASSACRE")
26 - THE SADISTIC EXPLOITS
TINY DESK UNIT (FROM D.C.)
STRICTLY LIMERANCE

APR. 1 - BRIAN BRAIN

EVERY WEDNESDAY NIGHT FEA-
TURES FREE ROCK DANCING
WITH DJ LEE PARIS.

NEW REGIME PRESENTS -- OMNI'S, AT 907
WALNUT ST. CALL 925-7799 FOR INFO.

¥3,900
バウハウス
# BAUHAUS
5月30日(月)毎日ホール 6:30pm

主催●ウドー音楽事務所
協力●ワーナー・パイオニア
協賛●ブリヂストンタイヤ株式会社

バウハウス
**BAUHAUS**
5月30日(月) 6:30pm
毎日ホール

1階 そ列 15 番 ¥3,900 **S**

# BAUHAUS
## ANNIVERS
### +The Patter
racecourse pa
sat·29··dec··

BACKSTAGE PASS

FRESH MUSIC PRESENTS
## GARY GLITTER
AND THE GLITTER BAND
## CLASSIX NOUVEAUX
DAVID DALE + COMPANY
## CUDDLY TOYS AND GUESTS
## BAUHAUS
LYCEUM, STRAND W.C.2.
7.30, THURSDAY, 10th APRIL

## bauhaus
THE SKY'S GONE OUT
# PASS
000006

STRAIGHT MUSIC
# BACK STAGE PASS
SORRY, BUT I NEED THIS!

Artist  Bauhaus
Date
Venue  MP.
Signature

B A

M A
AT-LIN
TICKETS £25
£300 ON THE D
WEAR A MASK

# LYCEUM
## BACKSTAGE PASS
Name
Artiste  BAUHAUS
Date
Authorised by

STRAIGHT MUSIC
# BACK STAGE PASS
THIS IS THE PLACE!

Artist  **BAUHAUS**
2 VAREG No 936 27 6 45

STRAIGHT MUSIC
# BACK STAGE PASS
GARAGE  CRASH!

Artist  BAUHAUS

ELECTRA-1
Festival per i fantasmi del futuro
Bologna 17 - 18 - 19 Luglio 1981

# UDO
ARTISTS, INC.
## BACKSTAGE PASS
DATE  58 5.30
SECTION  Bauhaus
NAME  Ann
ACCESS ALL AREAS

DER
O
PRO
artis
vent
date
sign

*Access
All
Areas*

*Lings*

AUHAUS

# BAUHAUS

F.C. IN JAPAN
THE UNDERPASS

bauhaus

access 6-7 □ □ inside 83

RY
on
50

1984 FUTURAMA

DANCE MACABRE
BAUHAUS

Zat. 6 dec. 1980
om 20 uur

Voorverkoop
180F

N° 001

FAC 51
THE HAÇIENDA

14 AUG 1982

REGULAR MU
PASS

BAU
HAUS

WE RESERVE ALL RIGHTS, AL

LUSU EN
BAUHAUS

Riverside
PASS

0000 0000 0

EVENT

BAND

SpecialPassSpecialPassSp
SpecialPassSpecialPassS
SpecialPassSpecialPassS
SpecialPassSpecialPassS
SpecialPassSpecialPassSp
SpecialPassSpecialPassSp
SpecialPassSpecialPassS

17

Leeds
Univents
backstage
Pass

BAUHAUS

Saturday 30th October 198

HAUS

GUEST

BALL
UM SAT. FEB. 20.
ROM ACME LINGS SPINADISC
PM WITH SUPPORT

SOUND & VISION

BAUHAUS

ROYAL COURT

★ ★ ★

STAGE CREW

SECURITY

Artist   BAUHAUS

Date   18 JUN 1981

Signature   M Daniels

BLOCK
CERT
TIONS

BAUHAUS

RADIO CITE 96

BACK STAGE PASS

LIVE

VIC

82

FINAL SOLUTIO

BACKSTAGE PAS

ARTIST

VENUE   11 DEC 19

SIGNED

## NICO

We first met Nico when she came by Playground Studios in London, where we were recording our second LP *Mask*. It was rather surreal to be hanging out with a member of The Velvet Underground, a band that was heavily inspirational to us all. Extremely charismatic and beautiful, with her distinctive Germanic brogue, I was quite in awe!

The second time that our paths crossed was at Fagins in Manchester, touring on the release of *Mask*. Nico was living in Manchester, sadly battling a heroin addiction. The promoter, Alan Wise, was acting as her manager at the time. Alan was a bit of a character. I recall that there was no sink to wash in backstage and after we presented this dilemma to Mr. Wise, he returned with a metal mop bucket half filled with murky water! I remember Daniel going ballistic at him!

During our sound check, we all noticed the arrival of Nico who sat in a booth while we ran through a few songs. Once our sound engineer, Peter "Plug" Edwards, was happy with the levels, we reacquainted ourselves with the legendary songstress. During our conversation, and probably instigated by Alan, a plan was hatched for Nico to join us during our encore to sing the classic Velvet Underground song, "I'm Waiting For The Man". With great enthusiasm, the four of us took our instruments back to the hotel to work out the song together. Daniel and David quickly set to the task of figuring out the chords, and Peter recalled the lyrics from memory (There was no Googling in those days).

The small club was packed to the gills and we played an electrifying set. Leaving the stage, drenched in sweat and catching our breath, we collapsed on to the floor of the tiny dressing room. Nico made her entrance and congratulated us on an amazing show. Suddenly Daniel came up with a great idea; that it would be much cooler to not have any grand introduction for Nico, rather, the five of us would just walk on stage and start playing. If looks could in fact kill, then Nico gave Daniel a look that had him dead and six feet under, with a bullet hole between his eyes! Needless to say, there was an introduction made. Daniel set things going with a chugging guitar about 100 beats per minute faster than the original. David and I joined in and after about thirty bars, Nico entered in with her characteristic slur; "Iiiiiiiiiiiiiiiiimmmmmmmmmmmmmmmmmm waiting for my mmmmmmmmaaaaaaannnnn!" A chill travelled down my spine as my mind was trying to process that I was actually playing a Velvet Underground song with Nico!

# ROYAL THEATRE & OPERA HOUSE

**Guildhall Road, Northampton NN1 1EA**

Box Office    0604 32533
Management  0604 38343
Stage Door    0604 34520

**Artistic Director MICHAEL NAPIER BROWN**
**Associate Director ANTONY LINFORD**
**General Manager ANTHONY McDONALD**

AM/JKM                       2nd March 1982

J. Haskins Esq.,
87 The Headlands,
Northampton,
NN3 2NZ

Dear Mr. Haskins,

First of all, I have no recollection of your letter before
Christmas, either of its arrival or its contents. If I had,
I would have answered it promptly. I must assume this to be
a lapse of memory on my part for which I can only apologise
unreservedly.

As for Sunday concerts, we are a repertory theatre presenting
our own productions six nights a week. Concerts and other
Sunday events are only a sideline with us and we can not
reasonably fit more than a half-dozen a year into our tight
schedule. We have a file bulging with details of artists
and entertainments anxious to fill those few dates and more
arrive in the post every week. To 95% of them we return the
standard answer: "details will be kept on file". This is
not prejudice, it is the supply of talent exceeding our
opportunities to present it.

With the exception of my regrettable failure to reply to your
last letter, I have not been remiss in answering communications
from Bauhaus. I had a long telephone conversation with a
gentleman whom I believed to be the group's manager back in
the Autumn. I explained to him that on the occasion of their
last visit (which was before my time as manager) some of my
front of house staff, who are mostly elderly, were dismayed
by the behaviour of a certain element in the audience. One
couple, for example, were reported as copulating in the circle
bar. Now, although the behaviour of a minority of fans can
not be laid at the door of the group, it is with the audience,
not the artistes, that the front of house staff have to deal.
As I rely upon their goodwill in working a seven, instead of
the usual six, day week when we have a Sunday concert on, and
as some of them had expressed a reluctance to work on evenings
that might attract the same audience, I felt it prudent to
leave a little more time for their memories to fade before
engaging Bauhaus again. I explained this to the gentleman I
spoke to in the Autumn and he fully understood my position.

continued overleaf/..

## THE ROYAL THEATRE & OPERA HOUSE

Always on the lookout for unique venues, something
off the beaten rock 'n' roll track, we were excited when
my father, Jack Haskins, secured us a show at our local
theater. The Royal Theater is a beautiful, highly decorative
Victorian theater dating back to 1884. In the 1930's my
Grandfather had the laborious task of driving Errol Flynn
from the stage door to various late night liaisons, but
Errol was dismissed from the production after he threw a
female stage manager down a stairwell!

As young lads, my parents took David and I there
to witness the great British Christmas tradition, the
Pantomime. Never would I have thought that some fifteen
years later, I would be on that same stage providing quite
a different form of entertainment.

On October 26th, 1980, the day of the show, we managed
to gain access to the prop room where we found just what

I am delighted that Bauhaus are going places.  Far from
us being "too grand" for them, I suspect that it will not
be very long before they are too grand for us.  In the
meantime I wish them every success.

Yours sincerely,

ANTHONY McDONALD
GENERAL MANAGER

we were looking for: an elaborately carved antique throne chair! This would be where "Count Murphy" would hold court as we performed our opening number, "Bela Lugosi's Dead".

The show was a huge success and I can recall all our parents coming backstage after the show to congratulate us. I think it was the first time that they had all met and apparently the Dads spent most of the night propping up the theater bar!

Around a year and a half later, on the group's request, my

Father wrote a letter to the theater manager to inquire about a return performance. The responding letter, displaying a very stiff and formal tone, basically denied us any chance of a heroic return. As deflating as that was, we were highly amused to read the main reason that the manager had chosen to keep us at bay. And I quote, "some of my front of house staff, who are mostly elderly, were dismayed by the behavior of a certain element in the audience. One couple, for example, were reported as copulating in the circle bar."

Performing at The Guildhall in our home town Northampton on May 26th,1979. I recall
being a bit self conscious about wearing my brand new white winkle picker shoes!

GIG INFORMATION.          TOUR:

TOWN: _LEICESTER_          DATE: SATURDAY 24TH APRIL 1982.
        APPROX 50 MILES FROM BIRMINGHAM.

| DETAILS | PHONE |
|---|---|
| PROMOTER: _UNIVERSITY OF LEICESTER STUDENTS UNION_   ENTS — | 0533 553760 |
| _UNIVERSITY ROAD, LEICESTER_   GENERAL — | " 556282 |
| LOCAL CONTACT:   SOCIAL SEC. — SIMON EDMONDS | " " |
| VENUE: QUEENS HALL, STUDENTS UNION BUILDING, UNIVERSITY OF LEICESTER FROM TOWN CENTRE – GRANBY ST – PASS RLY STATION – LONDON ROAD 3RD ON R. – UNIVERSITY RD. – 3RD L. TO HALL | |
| CAPACITY:   1200 | |
| TICKET PRICES:   £ 3 MAX | |
| STAGE DIMENSIONS:   30' × 25' × 4' | |
| PROSCENIUM ARCH:   NO | |
| OVERHEAD CLEARANCE:   18' | |
| FLYING FACILITIES:   2 FLYBARS – ONE FRONT STAGE, ONE MIDSTAGE | |
| BARRICADE:   NO | |
| SOUND WINGS:   2 PORTABLE RISERS 4' HIGH. | |
| MIX POSITION:   REAR OF HALL ON RISER @ 70' APPROX | |
| SPOTLIGHTS:   LOCATIONS ON BALCONY BUT NO SPOTLIGHTS SUPPLIED | |
| POWER SUPPLY:   3 × 60 + 1 × 60 | |
| DISTRIBUTION BOX:   STAGE LEFT | |
| GENERATOR:   —— | |
| LOAD IN/OUT:   THROUGH FRONT DOORS INTO HALL & UP RAMP ONTO STAGE | |
| STAGEHANDS:   6 – 8 | |
| UNION SITUATION:   —— | |
| FORK LIFTS /HOISTS:   —— | |
| PARKING, TRUCKS: ⎫ PARKING AREA NEAR FRONT OF HALL A FEW YARDS  CARS: ⎭   FROM LOAD-IN. | |
| HALL MANAGER:   —— | |
| STAGE MANAGER:   "NEBS" (KEVIN MEADOWS) | |
| ELECTRICIAN:   NICK CREE | |
| EMERGENCY CONTACT:   BRIAN MARCHANT   HOME | 551421 |
| SECURITY:   8 – PROFFESSIONAL | |
| CATERING:   O.K – TAKE·AWAY BROUGHT IN. | |
| LOCAL MUSIC STORES: STREET MUSIC, GOSSOP ST. MUSOS, EVINGTON RD. | 57490/58597 |
| DRESSING ROOMS:   2 DIRECTLY BACK STAGE WITH TOILET FACILITIES | |

Stage call: 12.30     sound check: 4.30     doors open: 7.30.

Show times: 8 – 8.30 HUNTS CAB     9 – 9.25 WET PAINT THEATRE COMPANY
                              10 – 11 BAUHAUS.

OTHER DETAILS:
(e.g.curfew,bye-laws etc.)

BAUHAUS HOTEL: HOLIDAY INN
                    ST. NICHOLAS CIRCLE
                    0533 – 51161

| GIG INFORMATION. | TOUR: | **BAUHAUS** |
|---|---|---|
| TOWN: NORTHAMPTON | DATE: SAT. 20 FEB 1982 | VAT. REG. No. 336 2766 45 |

| DETAILS | PHONE |
|---|---|
| PROMOTER: BAUHAUS c/o. HARRY ISLES 4. BADBY ROAD, NEWNHAM, DAVENTRY NORTHANTS | 03272.5032 (DAVENTRY) |
| LOCAL CONTACT: | |
| VENUE: LINGS FORUM. WESTON FAVELL CENTRE WELLINGBOROUGH ROAD. NORTHAMPTON | 0604 - 402833 (N'TON) |
| CAPACITY: 900. | |
| TICKET PRICES: £2.50 ADVANCE £3.00 DOOR | |
| STAGE DIMENSIONS: 20 x 24 x 4 — STAGEHIRE NOTTINGHAM | 0602 - 55126 |
| PROSCENIUM ARCH: NONE | |
| OVERHEAD CLEARANCE: 40' APPROX | |
| FLYING FACILITIES: NONE EXCEPT METAL ROOF TRUSSES | |
| BARRICADE: — | |
| SOUND WINGS: 8' x 4' x 4' | |
| MIX POSITION: AS REQUIRED (HALL 77' x 110') RISERS AVAILABLE 4 x 4 | |
| SPOTLIGHTS: NONE IN-HOUSE | |
| POWER SUPPLY: 3 x 60 | |
| DISTRIBUTION BOX: BEHIND STAGE ADJACENT TO DRESSING ROOMS. | |
| GENERATOR: — | |
| LOAD IN/OUT: OPPOSITE SIDE OF HALL FROM FOYER OFF PARKING AREA SMALL RAMP—UP&OVER DOORS INTO LOADING AREA APPROX 20 YDS ONTO FLOOR OF HALL - ONE LEVEL | |
| STAGEHANDS: 3 FROM 12 NOON | |
| UNION SITUATION: N.A. | |
| FORK LIFTS /HOISTS: NONE | |
| PARKING, TRUCKS: NEAR LOAD-IN (LOADING DOOR ARE ALSO FIRE EXIT SO TRUCKS MUST NOT OBSTRUCT DURING SHOW) CARS: AREAS NEAR FOYER, LOAD-IN & REAR OF HALL OR ON MAIN WESTON FAVELL CAR PARK | |
| HALL MANAGER: W. McKIM / RECREATION OFFICER — S. ROBERTSON | |
| ~~STAGE MANAGER~~: ADMIN OFFICER & DUTY OFFICER ON NIGHT MR RON DEAN | 0604 - 402833 |
| ELECTRICIAN: AVAILABLE IF REQUESTED IN ADVANCE | |
| EMERGENCY CONTACT: HARRY ISLES | 03272-5032 |
| SECURITY: 10-12 MEN FROM CONCERT SECURITY SERVICES, DUDLEY - ALAN WILLETT IN CHARGE. | 0384 - 59191/21186 |
| CATERING: LINGS CAFETERIA OPEN TO 1.30 P.M. DRINKS VENDING MACHINE IN FOYER CAFE & TAKE-AWAY IN WESTON FAVELL CENTRE TO 6.P.M - ROLLS FROM £14 BAR | |
| LOCAL MUSIC STORES: FUNKSHUN — 156/166 WELLINGBOROUGH RD. ALANS - 7. KETTERING RD, ABINGTON SQ. PETER GRAY 212A WELLINGBOROUGH RD. | 0604 - 34100 " 31129 " 31211 |
| DRESSING ROOMS: 2 CHANGING ROOMS WITH SHOWERS 2 TOILETS BUT NO MIRRORS TO REAR OF STAGE. | |

STAGE BUILDING - 9. A.M.

Stage call: 12. NOON   sound check: 4.30 P.M.   doors open: 7.0 P.M.

Show times: GENE LOVES JEZEBEL 7.30 - 8.05. "ROYSTON" (ILLUSIONIST) 8.10 - 8.20
BAUHAUS - 8.50 - 9.50

OTHER DETAILS: ————> SEE LINGS FORUM CONDITIONS OF HIRE
(e.g.curfew,bye-laws etc.) AVAILABLE FROM MANAGER.

LINGS FORUM STAFF ON DUTY — DUTY OFFICER - RON DEAN
2 BAR STAFF
1 RECEPTIONIST
2 RECREATION ASSISTANTS.

# B A U H A U S
## R.          E.          M.

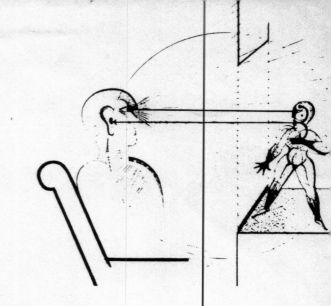

# T H U R S.
## 2     6     $5.

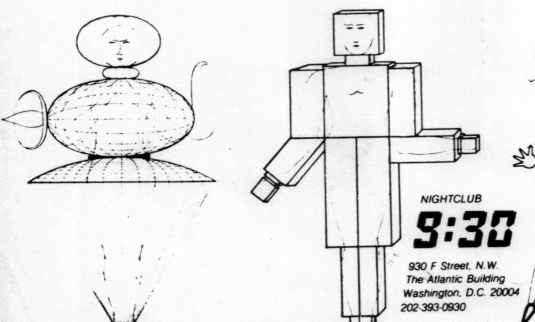

NIGHTCLUB
## 9:30

930 F Street, N.W.
The Atlantic Building
Washington, D.C. 20004
202-393-0930

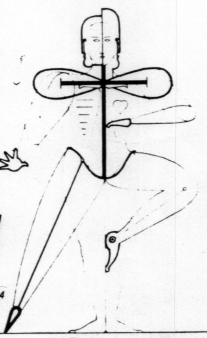

The Story Starts Here →

April 3rd or 4th? 1980 Bauhaus supporting Gary Glitter - Lyceum

I went with a couple of friends to see Gary Glitter mainly + also to see Bauhaus as a friend said they were old Adam + the Antz fans + I was into the Antz at the time. I was watching from the dance floor with a friend - pretty sure they did Double Dare first + we both thought they were great. Halfway through they did "Telegram Sam" + I was down the front + hooked.

During either this gig or the next (supporting Magazine) I met Amanda for the second time + asked her out (I met her at the Banshees at the Music Machine) I went out with her for the next 18 months - so my one serious girlfriend started out at a Bauhaus gig - how romantic.

May 1st 1980 Bauhaus supporting Magazine - Lyceum
It was a friends birthday + he was being driven to see Magazine I cadged a lift to see ~~Magazine~~ Bauhaus

May 10th 1980 Bauhaus supporting Magazine - Guildford
Local gig so I went up to see them Crisis were on first then Bauhaus, The Whitton punks were there with Water Pistol, ~~~~ that were squirted at Murphy, he offered one up on the stage he shit out, Murphy threw his strobe into the rather small audience it hit a girl - the only person in the place with Bauhaus on her jacket.

October 31st 1980 University of London -
Packed out gig I went with a mate Chris who was also into

a great gig.

~~~~ ~~~~ Tour with Birthday Party

Nottingham - Rock City. June 19th 1981
Went with Amanda - spent all night after gig in a doorway - fucking freezing.

Aylesbury - Friars June 20th 1981
Saw Dave outside gig, asked iff he remembered about guest list he said no but got us in. Got in an argument with about 6 Skinheads who were shouting when power failed I told them to shut up stayed in a well expensive hotel I payed for Amanda ₤24 I think.

Brighton - Jenkinsons June 21st 1981
I was down the front with Amanda, a load of Rockabillys started a fight. Stayed at Sussex University? After an argument with Amanda that night we split up, but remained 'friends' although only because I thought we'd get back together.

Reading - Not the university ~~cause~~ Top Rank?
Doors opened late as tyres slashed night before, had to take my boots off went down the front and smashed barriers down when Pete said) in my socks spent rest of gig on side of stage. Graham + Pete had a fight onstage. I went with Chris in his car he stopped going around this time + got into 'U2'

Lyceum London June 25th 1981
Packed out went down the front Amanda was annoyed as I went 'mad' + accidently punched her friend Racheal in the mouth

them - he used to like the Antz - During "God in An Alcove" (the fast bit) we went mad down the front (the first time of many in that part of the song) + Chris pulled the arm off my leather jacket which had Siouxsie on the back - Bauhaus written on the arm + collar.

? 20th 1980 - Rock Garden - London
    Supposedly a secret gig that was advertised by mistake, went all over London trying to get a ticket with Amanda. Eventually got one at the Rock Garden persuaded the cashier to sell us 2 (she was supposed to be saving them for when the doors opened) Christmas party with 'Fanny Cradock' supporting (back of Dark Entries cover), I swung on a bar + kicked Amanda's ex boyfriend in the head, Amanda said Murphy gave me a dirty look.

17th December 1980 - Venue London.
    Great gig - quite empty went with Amanda
Got a new Leather + painted the back with the design from Venue poster - took 7 hrs.
30th March 1981 - Heaven London
        as above but packed out

22nd May 1981 - Architects Association.
    Secret gig £10 to get in. Asked to see band, they tried to get us in for £5 if we only watched Bauhaus but no luck. I said I'd come from Walton + Harry said that wasn't very far to come. They said they'd put us on the list for Aylesbury. Amanda + I sneaked in downstairs + hid in the toilets for 2 hrs. Cleaners found us + thought something rude was happening, they didn't give us away though. When the doors opened we went in the bar about 12. Wog (a friend) + couple more turned up - apparently paying £2 to get in

2 nights Edinburgh Playhouse -
    Arranged my summer holidays at work to coincide,
took out £200 loan to pay for the trip went up on train with
Amanda, stayed in EXPENSIVE hotel off Princess street.

Stafford Bingley Hall -
    Caught train downthere, stayed in b+b. couldn't stay for
2nd night of Festival - Uk Decay were playing as I had work.
    Split up with Amanda completley after this gig, she stopped seeing
September 26th Leeds Queens Hall 'daze of future Past'-
    Queing up to get in  Scapy (Now Guitarist with Under 2 flags),
Tim (Bouncer at 100 club), Craig (Sex Gangs ex manager now Sunglasses
after Dark's manager) + I ran about 13 Northerners who had
knives as they calledus Cockney cunts. After gig stayedin Hall on
floor with Racheal (punched in the mouth at Lyceum) whom I started
seeing from then.

    MASK   TOUR.- Sent off For 2 tickets for every gig I went to.

October 22nd 1981 Reading University.-
    Arrived at Reading Station about 7, with Weg+2 others
after they demonstrated outside Spanish Embassy on behalf of
    Basque seperatists for money. I refused to join in but it was
still funny. Met Welshman for fial time as we shared a
taxi up there. We stayed on some girls floor, left 5 in
morning so her parents wouldn't find us. Went straight to work

Norwich University October 26th 1981
went with some girl  we were the only people on coach

## 37 ADAMS AVENUE

In 1980 we decided it would be a good idea to all live under the same roof, namely 37 Adams Avenue in Northampton, a terraced house very similar to the one that The Beatles lived in in the film, "Help." The difference being that ours wasn't four houses knocked into one, with all the latest fab, mod, luxurious interior design aspects. On the contrary, ours was cold, damp, grimy and haunted!. Daniel lived in the tiny attic room. He painted the walls and ceiling a dark grey and the floorboards black. He covered the floor with thick plastic sheeting as he was too impatient to allow the paint to dry before he moved in. In the two years that we lived there it never completely dried!

We were all on the dole at the time and so to avoid the stigma and guilt, I looked upon the weekly payments as an arts grant! However, it provided a very meager existence. Fine cuisine was not our strong point and with our limited budget, we all existed on a bland diet of rice and over cooked vegetables. Instead of storing our rubbish outside we used the larder instead. Consequently a family of rats moved in. We never used the living room as it had a very, very negative energy, and we were convinced that it was haunted by the ghost of some macabre crime. In an attempt to rectify this, we painted the entire room with a brighter color, but it still retained the atmosphere of a portal to Hell. Another idea to make it more inviting and cosy was to install wall to wall carpeting over the bare unfinished, floorboards. We asked our eccentric landlord if he could provide such but he suggested that a small rug would be a much better choice. He was obviously avoiding the expense and when we pressed him for the reason, he reasoned, in his thick Irish brogue; "When you lads have your parties, and you have too much to drink, you will need the space between the rug and the wall, to throw up in!"

Our friend's, John Barraclough and Glenn Campling lived next door but one, however, our other neighbours were not so friendly. The neighbour to the right of us for example was a large burly chap with a family of four and a very short fuse. He would be constantly yelling and banging on the partition wall for us to;" turn that bloody racket down!" On the occasions when the racket was not turned down, which were many, there would be a very loud banging on the front door. We were all terrified that he was going to kill us so no one was in a real hurry to greet him.

Our neighbour on the other side was an extremely nosey old aged pensioner. Whenever somebody came to our door she would immediately appear with a duster and proceed to clean her doorstep so that she could eavesdrop on our conversation. One day Daniel and I decided to play a prank on her. I came to the door in some sort of disguise and we both embarked on a fictitious conversation. Right on cue she came outside and began polishing her door frame. Our conversation was based around some anarchic plot to blow up the Queen in Buckingham Palace or some such crazy thing. Whispering very loudly, I inquired to Daniel if everything was ready and he assured me not to worry and that all the explosives were all primed and ready to go in our basement! I glanced in her direction to witness a look of concealed horror on her face. Stifling laughter, our conversation reached ludicrous heights, dropping words like "ballistic missiles" and "nuclear warheads". Eventually, the poor old lady, brimming with anxiety, was polishing the paintwork with such intensity that it began flaking off! I'm surprised that we weren't paid a visit from Scotland Yard, but those were happily more innocent times.

BAUHAUS RECORDING & TOURING SCHEDULE, MAY & JUNE 1981.

May 5th.-9th. (5 days, Tues-Sat.)                 Recording

May 18th- 22nd (5 days, Mon-Fri. )                    "

June 1st- 5th  (5 days, Mon-Fri.)                     "

June 8th-12th  (5 days, Mon-Fri.)                     "

The above dates have been booked at: PLAYGROUND STUDIO
                                     115-123, Bayham Street
                                     London NW1.
                                     Phone 01-267 7200

Engineer- Mike Hedges
Working hours are flexible and you can start and finish more or less
when you like but you should average at least 10 hours per day to make
the most economical use of the studio.
     Some time has been held at Jam Studio in case you find that Playground
does not suit you but it is more expensive and the sessions are not
arranged inthe way you want, you would also have to stick to a 1 p.m. to
midnight schedule.
ACCOMODATION - One twin room with bath & colour T.V. has been reserved
for the nights of 5th-8th and this willbe booked for subsequent weeks if
it proves satisfactory.
                    Grand Hotel
                    126, Southampton Row, WC1. phone 01-405 2006
Full English breakfast is included in the room charge.


June 18th. LIVERPOOL, Royal Court Theatre.    Bauhaus solo gig

     19th.  NOTTINGHAM, Rock City             "       "    "

     20th.  AYLESBURY, Friars Club            "       "    "

     21st.  OFF

     22nd.  OFF

     23rd.  GLASGOW, Tiffany's          .    Equal billing with Killing Joke.

     24th.  OFF

     25th.  BRADFORD, Tiffany's             "       "       "    "        "

     26th.  NEWCASTLE, Mayfair             "       "      "    "         "

     27th.  OFF

     28th.  Portsmouth, Locarno            "       "       "   "         "

     29th.  T.B.A. or OFF

     30th.  Hammersmith, Palais            "       "        "    "       "

N.B. These dates are not yet confirmed so there may be some changes, there
is a possibility of Brighton on 21st. or 29th. and a date in the midlands
on 27th.
Killing Joke are on tour solo from June 15th. and would link up with us
in Glasgow.
"Altered Images" are a possible supporting act for the joint dates or the
German band D.A.F.

Photo session by Stella Watts at Playground Studios during the recording of Mask

infO phone NORTHAMPTON ████ write ████ Duston Northampton

12" single **BeLA Lugosi's dead + boys**

SMALL WONDER RECORDS

From left to right; Pete Murphy, Graham Bentley and Daniel Ash attempting to recreate England's famous 1966 world cup victory, whilst on tour somewhere in Italy.

## IGGY POP

The stunning skyline of Manhattan revealed itself through a flickering strobe effect of the 59th Street bridge. Our first tour of The USA! After landing at LaGuardia we were now en route into the city, drinking in the sights and smells of Manhattan, and feeling every pothole in the well worn roads. Steam belched from the manhole covers and the rattle of the subway trains, combined with the car horns and sirens, blended together to form an anarchic avant-garde concerto. The cab eventually pulled up to the The Iroquois Hotel, (where all the bands stayed) on West 44th Street and where, as we discovered on entering our room, the unfortunate guests are outnumbered by an army of resident cockroaches!

After our tour manager Peter Kent had paid the cab driver, we dragged our luggage to the front desk to check in. While Peter was dealing with our reservation, I slipped away to check out the music drifting from the hotel bar. I poked my head around the corner and, as my eyes became accustomed to the dark surroundings, I made out an ancient crooner singing an old standard, seemingly for the millionth time. This charming and run down bar would be the stage for a couple of very exciting meetings.

Later that evening, we were all getting ready to go clubbing. New York City! The Big Apple! The energy of the city was palpable as a myriad of discordant sounds invaded our cramped quarters. We were all fired up and excited to hit the town. That is, all but one of us. Daniel had decided to have a quiet night in! It being an oxymoron, we couldn't get our heads round that idea. But no degree of persuasion could change his plans, so we eventually set off without him.

What we didn't know was that his evening in would trump ours by a massive degree! Daniel told us that soon after we left he decided to grab a quiet drink in the hotel bar. After ordering a Jack and Coke, to his astonishment, in walks no other than Iggy Pop, Glen Matlock and Mick Ronson! He literally couldn't believe what his eyes were seeing. After a while, a woman who was with Iggy came over to chat with Daniel. She told him that she had noticed him glancing towards them several times, and inquired if he was a fan. He told her that Mick and Iggy were two of his all-time heroes but that he didn't want to bother them. She reassured Daniel that it would be fine to meet them and eventually persuaded him to join them. Clocking the British accent, Iggy asked Daniel what he was doing in New York, and so he told him about our upcoming shows. After a couple of drinks, Iggy asked Daniel if he wanted to come up to his room where they were going to have a little party. After considering this invitation for one nanosecond, Daniel accepted and off they went.

Upstairs, drinks were fixed and Daniel sat fascinated as Iggy and Mick sparred back and forth about whose production skills were better, and other related topics. It was all conducted in an amiable way, and Daniel could tell that they were best friends.

As the night proceeded Iggy asked Daniel where he could hear our music and Daniel remembered that he had a copy of our single, "Terror Couple Kill Colonel", in our room. Iggy asked him to go get it and Daniel dutifully complied. Eventually, as with all good things, the party came to an end and Daniel returned to our room. As he sat alone, trying to process the surreal nature of the night's events, the three inebriated amigos returned from their conquest of Manhattan's underground club scene. As we excitedly recounted the night's events, Daniel listened patiently, waiting to reveal his unbelievable story. Of course we were all astonished and then wished that we had also stayed in for "a quiet night".

The following afternoon we all decided to visit the bar in the hopes that Iggy would be there. As we entered, our eyes fell upon the familiar face of a solitary figure sitting at the bar. Eying our prize, we all suddenly became very thirsty and duly sat down at the bar to order a round of drinks. Daniel said hi to his new found pal and introduced the rest of us as we attempted to appear cool and nonchalant. I then heard that old familiar languid baritone drawl of the man himself, "So this is the rest of the band, eh?" We responded in the affirmative and invited him to our show that night, at Tier 3 and Danceteria, one week later. He told us that he was leaving town that night but would try to make it to the latter. After some small talk he informed us that he had to get back upstairs to his room as Mick Ronson was waiting for him. We inquired if it might be at all possible to tag along. He gave us a wry smile and said his goodbyes.

Fast forward six days and we are now on stage playing to a packed house at Danceteria. A few numbers in and I hear a heckler yelling loudly above the music and can hear Peter giving back as good as he's getting. As Peter moved to the right I looked for the heckler and saw a guy jostling about down the front wearing a motorcycle jacket. It was Iggy Pop! The gig continued with Iggy and Pete launching verbal missiles at each other throughout our set. Afterwards, Iggy came backstage and congratulated us on a great show! He explained that he had a driver outside, and told him he'd only be about ten minutes, but as we were so good he decided to stay the entire set. I respectfully asked if I could take a shot of him and Peter on my new Canon camera and Iggy obliged. We exchanged some more banter and then Iggy announced that he was off to some "dark and dangerous S&M club," and then disappeared into the night.

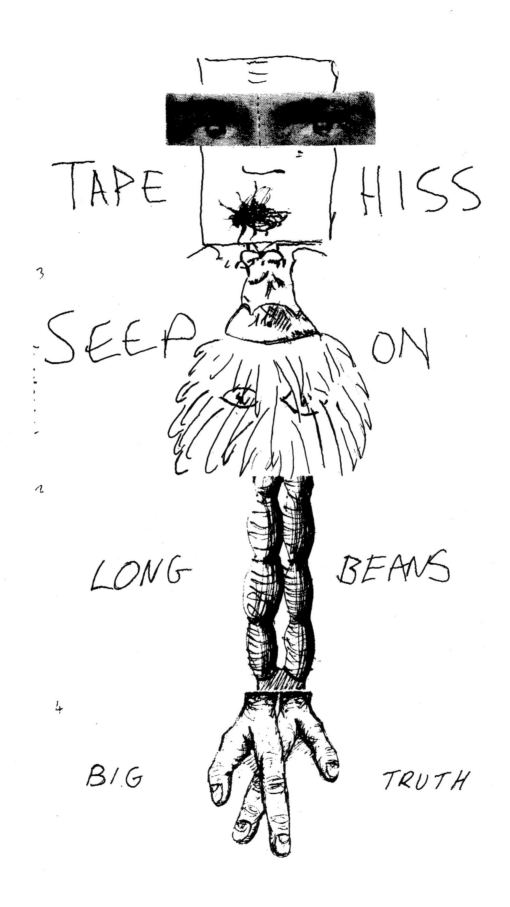

TAPE HISS

SEEP ON

LONG BEANS

BIG TRUTH

D. ASH

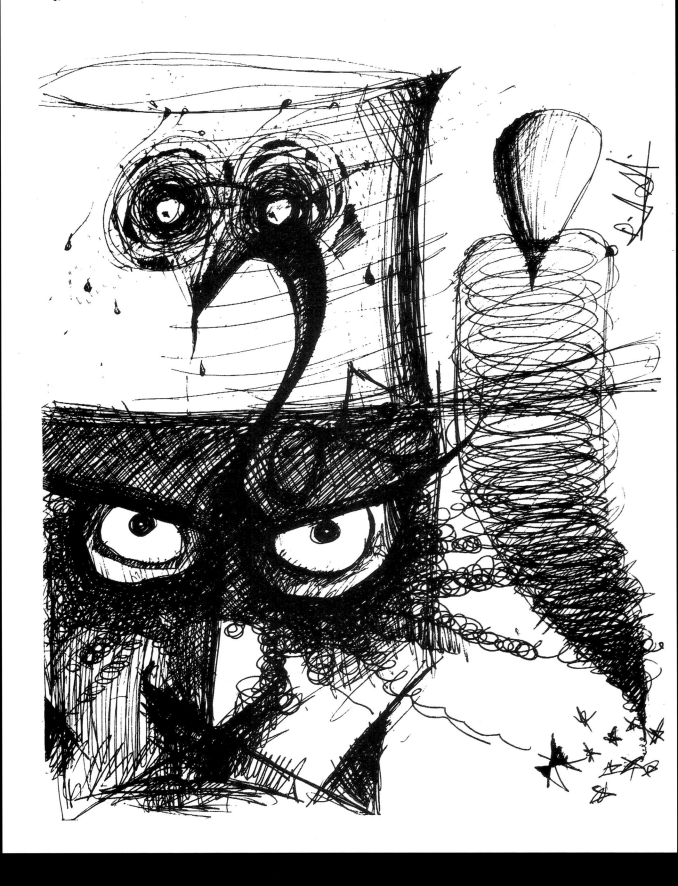

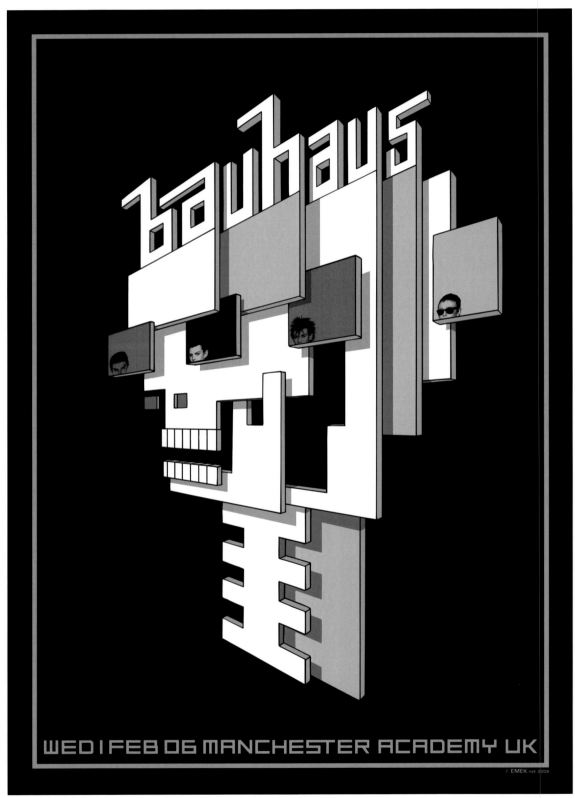

Poster Design: Emek X

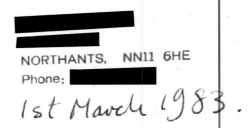

**BAUHAUS**
VAT. REG. No. 336 2766 45

NORTHANTS, NN11 6HE
Phone: ▮▮▮▮▮▮

1st March 1983.

Dear Mr. Davis,

thankyou for your letter, I apologise for not replying sooner but there always seems to be more things to fit into the day than I have time for. I will try to get you an up to date press kit next time I'm at Beggars Banquet, in the meantime here is a brief outline of the U.S. tour.

This was the first U.S. tour for nearly 2 years, the previous one having been from Feb to March 1981; it was also the first U.S. tour supported by an American record company, Beggars Banquet having only last summer completed a licencing deal with A&M. Bauhaus records were only available as imports prior to the release of the last album. The main difference this made to the tour was that we could lose far £ more money than on our last tour and we had properly organised press coverage. Bauhaus are still at the stage where foreign tours are a purely promotional exercise in that costs far exceed earnings and the best one can do even in the more accessible market of Europe is to break even. It may surprise you to learn that it was not until our last British tour in October that we could ever show a profit from a tour in this country.

But to return to the U.S. tour, we started off on the East Coast, doing club dates in Long Island, Philadelphia, Baltimore, Trenton & Boston as well as several gigs in the New York area. The response to the band was generally good but some of the places we played were so small that it was a very depressing experience for the band after having just completed a sell-out U.K. tour to find themselves playing to audiences as small as two hundred people. We did two dates in Canada, at Montreal & Toronto where we sold out venues holding about 500, but we have always been stronger in Canada than the U.S. and have had record licences there for a couple of years. On to Detroit and Chicago, where we played two good gigs, and then Minneapolis which was very small again. From here we flew to the West Coast, the first time for the band. for three nights at the Roxy in Los Angeles. Here the response was very encouraging, we sold out the first two nights and almost the third as well as doing some valuable press and radio promotion set up by A & M records who are based in L.A. The tour finished in ~~Berkeley~~ San Francisco with two gigs, the first in the town centre was a sell-out in a large club but the second in a smaller club in Berkely was less good both in terms of audience response & attendance.

Since ~~the~~ Christmas the band have been kept busy with recording sessions both for the next single, due out on March 18th or 25th, and for a David Jensen show. The latter was recorded a couple of weeks ago and should be going out on the air in the next few weeks. There was also a Top of the Pops appearance a few weeks ago with the "Lagartija Nick" single which went straight down from 44 to 46 immediately after. The next single is

to have a promotional video to support it
and the arrangements for the shooting of
this are currently taking up quite a bit of time.
Peter Murphy has been doing a new Maxell
Tape ad. for T.V. and ~~Peter~~ David & Danny
have both been spending time on individual
recording activities. The Band will be starting
their next L.P. on March 21st and then
will keep them busy for a month with
a break in early April for a short trip to
France to play at the Bourges Festival, a
club in Lyon and the "Palace" in Paris. A
trip to Japan is in the pipeline for the end of
May with a possibility of some dates in other
exotic places on the way. The New
album will be released in mid June to
coincide with this years U.K tour, leaving the
Autumn clear for European dates, an area
we have neglected (apart from an Italian
tour last year) for almost 2 years.
    I realise this is a very sketchy account of
Bauhaus's activities, but I would need to write
at least a few thousand words more to cover
things properly. If you would like more details
or clarification of anything please phone me
                        Yours Harry Isles.

HARRY ISLES.

71

Drawing that I made depicting my first impressions of Manhattan. It would appear that I found it all too overwhelming.

STEREO
8297

242
NEW WAVE

TOP
ALBUM

bauhaus
THE SKY'S GONE OUT

ALIF 4 AD

STEREO
□□ DOLBY SYSTEM

BAUHAUS
THE SKY'S GONE OUT

LOWDOWN

bauhaus
the sky's gone out

B A U H A U S

BURNING FROM THE INSIDE

LOWDOWN
LOW
PRICE
SPECIAL

B A U H A U S

SWING THE HEARTACHE
THE BBC SESSIONS

GOLDEN
GL

STEREO
GL 1452

BAUHAUS
BURNING FROM THE INSIDE

NEW WAVE
GROUP

C-60 C-60 C-60

Melodies
M - 10133

BAUHAUS
THE SKY'S GONE OUT
VOL. 1

bauhaus
the sky's gone out

NEW WAVE

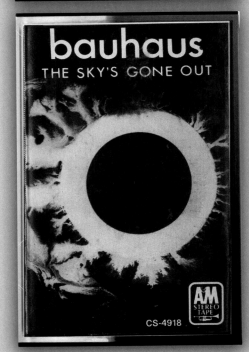

bauhaus
THE SKY'S GONE OUT

A&M
STEREO
TAPE

CS-4918

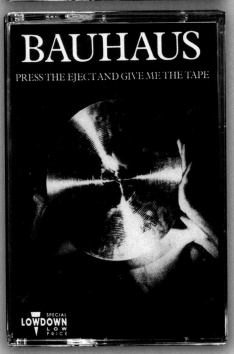

BAUHAUS
PRESS THE EJECT AND GIVE ME THE TAPE

LOWDOWN
LOW
PRICE
SPECIAL

BAUHAUS
MASK

BAUHAUS

Beggars
Banquet

BAUHAUS
MASK

BAUHAUS

Beggars Banquet

BAUHAUS
THE SINGLES
1981-1983

BAUHAUS
THE SINGLES

1981-1983

DOLBY SYSTEM

Double Play Tape
Includes 2 Albums

BAUHAUS

The Sky's Gone Out

Press The Eject And Give Me The Tape

RECORDED LIVE IN LIVERPOOL AND LONDON

Beggars Banquet

BAUHAUS
IN THE FLAT FIELD

CrO₂ Chromedioxide Cassette

bauhaus

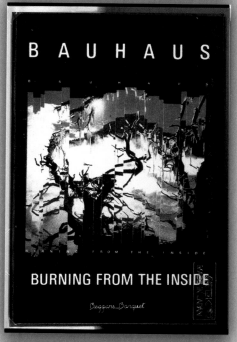

B A U H A U S

BURNING FROM THE INSIDE

Beggars Banquet

B A U H A U S

£5
UNDER A FIVER

SWING THE HEARTACHE
THE BBC SESSIONS

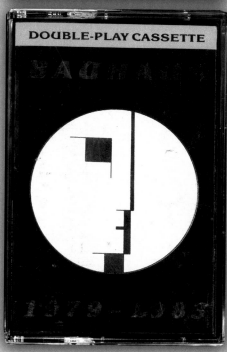

DOUBLE-PLAY CASSETTE

BAUHAUS

Melodies
M-10134

BAUHUS
PLAY VERY LOUD VOL. 2

bauhaus

NEW WAVE

Photo: Howard Rosenberg

## IN THE FLATFIELD

Southern Studios in Wood Green London was owned by a reclusive maverick by the name of John Loder. The control room was in a converted garage and the recording room was the front room of the adjoining terraced house. In this rather unusual setting in the summer of 1980, we recorded our first LP, "In The Flat Field".

The recording room had a baby grand piano that we used to good effect on the song entitled "Nerves". Not only in the conventional way of playing the keys, but also by scraping all manner of metallic objects, stolen from his kitchen, over the strings. Fortunately, the engineer, Tony Cook, seemed to encourage this type of spontaneous avant-garde behavior. However, Sue, the wife of John, was probably of a different persuasion. Not only was all her kitchenware inside the piano, but her vacuum cleaner was also otherwise employed. Her patience was further tested when all the neighbours began complaining about an extremely loud banging noise. To create a dynamic percussive effect for the song, "Nerves" I decided to slam the kitchen door as hard as my skinny arms could manage. This operation was quickly aborted when Sue, to her dismay, discovered a large crack in the kitchen wall.

There is one particular experience whilst recording that LP that is burned into my mind. During the mixing of "Stigmata Martyr", we decided that it needed another element and came upon the idea of using choral music to play all the way through the song. One of us was sent on a mission to procure some Christian choral music, and duly returned with a vinyl LP. I believe we tried it playing forwards at first, but it just didn't work at all. "What about playing it backwards?", one of us suggested. To achieve this effect, John removed the two inch reel of tape, placed it on the machine backwards, so that it played everything back to front. Then he recorded the choir music to the tape. After reversing the entire process, so that we were listening to the song in the normal fashion, the choir music played back in reverse.

As soon as he started rolling the tape, the results were astonishing... in more ways than one! It sounded perfect! Very dark and very spooky! However after about ten seconds, Tony began experiencing technical problems. Certain tracks were not playing back although he could see the meters moving. Then the playback machine just stopped! We all looked at each other with concern and began to ponder the possible consequences of what happens when one reverses Christian music. Tony pressed play and the song began running again but then the studio lights started flickering on and off! At this point we were all beginning to feel seriously uneasy. Tony informed us that nothing had ever happened like this in all the years he had been working at the studio and he had no explanation. We decided to take a break, get out of the control room sharpish, and return later, once the mischievous spirits had had their fun.

(Opposite) Peter and David at Southern Studios recording the dual piano part for the song entitled Nerves from our first LP, *In The Flatfield* / Photo by Kevin Haskins

Daniel using the piano to tune his saxophone before recording his part on the song entitled, "Dive", from our first LP, *In The Flatfield*

Kevin working on achieving the perfect drum sounds at the beginning of the recording sessions for our fist LP, entitled, *In The Flatfield*

# Gothick as a brick

**BAUHAUS**
**In The Flat Field (4AD)**

CROSSOVERS — those points where two subcultures mingle and merge — are interesting to observe, but generally not a lot of fun to listen to, the hybrid possibilities being limited and rigidly predetermined.

At the moment, we're in the throes of a hard punk/moderne monochrome crossover, with bands like Killing Joke, Bauhaus and (possibly) ClockDVA on the verge of tapping a potentially massive market opened up by the earlier efforts of such as Siouxsie And The Banshees, Adam And The Ants, and even Joy Division. To these ears, there's a palpable qualitative difference between these two groups of groups, as there is between the Sex Pistols and the Cockney Rejects — something like the difference between art and artifice, but not quite.

'In The Flat Field' is the first Bauhaus album, and I wouldn't be at all surprised to see it storming up the "alternative" charts, at the very least. It oughtn't to.

I must admit to a passing liking for their three singles — I was even prepared to overlook their taking their name in vain (I mean, what the hell has their Gothick-Romantick pseudo-decadence got to do with the stripped, no-nonsense principles of the Bauhaus?) — but over the length of an album, their limitations and endless pretence are just too much to take.

'In The Flat Field' is nine meaningless moans and flails bereft of even the most cursory contour of interest, a record which deserves all the damning adjectives usually levelled at grim-faced "modernists". It's doom for doom's sake, that most miserable of cudgels with which to clout your consciousness.

If nothing else, this serves to shed some light on the punk/moderne crossover audience, a group of people who, in their taste for excessive tribal plumage and dismal, doom-laden music, are more closely related to the heavy-metal hordes than they'd like to believe. And Bauhaus are nothing more than a hip Black Sabbath. Really.

Personally, I couldn't give a toss, not feeling much affinity with many other human beings in general, and certainly not with any tribal group. I just wish the music on this record had been more *interesting,* more *original,* and less reliant on the obvious strokes.

Ah well. Their singles showed Bauhaus weren't devoid of an idea or two; this album shows they've used them both up.

**Andy Gill**

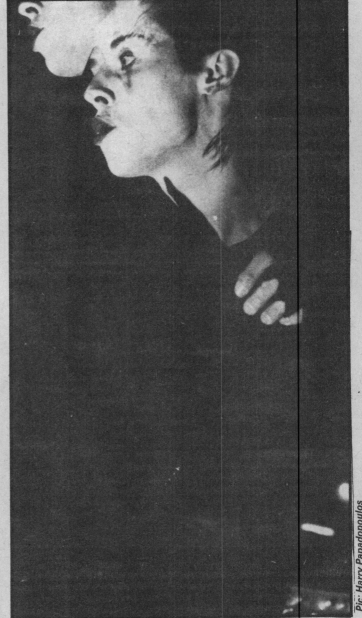

Pic: Harry Papadopoulos

*Bauhaus present the two-headed look — moderne chic for after the bomb.*

# BAUHAUS

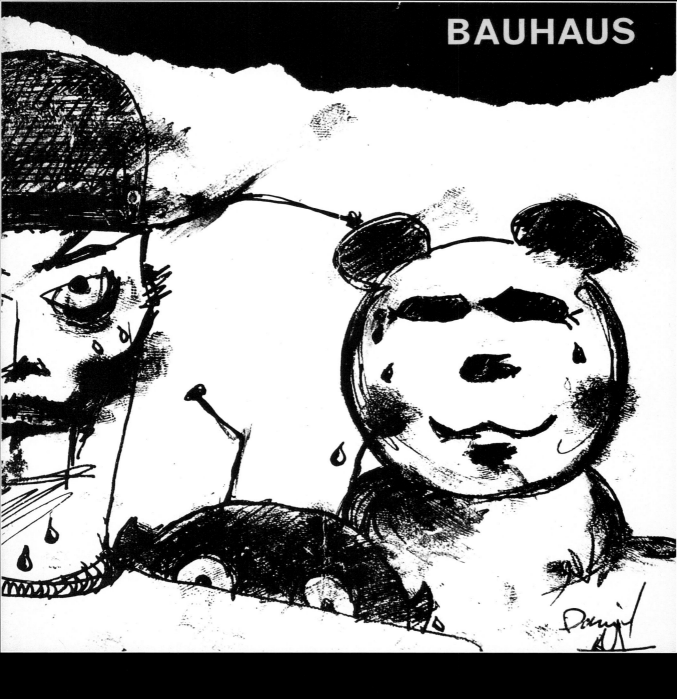

BAUHAUS

Mask / Beggars Banquet / 1981

The Sky's Gone Out / Beggars Banquet / 1982

B A U H A U S

B U R N I N G   F R O M   T H E   I N S I D E

Burning From The Inside / Beggars Banquet / 1983

# bauhaus

Bela Lugosi's dead

*bauhaus*

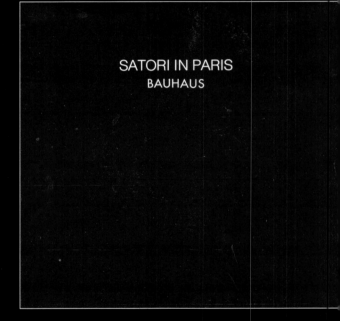

SATORI IN PARIS
BAUHAUS

# BAUHAUS

the
passion of lovers

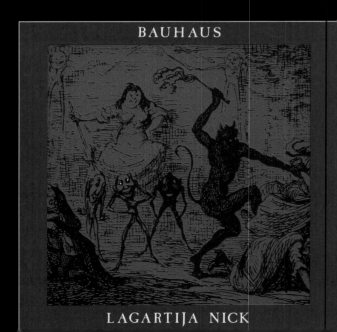

BAUHAUS

LAGARTIJA NICK

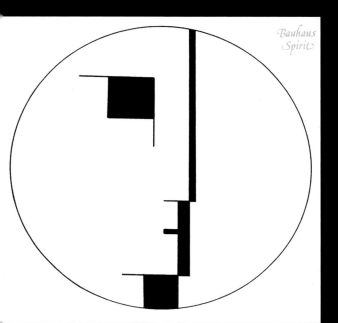

BAUHAUS
kick in the eye
searching for satori e.p

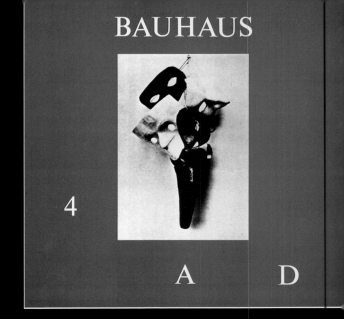

BAUHAUS

4

A          D

BAUHAUS
1979 1983

1979 1983

DOUBLE DARE          IN THE FLAT FIELD          DARK ENTRIES          STIGMATA MARTYR          BELA LUGOSI'S DEAD
TELEGRAM SAM   ST. VITUS DANCE   A SPY IN THE CAB   TERROR COUPLE KILL COLONEL   THE PASSION OF LOVERS   MASK

**bauhaus**
live in the studio 1979

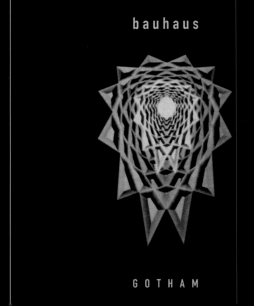

bauhaus

GOTHAM

BAUHAUS

GO AWAY WHITE

## PARANOIA PARANOIA

Founded by Brothers Kingsley and Charles Ward in 1963, Rockfield Studios in Monmouth, Wales became the world's first residential studio. Formerly a farm, it became a premier world class studio where the likes of Hawkwind, Queen, Adam and the Ants, The Damned, Iggy Pop, The Stranglers, Robert Plant, Oasis, Paul Weller, XTC, New Order, Suede, Pixies and The Cure all made some of their finest recordings.

We had been here before to tape the Spirit single and again to record our third LP The Sky's Gone Out which actually began on my 22nd Birthday, but we came back again in September to record a new single; Silent Hedges. As always, we had enlisted the assistance of Derek Tompkins who engineered our first iconic single, Bela Lugosi's Dead. Derek chose the only bedroom on the ground floor of the house that we were staying in which may have been an error of judgement as we were prone to stay up all hours after each session, blasting music well in to the night, and playing pool adjacent to his lodgings. Still, somehow he was usually able to sleep through the racket and goings on. After a long days' work and in order to relax we had a penchant for imbibing in what we termed as "whacky backy" and usually listening to late Beatles and a good smattering of dub reggae from the likes of Mikey Dread, Tapper Zukie and Lee Scratch Perry.

Stoned out of our brains, we happened on the idea of trying to scare Derek and record the proceedings on Glenn Campling's boom box. We all set off out of the back door to skirt around the house to arrive at Derek's window, where we proceeded to make ghost noises and rattle on his window. Upon

hearing, "what the bloody hells going on?" emanating from Derek's abode, we all sped off back in to the house, Daniel began singing "Paranoia, Paranoia Da Da Da Da Da..." Once inside we carried on singing and then someone started a frantic game of pool... you can hear the balls smashing about on the pool table on the recording. The following evening, after Derek had retired for a hopefully peaceful night, we came upon the idea of using the recording for a "dub mix". Many bands around that time, influenced by the reggae culture that infused their teenage years, would make dub mixes, usually of their A sides. As we had just taped "Silent Hedges" we used that for the template and transferred the boom box recording on to the multitrack tape. The engineer, Neil Black, had set up a bunch of delays for us to utilize, we all took our places at the desk. As the tape rolled we would mute and then un-mute certain tracks and bring in delays on others. Sometimes these dub mixes took us several hours to get right, as it was a very spontaneous and organic process. And that is how the song, Paranoia Paranoia was born. One lovely unexpected element is the pedal steel guitar right at the end. Because our record company was prone to penny pinching, instead of paying for brand new multi-track tapes, they elected for us to use previously used ones. Normally the prior recordings were completely wiped, however a small snippet of a pedal steel guitar was left on one track of the tape. It added an unexpected and whimsical end to the final mix, we thought that its incongruous nature was very Bauhaus! Silent Hedges was eventually dropped as a single release in favour of Ziggy Stardust. The aborted artwork idea by David J can be seen above.

VERA

**bauhaus**

VOORPROGRAMMA ZEV

23 NOVEMBER
ZAAL OPEN: 21.00 UUR
ENTREE: ƒ 6,    VOORVERKOOP:
N.l. :ƒ 7,50  ELPEE, GROEF, CIRKEL

# OUT NOW

## DARK ENTRIES

**SINGLE ON 4AD RECORDS**

PIC SLEEVE

ORDER FROM WEA

BEG 37

# bauhaus

Dear Sirs

We refer to the single 45 rpm record which you have agreed to record and deliver to us consisting of the "A" side entitled "DARK ENTRIES        " and "B" side entitled " UNTITLED        " ("the Single")   We also refer to the recording agreement between yourselves and Beggars Banquet Records Limited ("Records") attached to this letter ("the Agreement")   In consideration of the sum of one pound (£1) which we have paid you on signature hereof (receipt of which you hereby acknowledge) you hereby grant and assign to us the same rights in the Single as you grant to Records in respect of masters as defined in the Agreement   You agree to pay all recording costs in connection with the Single and to indemnify us in respect of all such payments  (We agree to pay the cost of recording the Single which shall be recoupable from royalties otherwise payable to you hereunder)   We shall pay to you royalties in respect of sales of the Single calculated and paid at the rate and in accordance with the provisions of the Agreement for masters delivered to Records in the Initial Period   You further grant to us the unrestricted right to exploit your name biography and likeness in connection with promotion and sale of the Single   We shall have the right within three months after the release of the Single to call upon you to record and deliver to us either a second single or a long-playing album of your performances ("the Second Record") and all the provisions hereof in respect of the Single shall apply to the Second Record save that

we shall pay the cost of recording the Second Record by way of an advance against royalties payable to you hereunder

In consideration of the payment to you by Records of one pound (£1) receipt of which you hereby acknowledge you hereby agree that Records shall have the right to give notice to you bringing the Agreement into effect at any time within three calendar months after release of the Second Record in the UK and on giving such notice the Agreement shall come into full force and effect and the term thereof shall commence as of the date of such notice

It is agreed for the avoidance of doubt that if the Agreement takes effect neither the Single nor the Second Record shall be treated as being in fulfilment or part fulfilment of the product commitment mentioned in the Agreement and if the Agreement comes into effect you agree to execute such further documents as we or Records may reasonably require including such inducement letters as Record's distributor may require

Would you please sign below where indicated to show your acceptance of these terms

Yours faithfully                              Accepted and Agreed


.............................                 .............................
for and on behalf of
Beggars Banquet Limited
trading as AXIS RECORDS

# DARK ENTRIES

Peter Kent was on the phone to Geoff Travis at Rough Trade records and, by chance, Geoff was playing a demo cassette from a band that he had recently received in the mail. Peters ears pricked up and immediately inquired about the music that was playing in the background. Geoff told him that it was a band called Bauhaus and that he didn't feel the music was a good fit with the label's aesthetic. Within a few days Peter Kent was on a train to Northampton to meet with us.

Under the larger umbrella of Beggars Banquet Records, Peter ran a label together with Ivo Watts - Russell called Axis Records, which soon had to change its name to 4AD when it was brought to their attention that another label was already using the same name. Peter was a tall, elegant man with a gentle disposition, whilst Ivo was somewhat shy, intellectual, thoughtful and softly spoken. We all felt a positive connection with Peter and Ivo and, coupled with the offered salary of £200 per month each, we couldn't sign the contract fast enough! We were sad to leave Small Wonder, but Pete Stennett actually felt that we needed the financial support of a larger label in order to further our career. However, as was typical of the times, it was not a very good contract. We did consult with a lawyer at the Musicians Union which was all we could afford, but the phrase, "you get what you pay for" has never ever had more meaning to me. However, leaving behind the stigma and poverty of living on the dole, coupled with the fact that we were now professional musicians, meant the world to us.

4AD released our second single "Dark Entries" in early January 1980 and it immediately climbed to the top of the Indie charts.

Peter "Plug" Edwards and Daniel Ash cruising in Los Angeles. Photos taken en route to in store appearance at Vinyl Fetish record store. / Photo: Kevin Haskins

Peter and Kevin atop The Empire State building in New York.

## BILLY'S

During January and February, 1980, we landed a five night residency at a club called Billy's in Soho, London. The club stands on the site where King Charles II would visit his mistress, Nell Gwynne, and in the 30's it housed the radical Gargoyle Club which attracted the likes of Noel Coward, Francis Bacon and Tallulah Bankhead. I guess you could say that we were in good company! Soho hadn't changed all that much during the 1980's, as all brands of entertainment were contrived to ruffle the feathers of conventional society. Inhabited by artists, strippers, bohemians and voyeurs, it was an intoxicating locale for four young lads still wet behind the ears.

Billy's was housed in the basement at 69 Dean Street which hosted a different club every night of the week. Photographer Derek Ridgers, who we did a session or two with back in the day, coined the perfect quote about Billy's: "Like walking into a Hieronymus Bosch painting: furtive but lively with a dedication that's never been equaled since." Only a month before, we had played another Soho venue, the legendary Marquee club. Supporting Doll By Doll, we were actually fined one pound a minute for playing over time. As we wanted to play to as many people as possible, we went past our allotted time. We ended owing the promoter about twenty pounds.

As each night progressed at Billy's, we attracted more and more followers clad in black leather and lace, witnessing the seeds of the Gothic movement

beginning to germinate. There we were, standing at the beach head, unwittingly inventing an entirely new genre of music.

On one particular night, as we stormed through our set, I was convinced that I spied Tony Wilson and Ian Curtis at the bar. It transpired that Joy Division were in London recording their second album *Closer* at Britannia Row in Islington. After our set, we approached Ian who told us that Tony had left early because of his dislike of bands that wear makeup. Ian went on to tell us that he enjoyed our set and was inspired to see us play live after hearing our records. It came as quite a shock, just three months later, when we learned, with great sadness, that he had taken his own life.

The band standing outside a hardware chain store in Germany that to our surprise happened to be called Bauhaus.

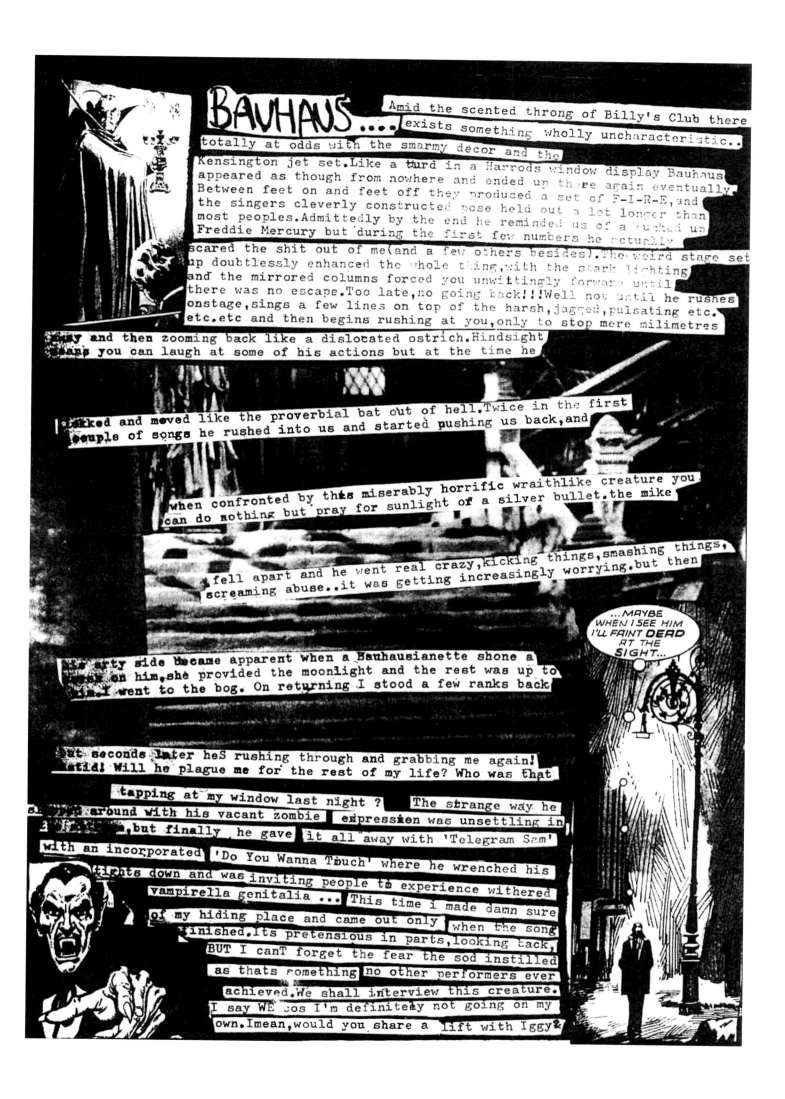

# BAUHAUS....

Amid the scented throng of Billy's Club there exists something wholly uncharacteristic.. totally at odds with the smarmy decor and the Kensington jet set.Like a turd in a Harrods window display Bauhaus appeared as though from nowhere and ended up there again eventually. Between feet on and feet off they produced a set of F-I-R-E, and the singers cleverly constructed pose held out a lot longer than most peoples.Admittedly by the end he reminded us of a pushed up Freddie Mercury but during the first few numbers he actually scared the shit out of me(and a few others besides).The weird stage set up doubtlessly enhanced the whole thing,with the stark lighting and the mirrored columns forced you unwittingly forward until there was no escape.Too late,no going back!!!Well not until he rushes onstage,sings a few lines on top of the harsh,jagged,pulsating etc. etc.etc.and then begins rushing at you,only to stop mere milimetres away and then zooming back like a dislocated ostrich.Hindsight means you can laugh at some of his actions but at the time he

looked and moved like the proverbial bat out of hell.Twice in the first couple of songs he rushed into us and started pushing us back,and

when confronted by this miserably horrific wraithlike creature you can do nothing but pray for sunlight of a silver bullet.the mike

fell apart and he went real crazy,kicking things,smashing things, screaming abuse..it was getting increasingly worrying.but then

...MAYBE WHEN I SEE HIM I'LL FAINT DEAD AT THE SIGHT...

the arty side became apparent when a Bauhausianette shone a spot on him,she provided the moonlight and the rest was up to him.I went to the bog. On returning I stood a few ranks back

but seconds later heS rushing through and grabbing me again! stid! Will he plague me for the rest of my life? Who was that tapping at my window last night ?   The strange way he slithered around with his vacant zombie expression was unsettling in itself,but finally he gave it all away with 'Telegram Sam' with an incorporated 'Do You Wanna Touch' where he wrenched his tights down and was inviting people to experience withered vampirella genitalia ... This time i made damn sure of my hiding place and came out only when the song finished.Its pretensious in parts,looking back, BUT I canT forget the fear the sod instilled as thats something no other performers ever achieved.We shall interview this creature. I say WE cos I'm definitely not going on my own.Imean,would you share a lift with Iggy?

Bauhaus performing at Tier 3, New York, September 5th, 1981. / Photos: Eugene Merinov

Various members of Bauhaus road crew.

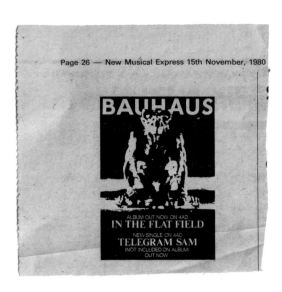

**BAUHAUS**

ALBUM OUT NOW ON 4AD
**IN THE FLAT FIELD**

NEW SINGLE ON 4AD
**TELEGRAM SAM**
(NOT INCLUDED ON ALBUM)
OUT NOW

BRISTOL HIPPODROME
(0272) 299444
£6.00, £5.00, £4.00, £3.00

FINAL SOLUTION PRESENT
**MAGAZINE**
**BAUHAUS**
**MANICURED NOISE**
**THE LAST DANCE**

73⁰ THUR MAY 1, LYCEUM, STRAND, WC²

TUES, APRIL 29, TIFFANYS, GLASGOW

FRI, MAY 2, GUILDHALL, NORTHAMPTON

MAY 6, DIGBETH HALL, BIRMINGHAM

WED, MAY 7, TRINITY HALL, BRISTOL
BAUHAUS SUPPORT EXCEPT* MANICURED NOISE

**BAUHAUS**
GUEST
**MASK BALL**
AT-LINGS FORUM SAT. FEB. 20.

TICKETS £2.50 ADVANCE FROM ACME LINGS SPINADISC
£3.00 ON THE DOOR 7PM TO 10PM WITH SUPPORT
WEAR A MASK!

**BILLY'S**
69 DEAN STREET, W.1.
9 pm / 3 am
BEER ½ PRICE BEFORE 10.30.

Tuesday 5th                      Admission £2
**KILLING JOKE + T.B.A.**
Wednesday 6th
**BAUHAUS + T.B.A.**

Thank you for writing, it is always encouraging when
interest of this nature is shown. We hope that the notes
enclosed answer your questions.
Bela Lugosi is dead, BAUHAUS on the other hand...

**OUT NOW**
**DARK ENTRIES**
SINGLE ON
4AD RECORDS
PIC SLEEVE

BEG 37

**bauhaus**

*bauhaus*

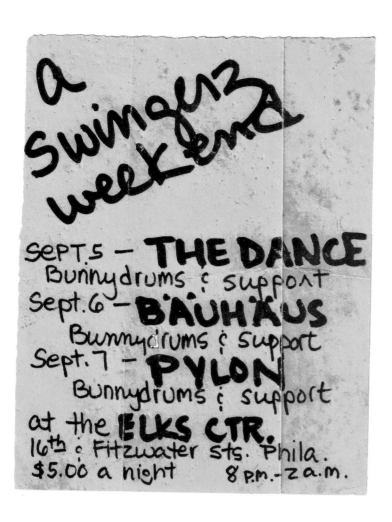

a Swingers
weekend

Sept.5 — THE DANCE
Bunnydrums & support
Sept.6 — BAUHAUS
Bunnydrums & support
Sept.7 — PYLON
Bunnydrums & support
at the ELKS CTR.
16th & Fitzwater sts. Phila.
$5.00 a night        8 p.m.—2 a.m.

FUTURAMA · 3
New Bingley Hall — Stafford 1981
SATURDAY 5th SEPTEMBER
GANG of FOUR
BAUHAUS
the HUMAN CONDITION
(JAH WOBBLE : JIM WALKER : ANIMAL)
THE PASSIONS
THEATRE OF HATE
KING PLEASURE
ROBERT & L.A. of SHOCK
HAVANA LET'S GO
THE SOUND ★ FELT
23 SKIDOO ★ THE LINES

★ FATAL CHARM
REVENNA AND THE MAGNETICS
FLOCK OF SEAGULLS
PONDEROSA GLEE BOYS
ANOTHER COLOUR

**S**HOX: "No Turning Back" (Axis 4)/BEARZ: "She's My Girl" (Axis 2)/BAUHAUS: "Dar Entries" (Axis 3)/Collectors' items already! Within the same week of release, Axis are having to withdraw all the above. They hadn't done their homework properly because there was already in existence an Axis Records Ltd owned by a certain Nigel Thomas. The new label is 4 A.D. Despite that, it's an auspicious start. (Well, what else do you expect from an offshoot of the ludicrously successful Beggar's Banquet?) Shox give straightforward pop the new electronic twist (and shout). Fresh and naturally home-made, like the Human League once upon a time. Bearz are equally appealing, with neo-psychedelic vocals over an attractively lumpy melody. Bauhaus, much beloved by Win Wenders' cameraman, Martin Schuller, ride an I-styled insistent rhythm with decidedly post-modernist style and a lot of confidence. A surprisingly strong dance record.

FINAL SOLUTION PRESENT
CLASSIX
NOUVEAUX
BAUHAUS
SECTION 25
PLAIN CHARACTERS

7.30, THURS, 20th MARCH
ELECTRIC BALLROOM
184 CAMDEN HIGH ST. NW1

FINAL SOLUTION RECORDED MUSIC
MAN IN THE RAILINGS

BILLY'S
69 DEAN STREET, W.1.
9 pm / 3 am
BEER ½ PRICE BEFORE 10.30.
Tuesday 19th February
FASHION
Wednesday 20th February
BAUHAUS

BAUHAUS

15 OCT·Bristol                          Granary
16 OCT·Bournemouth         Stateside Centre
18 OCT·Middlesborough        Rock Garden
20 OCT·Leeds                           [TBA] Venue
21 OCT·Scarborough                Penthouse
22 OCT·Manchester                       Rafters
23 OCT·Derby                                  Ajenta
24 OCT·Dudley                                  J.B's
25 OCT·Liverpool                            Bradys
26 OCT·Northampton          Royal Theatre
31 OCT·London              London University

LP OUT SOON ON 4AD

IN THE FLAT
FIELD TOUR

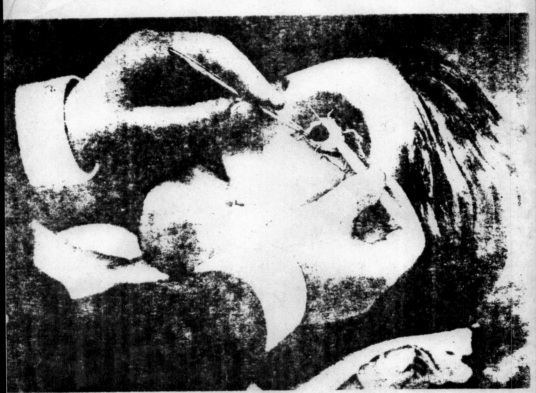

# b a u h a u s

1. The Old Five Bells — Sat 28ᵗʰ April
2. Corndolly Club (Oxford) Mon 30ᵗʰ April
3. Hitchin Polytechnic (with Sat 5ᵗʰ May
   Adam + the Ants)
4. the Paddock (with John Peel) Sat 16ᵗʰ June

# BAUHAUS

**marquee**
90 Wardour, St. W.1 | 01-437 6603

FRI. 7th SEPT
with Gloria Mundi

+ the Paddock 8th sept.

+ The Nags head 23rd Sept.
(Wollaston)

BERKELEY

Nightclub and

1333 University, Be

# BAUH

## MARTINI

# D

**MINORS WELCOME!**

TWO DRINK MINIMUM

ADVANCE TI

QUARE
estaurant
ley 849·3374

HAUS

SHOWTIME 9:30

ANCH

C.16

THURSDAY

BASS & TICKETRON

## PURPLE PIE PETE

Peter was performing a death defying dance, twenty feet up on the top of a huge old industrial boiler. As I surveyed him from below, his winkle pickers in full flight, I felt very content to be on terra firma. Over the course of the band I would often marvel at his fearless attitude, as he would think nothing of spontaneously climbing up fifty foot high theater curtains or balancing precariously atop PA speakers. It's a real miracle that he was never seriously hurt.

We were shooting our first video, directed by Mick Calvert and punk dread Don Letts, for our fourth single, a cover of "Telegram Sam", originally by T Rex. I was excited to work with Don, as he was an icon in the early punk rock scene, which had been such a huge influence on me. Don went on to make several music videos and award winning documentaries as well as forming Big Audio Dynamite with Mick Jones, formerly of The Clash. Though it wasn't the first time that I would have met Don. That was at his very cool clothing store called Acme Attractions on The Kings Road in London. As a sixteen year old kid, I would take the train on a monthly pilgrimage to London to acquire new punk rock threads. At that time I wasn't aware of Don's involvement with the Punk movement, so to me he was just the cool looking Rastafarian guy behind the counter. Coming from a very closeted small town upbringing, it was a big deal to me back then to go down to "The Smoke" on my own. When I would

enter a clothing store I used to feel overwhelmed by all the choices and would have no idea what to buy. I would spend ages trying on this and trying on that, but on this trip I eventually settled on a pair of vintage turquoise wrap around shades and multi colored flecked zoot suit trousers. Don was probably glad to see the back of me.

I relayed this story to Don when we all visited his high-rise flat in London for a pre-production meeting for the video. I also recall during the meeting that we were all a bit distracted by a scantily clad member of one of my favorite bands, The Slits, moving seductively around the flat.

Filmed in the boiler room of a disused public bath house in Fulham, the video captured the intense energy of the band along with Peter's formidable showmanship, and electric dance moves. In one shot, we solicited an impromptu performance from a lovely elderly woman who worked in the bath house. Cupping Peters chin, she gazed lovingly into his eyes miming the line, "You're my main man!" In another scene we see Peter's large looming shadow, dancing frenetically on the surface of the basement wall; another homage to expressionistic film. The last shot is of Peter "air dancing", hanging by his hands from an iron chain, that just happened to be dangling above the boiler that he was standing on. Unconcerned for his safety, he just took a leap, and went for it.

# TO-NIGHT....
## BAUHAUS

# SESSION

# JOHN PEEL SHOW

# RADIO 1   10·00 P.M

THURSDAY 3rd                    BAUHAUS

John Peel Photo credit: Chalkie Davies

## JOHN PEEL

The radio DJ John Peel was a savior to every music lover in Britain and, with the inception of the Internet, eventually to the world. He began broadcasting in 1967 on the pirate radio station Radio London and then moved to his permanent home, The BBC. During the 70's and beyond, the only way to hear music in the UK was on the BBC or pirate radio. Unfortunately the majority of playlists on the BBC consisted of atrocious boring pop or bland middle of the road music. However, John always had his ear pressed firmly to the ground and his taste was impeccable. At the age of 16, when I began art school, I would faithfully listen every night from 10:00 PM to midnight on my tiny transistor radio, and that's where, for example, I first discovered punk rock. John Peel's show was a shining beacon in an otherwise dull sea of bland mediocrity.

On September 23rd, 1979, John Peel DJ'd one of our early shows at The Nags Head Wollaston, just outside of our home town of Northampton. We took advantage of this situation by presenting him with a copy of our recently released single, "Bela Lugosi's Dead". Two months later, we were all huddled around our radio in the freezing kitchen of the house we all shared. We had tuned in to the John Peel show and were listening to "Bela Lugosi's Dead" coming out of the radio! To us, this was remarkable! Our music actually coming out of the radio! I felt so excited! The dream that I had held so close since hearing so many of my favorite artists on the radio, was beginning to take shape. After all the years of slogging around the pubs and working men's clubs, it finally felt like it was starting to pay off. After "Bela" ended, we hung on to every word that John Peel said. It was a benchmark moment that I will never forget.

Inspired by this, we all decided to pay him an unsolicited impromptu visit at Broadcasting House during his live broadcast. At around 10pm, we nervously entered the huge lobby and asked the receptionist if we could pay John a visit, as we had a very important record for him. This was our 7" follow up single to "Bela" entitled, "Dark Entries". I think that she was touched by our naivety and brazenness and told us that she would see what she could do. I don't think we really expected to be invited up, but moments later we were delighted as we were escorted upstairs by a BBC security guard. John received his uninvited guests with warmth and charm, even sharing his fine bottle of red with us. It was exciting and also very surreal to actually witness a visible representation of his marvelous radio show. All too soon the visit was coming to an end and in his usual understated drone, he uttered the words with which he ended most of his shows, "Well that's the end of tonight's program, thank you for listening, good night and good riddance!" We left him with our latest unreleased single and thanked him profusely.

He must have enjoyed our company, as a couple of months later on December 4th we were booked to record a "Peel session" at the BBCs Maida Vale Studios. A complex of seven studios and a maze of claustrophobic corridors, the studios in Maida Vale date back to 1946. The history therefore is quite palpable, and as I walked around the dusty corridors I could almost hear the ghostly sounds of the Radiophonic Workshop and the early Beatles, Bowie and Hendrix sessions. It's a very vibey place and I can hear that influence ingrained in all our recordings there.

The session itself was a very exciting and also nerve wracking prospect, as bands only had eight hours to record and mix four songs. There was no time for error. This infused the session with a tension and urgency, and any odd improvisations were usually kept in adding a spontaneous aspect to the recordings.

The BBC has a reputation for being a quite uptight British institution. It was only twenty years before our session that radio announcers were required to wear a suit and tie when nobody could even see them! There were also strict Union rules that came to our notice when Daniel proceeded to repair a power cable. He was immediately stopped by our engineer and we had to wait over half an hour for a union electrician to arrive to perform a simple task that only took one minute.

The spirits of studio MV4 had our backs as the session went really well recording the songs "A God In An Alcove", "Spy In The Cab", "Telegram Sam" and "Double Dare". This version of "Double Dare" was licensed from The BBC for our first LP as, try as we might, we could not match the spontaneous energy of this particular recording. In fact it was only a few weeks previous to this Peel session that we had actually aborted a recording session mid way through whilst attempting to tape this very same track. The Peel session was broadcasted on January 3rd 1980.

BAHAUS - Detailed Schedu.. [?] .. March. 1982.

Mon.8th. Mixing at Morgan Studios, 167, Will[...] Rd. N.W.10, - 459 7244
arrive about 12 noon to allow t[...] [...] if needed.

Tu .9th. Backing track recording for T.O.T.P. at C.T.S. Studios, Engineers
Way, Wembley. - 903 4611.(North side of Wembley Arena, also called
the Music Centre.) Arrive at 2.00 p.m. Studio 2.
OR - Mixing at Morgan if not on T.O.T.P.

Wed.10th. Re Recording Bela Lugosi at Morgan Studios for use in Bowie film,
Musical Director Howard Blake in Charge of session. Gear will be
loaded in by 11.30a.m. and you must be ready to start at 12. noon.

Th. 11th. If on T.O.T.P. you will be at B.B.C. Television Centre (Wood Lane
W 12. - near White City) all day. Exact times will depend on your
position on the bill and will be advised later. Programme goes out
live thisweek.
OR - Mixing at Morgan.

Fri.12th. Mixing at Morgan Studios.

Sat.13th. John Peel Session at B.B.C. Maida Vale Studios, Delaware Road, W.9.
Studio 4. Producer Dale Griffin.        580 4468.
Gear arrival 12.30 p.m. Band must arrive by 2.00 p.m.

Band hotel allweek: Nayland Hotel, 134 Sussex Gdns. W2. 723 8275

Gear - will be loaded out of Roadmender Monday evening or Tuesday morning,
if we are not on T.O.T.P. gear will be loaded into Morgan on Tuesday
and the van returned to Northampton. Gear can then be loaded out of
Morgan on Saturday morning for the Peel session at Maida Vale  and
returned to the roadmender on Sunday. If we are on T.O.T.P. van will
take gear straight to C.T.S. arriving about 12.00 noon Tuesday and
stay in London all week.


Schedule: W.E. Sat. 20th. March.

Mon.15th. Photo session with Stella, on location in Peak District.
Transport and times to be arranged.

Tue.16th. Photo session with Mitch Jenkins and Graham Trott, on location at
Castle Ashby in the afternoon and in the Chronicle and Echo studio
in the evening. (this session may need to be re-scheduled if TOTP
comes up this week to allow for recording of backing track.)

Wed.17th. T.O.T.P. ? (Pre-recorded this week)

Th. 18th. Rehearsals atRoadmender (or re-scheduled photosession from Tuesday)

Fri.19th.        "        "        "

RECORDING OF LILLIES ON CHICAGO TAPE - TAKE ALL BAUHAUS
TAMBORINE FOR PEEL SESSION.                        TAPES.

## morgan

**RECORDED AT +4dB ABOVE AMPEX REF LEVEL ON SCOTCH 256 320 nWb/M**

| | | |
|---|---|---|
| artiste | BAUHAUS. | 30/1/82 |
| client | BEGGARS BANQUET | CCIR-4dB |
| engineers | MIKE HEDGES/CHARLES | 15 IPS |
| studio | ONE. | |
| producer | MIKE HEDGES. | ✓ |

| | 24 | MONO | | AT HEAD | 1KHz 10KHz 63Hz O'VU | |

| title | | | time |
|---|---|---|---|
| ① A KICK IN THE EYE | WHITE FL/RED EL | | 3:35 |
| ② BELA LUGOSI IS DEAD | WHITE FL/RED EL | | 6:24 |
| | TOTAL TIME | | 9:59 |

---

## morgan

| | | |
|---|---|---|
| artiste | BAUHAUS | date 24/3/82 |
| client | BEGGARS BANQUET | rec by NAS |
| engineers | JEFF/ | speed 15 IPS |
| studio | ONE | |

ROUGH MIXES

| dolby | yes | no | frequency run | | | | | | | | | |

| quad | 4 track | | | | | main system | | | |

| title | | time |
|---|---|---|
| ① SPIRIT | | |
| (2) SILENT HEDGES | | |
| ③ SPIRIT IN THE SKY 2-55. | | |

MASTERED BY

**Tape ONE**
01 580 0444

Date 20.10.83
Room ONE
Eng. Scott

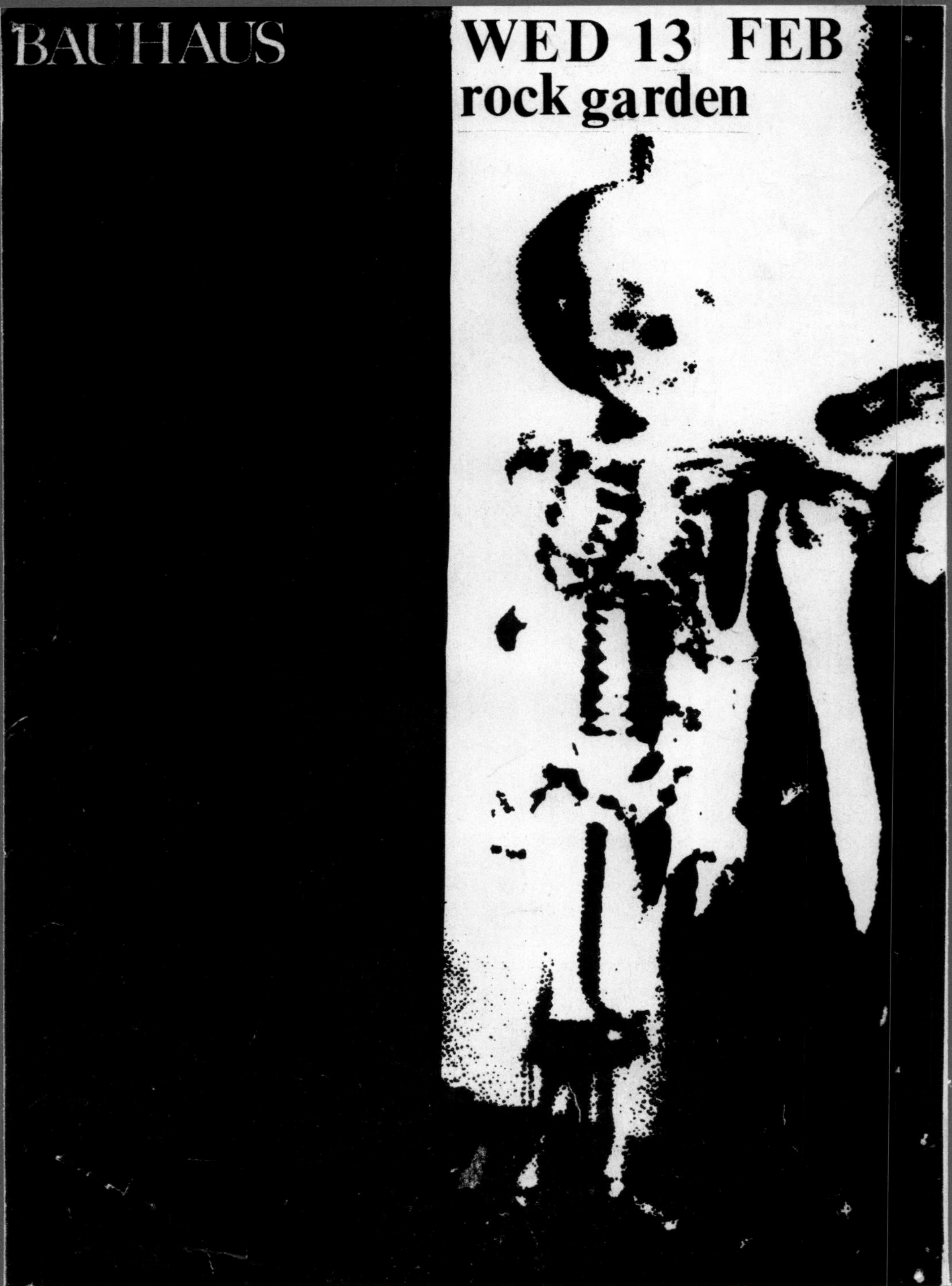
BAUHAUS
WED 13 FEB
rock garden

# bauhaus

infO phone    NORTHAMPTON 51307    write    21 Cotswold Avenue
Duston Northampton

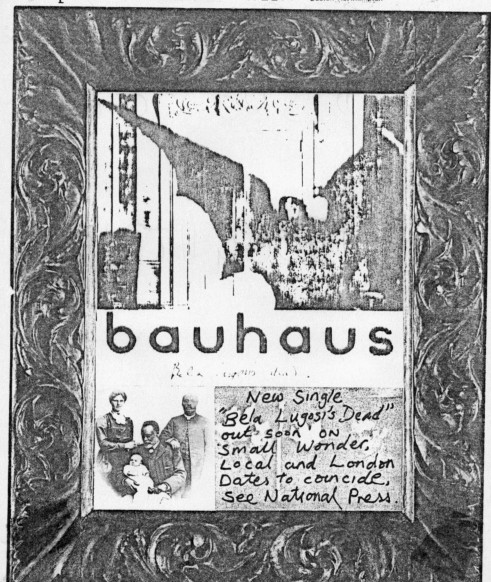

bauhaus

New Single
"Bela Lugosi's Dead"
out soon on
Small Wonder,
Local and London
Dates to coincide,
See National Press.

11th April, 1981 New Musical Express — Page 49

**Bauhaus**
**Clock DVA**

**Heaven**

I DIDN'T really fancy enduring the hell-hole of a sardine-packed Heaven, but the ghost of Bela Lugosi beckoned and I duly followed.

Catching a mere ten minutes of Clock DVA's set doesn't really authorise passing off the ~~~~ions as ~~~~

improvements on the rest of the set. The last, particularly, proved to be a spectacular climax, showing up the depressing inadequacy of the production on 'In The Flat Field'.

But anyway, when you children have quite finished, let us look up to Scotland for our next musical direction. The passion is on Postcard, and we must bring it down south before we all become (non-danceable) showroom dummies.

**Barney Hoskyns**

No 157

**Peerford Limited**
Shepperton Studios,
Shepperton, Middlesex
Chertsey (09328) 62611

"THE HUNGER"
- an MGM Production

# BAUHAUS

## New Single

## Kick in the eye
### (searching for satori) E.P.

12" E.P. (remixed version)
Includes 3 new unreleased tracks

Also available 3 track 7"

Appearing at the Old Vic 24 Feb

FINAL SOLUTION

BACKSTAGE PASS

ARTIST ........................

VENUE ........................

SIGNED ........................

STRAIGHT MUSIC PRESENTS

# BAUHAUS

VIC GODARD & SUBWAY SECT | THE BIRTHDAY PARTY

LYCEUM
STRAND, WC2 | THURSDAY 25th JUNE at 7·30

TICKETS £3·00 (INC. VAT) ADVANCE LYCEUM BOX OFFICE, TEL: 836 3715, LONDON THEATRE BOOKINGS, SHAFTESBURY AVE., TEL: 439 3371; PREMIER BOX OFFICE, TEL.: 240 2245, OR ROCK ON RECORDS, 3 KENTISH TOWN RD., NW1, TEL: 485 5088

BAUHAUS

Please can you supply 2 signed
photos & any publicity material
on Bauhaus for a schoolboys
essay on the group?

Best wishes.
Miss ZZZZ

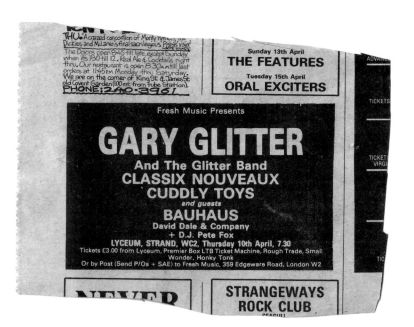

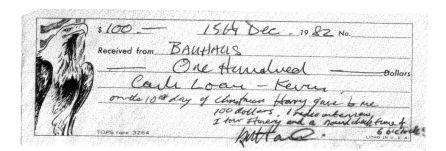

→23 →23A →24 →24A

→29 →29A →30 →30A

→8    →8A    →9    →9A    →10
KODAK SAFETY FILM 5063    KODAK SAFETY FILM 5

→14    →14A    →15    →15A    →16
SAFETY FILM 5063    KODAK SAFETY FILM 5063    KOD

→20    →20A   Y 7 3 7   →21A    →22
KODAK SAFETY FILM 5063    KODAK SAFETY FILM 506

Candid moments captured by Jean Ramsey during the filming of the video for "She's In Parties" / Photos: Jean Ramsey

FINAL SOLUTION PRESENT

# ꞊MAGAZINE꞊
## BAUHAUS
### PLUS GUESTS

7.30, MAY 5, WELLINGTON CLUB, HULL

TICKETS £2.00 ON THE NIGHT

Final Solution's distinctive show fliers.

BAUHAUS - U.K. TOUR OCT/NOV '81

| TOUR RECEIPTS. (NET V.A.T) | £ 15,173. — |
|---|---|

COSTS

| | |
|---|---|
| COMMISSION DUE TO WASTED TALENT | 2,489.22 |
| COMMISSION TO H.I. | 2,276.13 |
| EQUIPMENT - REPAIRS, HIRE & PURCHASE. | 6,314.27 |
| HOTEL BILLS - INCLUDING SOME PHONE CHARGES | 2,004.88 |
| FUEL, FARES, VAN & MINIBUS RENTAL (TRUCK INCLUDED IN P.A.) | 1,996.20 |
| OTHER PHONE & POSTAL CHARGES | 157.18 |
| WAGES & PER DIEMS | 2,502.11 |
| SUNDRIES | 179.11 |
| STAGE REHEARSALS 3 DAYS @ £25 | 75.— |
| V.A.T ON COSTS. | 572.98 |

| | |
|---|---|
| TOTAL | £ 18,567.08 |
| LESS PORTION OF LIGHTING HIRE CHARGED TO EUROPE | 500.— |
| | 18,067.08 |
| DEFICIT | £ 2,894.08 |
| MERCHANDISING REVENUE SET AGAINST DEFICIT | 1098.66 |
| FINAL DEFICIT. | 1795.42 |

| | |
|---|---|
| V.A.T. COLLECTED ON £15,173. — TOUR RECEIPTS | £ 2275.95 |
| RECOUPABLE V.A.T. PAYED OUT ON TOUR - APPROX | 572.98 |
| DUE TO V.A.T. OFFICE (APPROX) | 1702.97 |

1981 UK TOUR ACC.

# European Tour Account.

## COSTS.

| | | |
|---|---:|---:|
| EQUIPMENT - REPAIR, REPLACEMENT & RENTAL. £ | 437 | 13. |
| TRANSPORT - FUEL, FARES, FERRIES, VEHICLE HIRE | 2305 | 77 |
| HOTELS | 1330 | 09 |
| PHONE CHARGES, INCLUDING PART OF U.K. PHONE BILL | 201 | 56 |
| WAGES & PER DIEMS (P.D's APPROX £1680) | 2797 | 87 |
| CARNET & INSURANCE CHARGES | 357 | 82 |
| AGENCY COMMISSION | 857 | 81 |
| MANAGEMENT COMMISSION (INCLUDING £51.14 COLOGNE OUTSTANDING) | 746. | — |
| OTHER ITEMS | 132. | 08 |
| V.A.T. ON U.K EXPENDITURE | 229. | 52. |
| TOTAL. £ | 9395 | 62. |

PLUS SOME LIGHTING HIRE & FERRY CHARGES
NOT YET INVOICED.

## INCOME

| | | |
|---|---:|---:|
| GIG RECEIPTS FROM BELGIUM £ | 1,800 | — |
| GIG RECEIPTS FROM HOLLAND (Fl. 7250 @ 4,8) | 1,510 | 42 |
| RADIO RECORDING FEE HOLLAND (Fl 500) | 104 | 17. |
| GIG RECEIPTS FROM GERMANY (6000D.M @ 4.4) | 1363 | 64 |
| GIG RECEIPTS FROM PARIS | 300. | — |
| TOUR SUPPORT FROM BENELUX LICENCEES | 1000. | — |
| " " " GERMAN LICENCEE | 1000. | — |
| V.A.T ON FOREIGN LICENCEES TOUR SUPPORT FROM B.B. | 300. | — |
| TOTAL. £ | 7378 | 23 |

## TOUR LOSSES

| | | |
|---|---:|---:|
| | 2017 | 39 |
| £ | ~~1957~~ | ~~56~~ |
| ALREADY PAID ON BEGGARS BANQUET AMEX CARD £898.43 | ~~838~~ | ~~60~~ |
| BALANCE | 1118 | 96 |

~~NEED~~ NES

WED - CHRONIC ECHO.

FRI PRACTISE.

called "Trabant" They appeared to come in various shades of muted colors. I recall being fascinated by the occupants. Generally, miserable looking East Germans who also appeared to come in various shades of muted colors. In stark contrast were the West Germans, cruising by proudly in their opulent Mercedes sedans. Our soundtrack for the journey was the B side o Bowie's Low album which was the perfect underscore.

Everything was going fine until we happened to take a wrong slip road into a small East German town. It was like we had suddenly time travelled back 30 years! I recall looking at shop window displays which resembled 1940's vintage fashion stores and we were attracting some shocking looks of bewilderment from the local townspeople. Fortunately we were able to quickly re-join the autobahn without police intervention. It was somewhat of a relief to arrive at Checkpoint Bravo which was operated by British, French and American military police.

## SLIP ROAD SLIP UP

November 25th, 1980 found us playing "Ratinger Hof" in the West German city of Dusseldorf. During World War II and largely due to its many steel factories and chemical works Dusseldorf was the unfortunate target of a strategic bombing campaign by the RAF. In 1942 much of the city and its infrastructure were destroyed almost overnight having taken direct hits from the 700 tons of bombs that were dropped by over 350 Halifax and Lancaster's deployed from RAF Bomber Command. By the end of the war, 50% of the city was levelled with only 10% of its buildings left untouched. By the time we paid our visit, you could still see evidence of bomb damage, however the battered City spawned a healthy music and arts movement, generating some ground-breaking bands such as Kraftwerk and Neu!.

Ratinger Hof was a cosy pub that was the epicenter for the cities punk rock scene and our performance was met with great enthusiasm by the local kids. Our next gig the following evening was a five hour drive away at the SO36 in West Berlin and at that time in history, one had to navigate through the Soviet controlled East Germany to get there. When we arrived at Checkpoint Alpha near Helmstedt we had to go through passport control with its lookout towers manned by armed soldiers, it was a little intimidating. We were allowed two to four hours to complete the remaining 110 mile journey, instructed to maintain a speed of 40MPH and to not leave the autobahn. If we did not arrive in time then the military police would come looking for us.

Once through the checkpoint we passed a menacing looking Russian tank with it's gun strategically pointing to the West. The next thing we noticed were the funny looking little East German cars

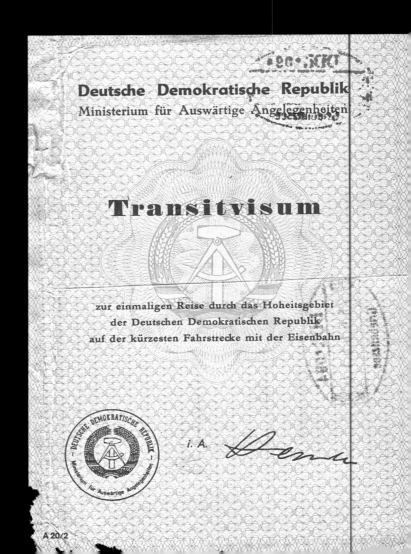

Deutsche Demokratische Republik
Ministerium für Auswärtige Angelegenheiten

# Transitvisum

zur einmaligen Reise durch das Hoheitsgebiet
der Deutschen Demokratischen Republik
auf der kürzesten Fahrstrecke mit der Eisenbahn

i. A.

A 20/2

**Ceremonies in the Dark**

# BAUHAUS

## Vorgruppe: ZEV

**Dienstag,**
**25. Nov.**
20.00 Uhr

**Düsseldorf** Ratinger Hof,
Ratinger Str.

nur Abendkasse

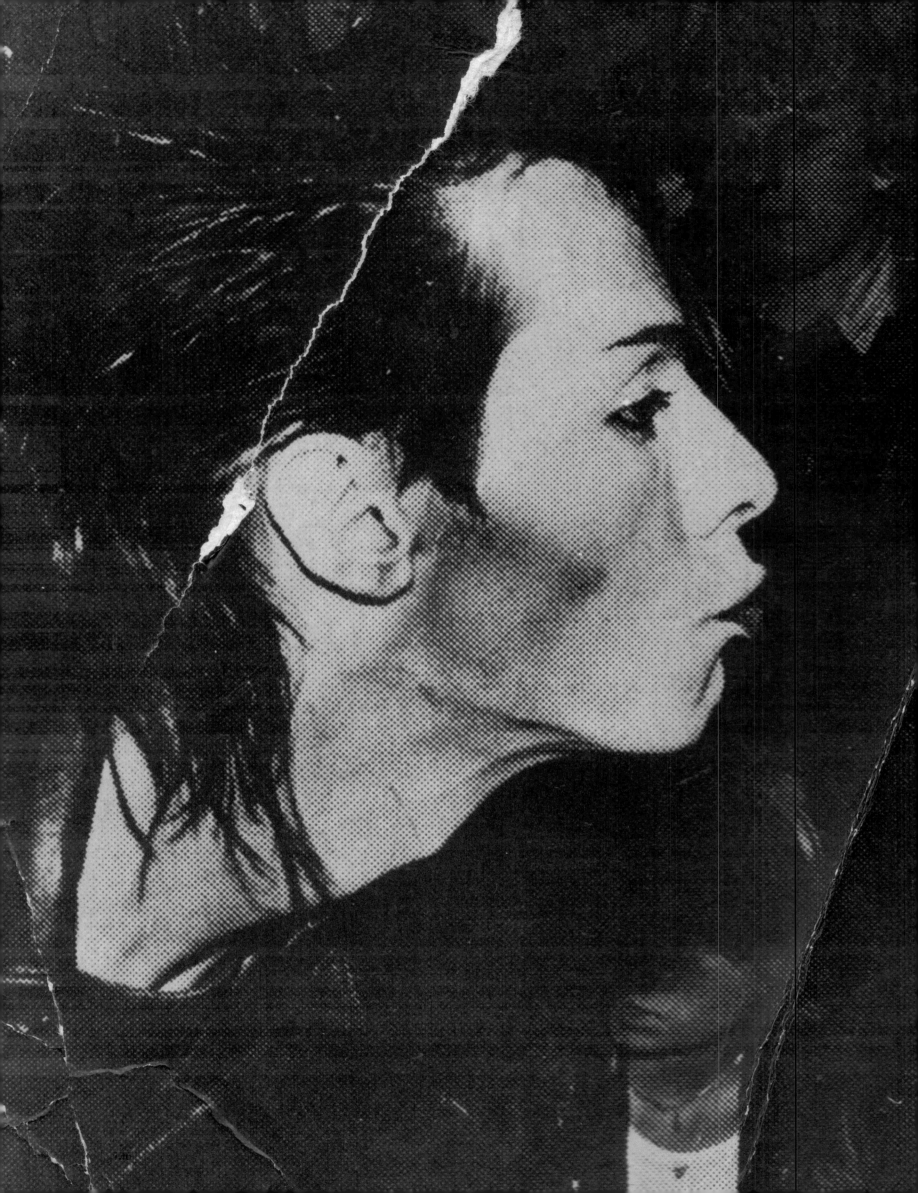

**Blue Moon + ZENSOR** *presents*

# Bauhaus

Electronic New Wave / (England)

## The Giants Rock-a-Billy
Berlin Südstaaten

## White Russia Sibirien Rock

## Emirat 030

Attraktiv – Preiswert – Musik

# S.O.36 28.3. 80

## Mer Haba

## Oranienstraße 190

Karten nur bei ZENSOR + Blue Moon  Belziger Straße 23
Vorverkauf 10,00 DM   Abendkasse 12,00 DM

the front row, giving them a stern warning and throwing them back into the pit. This quelled the onslaught for most of the show and we managed to finish our set unscathed.

At the SO36 the dressing room was situated half way down the hall so to access it, one had to walk, or in our case, run through the audience. Well the Teddy Boys knew this, and on our way back there, they attempted to attack us! We managed to arrive relatively intact, along with the promoter and our two-man crew. At the rear of the dressing room was a big stack of wooden chairs. To our surprise, the promoter suddenly began smashing them to bits! Had he gone mad? We soon learned the reason for his bizarre behavior when he gave each of us a chair leg to use as a defensive weapon!

Grabbing the door handle he struck a rather dramatic commando like pose, yelled, "Eins, Zwei, Drei, Vier...and boom! We were now running through the audience towards the exit, wielding our makeshift clubs! Thankfully, the Teds were too alarmed to engage and we made it safely to a waiting mini bus. We endured a rather frigid journey back to our lodgings though, as they had smashed every window on our bus.

### EINS, ZWEI, DREI, VIER!!!!

The SO36 Club is situated in Kreuzberg, Berlin, in the heart of the Turkish Quarter. During the 70's, it was a squat which morphed into a legendary punk rock venue. David Bowie and Iggy Pop were often seen there during the time they were living in Berlin. Today it has been renovated, but back then it was cold, bare bones, rough and ready. The first time we played there was on the second gig of our

first European tour on March 29th, 1980 and it was quite a memorable experience.

Unfortunately, there was a certain element in the crowd who had come only to listen to one of the local support bands, The Giants, who were a Rockabilly band. The Teddy Boys were yelling profanities and threatening the kids who had come to see us. As they became more and more aggressive, our one and only roadie, Tony, began pulling the trouble-makers out of

Ticket stub from the second Bauhaus performance at SO36 on 26 Novermber 1980.

(Above) Show flier for the 28 May 1980, at SO36

(Opposite) Peter Murphy performing at SO36 Club in Berlin.

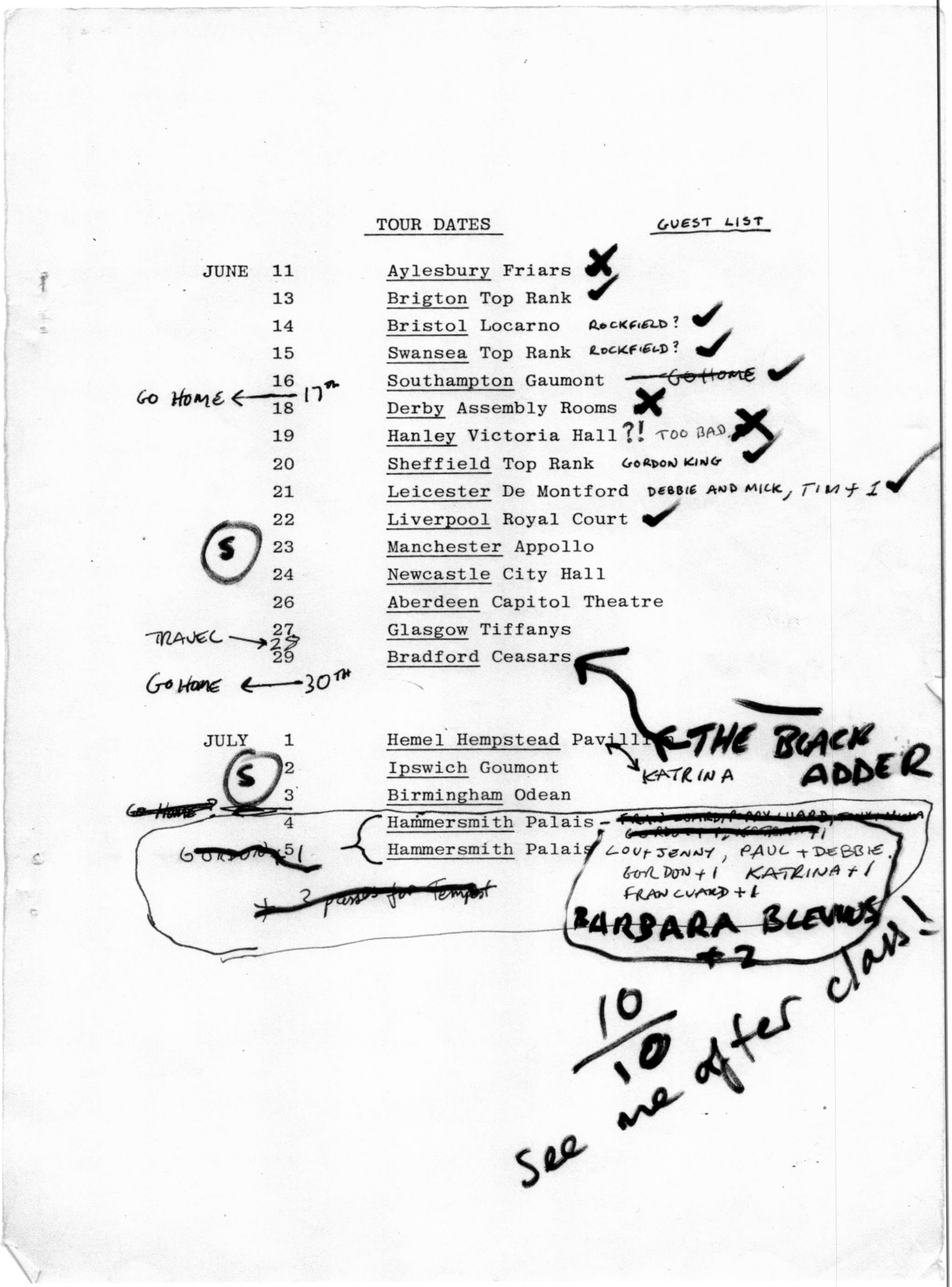

|  | TOUR DATES | GUEST LIST |
|---|---|---|

**JUNE 11**    Aylesbury Friars ✗

**13**    Brigton Top Rank ✓

**14**    Bristol Locarno   *ROCKFIELD?* ✓

**15**    Swansea Top Rank   *ROCKFIELD?* ✓

*GO HOME* ← **16** *17ᵗʰ*   Southampton Gaumont ~~*GO HOME*~~ ✓

**18**    Derby Assembly Rooms ✗

**19**    Hanley Victoria Hall *?!* *TOO BAD* ✗

**20**    Sheffield Top Rank   *GORDON KING*

**21**    Leicester De Montford   *DEBBIE AND MICK, TIM + 1* ✓

**22**    Liverpool Royal Court ✓

Ⓢ **23**    Manchester Appollo

**24**    Newcastle City Hall

**26**    Aberdeen Capitol Theatre

*TRAVEL* → **27 28**   Glasgow Tiffanys

**29**    Bradford Ceasars

*GO HOME* ← *30ᵗʰ*

**JULY 1**    Hemel Hempstead Pavilion *THE BLACK ADDER*

Ⓢ **2**    Ipswich Goumont   *KATRINA*

**3**    Birmingham Odean

*Go Home?* **4**   Hammersmith Palais

*GORDON* **5**   Hammersmith Palais

*LOU + JENNY, PAUL + DEBBIE. GORDON + 1 KATRINA + 1 FRAN CUARD + 1*

*BARBARA BLEVINS + 2*

*+ 3 passes for Tempest*

$\frac{10}{10}$ *see me after class!*

Notes that I made on our 1983 UK Tour itinerary. Aside from reminders of who to add to my guest lists, It appears that I was a big fan of the highly successful comedy show; The Black Adder!

It looks like the pressure of the tour was getting to me! Drawing on blank page of the 1983 UK Tour itinerary.

the **FAN** presents a series of concerts at one of the best halls in YORKSHIRE!

# UNITY HALL WAKEFIELD

UNITY HOUSE opposite WAKEFIELD WESTGATE STATION     phone : 75719

---

**SUNDAY 4th MAY**
DOORS OPEN 7.30pm.

COME OUT FROM UNDER THE FLOORBOARDS!
**MAGAZINE**
NEW L.P. ON Virgin "THE CORRECT USE OF SOAP"

with guests 'BAUHAUS'
AND LOCAL GUESTS **STRANGER THAN FICTION**

TICKETS £2.00 from FAN CLUB or UNITY HALL

---

**FRIDAY 16th MAY**
DOORS OPEN 7.30pm

**THE ONLY ONES**
EXCELLENT NEW L.P. "BABY'S GOT A GUN" OUT NOW ON C.B.S.

TICKETS £2 AS A... WITH WASTED YOUTH

---

**THURSDAY 22nd MAY**
DOORS OPEN 7.30pm
TICKETS £2.00

Heavy Metal!
SHEER GREED   SHEER GREED   **Girl**   SHEER GREED

DICKEN FROM MR... with AND BROKEN HOME

Jet RECORDS   SHEER GR... JET LP22 ... JET C...

---

**THURSDAY 29th MAY**
DOORS OPEN 7.30pm
TICKETS £2.00

# THE HUMAN LEAGUE
with guests 'the SCARS'

A TRACK EP 'Holiday 80' OUT ON Virgin
TRACKS: MARIANNE, DANCE VISION, BEING BOILED, ROCK'N'ROLL NIGHTCLUB

---

SINGLE No 20. L.P. No 5.

**WEDNESDAY 4th JUNE**
TICKETS £2.50

**SAXON**
with guests **TYGERS OF PAN TANG**

---

**FRIDAY 6th JUNE**
DOORS OPEN 7.30pm

**toyah**
with her special guests:
TICKETS £2.00

FINAL SOLUTION PRESENT A BENEFIT IN AID OF RELEASE

# DOLL BY DOLL
## BAUHAUS
## Z-HEADS
7.30PM, FRI, MARCH 7TH
### PORCHESTER HALL
### PORCHESTER RD, W.2
£1.50

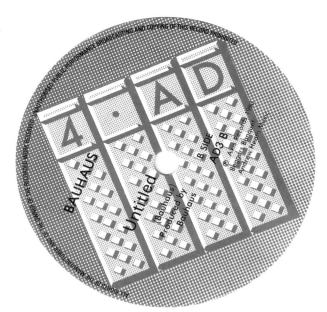

# BAUHAUS
## IN THE FLAT FIELD
## Album Out Now

Also 12" Single
now available
with bonus track
— both on 4AD

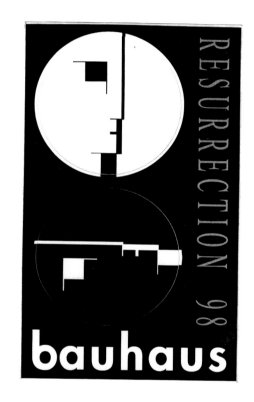

RESURRECTION 98

bauhaus

# BAUHAUS
# ANNIVERSARY
+ The Patterns
racecourse pavilion
sat·29··dec··£1-50

Cover of my copy of our 1983 UK Tour itinerary that I lavishly embellished during down time.

THUNK!
DEAD!

SCREEEEK

GLASS

OR IT'S AL

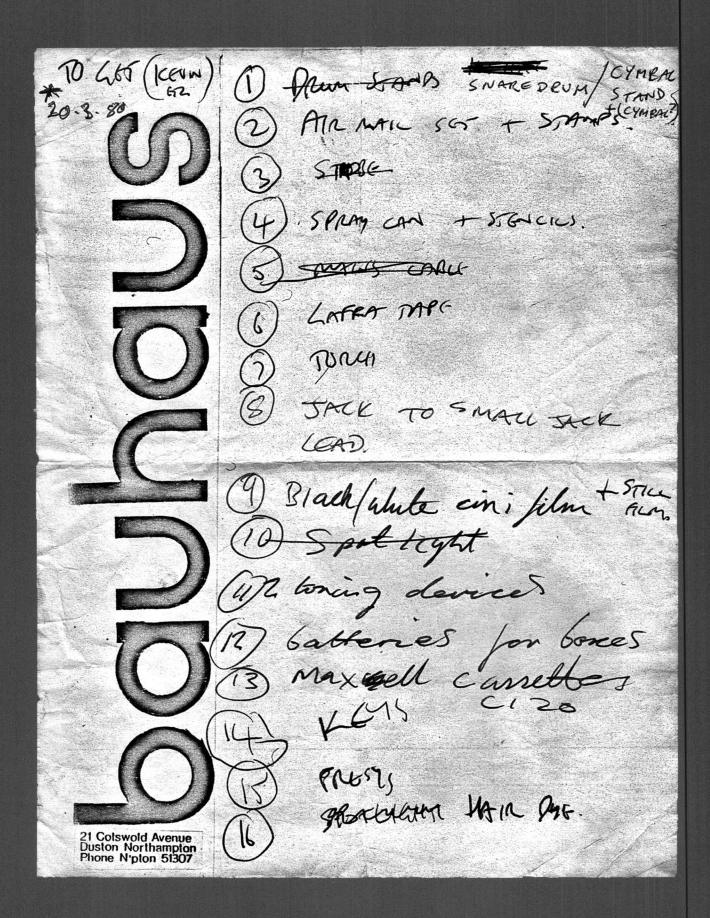

**TO GET (KEVIN GTZ)** *
20.8.80

**bauhaus**

21 Cotswold Avenue
Duston Northampton
Phone N'pton 51307

1. ~~DRUM STANDS~~ ~~SNAREDRUM~~ / CYMBAL STAND (CYMBAL?)
2. AIR MAIL SG5 + STANDS.
3. ~~STROBE~~
4. SPRAY CAN + STENCILS.
5. ~~MAINS CABLE~~
6. GAFFA TAPE
7. TORCH
8. JACK TO SMALL JACK LEAD.

9. Black/white cine film + STILL FILM
10. ~~Spot light~~
11. toning devices
12. batteries for boxes
13. Maxwell cassettes C120
14. KEYS
15. PRESS
16. ~~SPOTLIGHT~~ HAIR DYE.

Milli and Graham Bentley

## THE OLD MEN OF DEN HAGUE'

Considering it was their first and last show, "The Old Men of Den Hague" was a rather short lived enterprise, but it will go down in the annals of rock and roll history as being the fastest assembled band to play a live show.

As part of Bauhaus' European Mask Tour, our agency had arranged five double headlining shows with a band called The Passions who had scored a top 30 hit in January with "I'm in Love with a German Film Star". Double headlining usually means that the bands take turns at headlining, however, The Passions insisted on headlining at each and every show. This happened to backfire because almost half of the audience ended up leaving during their set. Consequently at our fifth and last show booked with them at the Paard Van Troje (Trojan Horse), on November 21st 1981, The Passions were a no show.

A support band was quickly assembled from assorted members of Bauhaus, our road crew and our audience. On bass guitar was then Bauhaus roadie Glenn Cam-

pling, on guitar was Bauhaus lighting designer Graham Bentley, on vocals Bauhaus fan Milli (flying by the seat of his pants), and Peter Murphy sat in on drums, until he got bored that was. Apparently my contribution to the performance was an attempt to pull down Graham's trousers as he was playing, which resulted in him falling to the floor as he took a swinging kick at me to fend me off while Glenn channelled Peter Hook style bass lines. The ten minute "set" consisted of a brief raucous trawl through The Residents "Constantinople", followed by an improvised original; "Ere Comes the Weekend", a very fleeting but soon aborted attempt at The Animals "House of the Rising Sun" was also initiated as Graham knew the opening Am chord!.

They deserve a tip of the hat as somehow, this somewhat shambolic "band" managed to procure an encore without actually leaving the stage! They delivered "Kevin was a Cowboy" with Milli providing a fabulous impromptu lyric set to "Wild Thing" style guitar and bass riffs from Graham and Glenn, Peter had, by this stage, vacated his drum stool.

*yes lad's z think that you'll really benefit from this tour!*

BAUHAUS

ITALY, APRIL/MAY 1982

| | |
|---|---|
| 29 April | PALERMO, Teatro Dante |
| 30 | MESSINA, Teatro Garden |
| I May | TARANTO, Toursport Club |
| 2 | DAY OFF |
| 3 | MILAN, Odissea 200I |
| 4 | BOLOGNA, Puntoacapo Club |
| 5 | LIVORNO, Teatro Odeon |
| 6 | FLORENCE, Tenax Club |
| 7 | ROME, Teatro Trianon |

*THAT'S ROCK N'ROII AARey!*

CONTACTS

Harry Isles (Manager)
▓▓▓▓▓▓▓▓▓
Newnham
Northants
Telephone: ▓▓▓▓▓▓▓▓

Ian Wilson (Agent)
c/o Wasted Talent
▓▓▓▓▓▓▓▓▓▓▓▓
London W2
Telephone: ▓▓▓▓▓▓

Martin Mills (Record Company)
c/o Beggars Banquet
▓▓▓▓▓▓▓▓▓
London SW 5
Telephone: ▓▓▓▓▓▓

Fran Tomasi (Promoter)
▓▓▓▓▓▓▓▓▓
Bologna
Italy
05I/237I43

Local Promoter as per following info.

Giovanni Natale (Italian Licensee)
Italian Records
▓▓▓▓▓▓▓▓▓
Bologna 40I23
Telephone: ▓▓▓▓▓▓

— I WAS TALKING TO JOE THE
OTHER DAY.
IAN'S OK AS WELL.

WEDNESDAY 28 APRIL

TRAVEL DETAILS

Luton - Milan

Tickets to be taken at 13.30 pm
from the special desk

(British Airtour Flights/for Sainteseal/
Alicvacanze)

Depart Flight NO OM/614    3.00 pm
Arrive  Milano Malpensa    5.45 pm

HOTEL INFORMATION

BAND AND CREW

Hotel Rex
Via Marco D'Agrate 34
Milan

TELEPHONE

02 533715

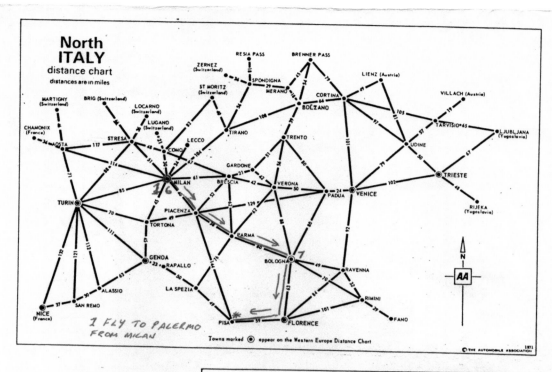

# North ITALY
## distance chart
distances are in miles

MARTIGNY (Switzerland)
CHAMONIX (France)
BRIG (Switzerland)
LOCARNO (Switzerland)
LUGANO (Switzerland)
ST MORITZ (Switzerland)
ZERNEZ (Switzerland)
RESIA PASS
SPONDIGNA
MERANO
BRENNER PASS
CORTINA
BOLZANO
LIENZ (Austria)
VILLACH (Austria)
TARVISIO=65
LJUBLJANA (Yugoslavia)
AOSTA
STRESA
LECCO
COMO
TIRANO
TRENTO
UDINE
TRIESTE
RIJEKA (Yugoslavia)
MILAN
GARDONE
BRESCIA
VERONA
PADUA
VENICE
TURIN
PIACENZA
TORTONA
PARMA
BOLOGNA
RAVENNA
GENOA
RAPALLO
RIMINI
FANO
ALASSIO
LA SPEZIA
SAN REMO
NICE (France)
PISA
FLORENCE

1 FLY TO PALERMO
FROM MILAN

16

N
AA

Towns marked ⊙ appear on the Western Europe Distance Chart

© THE AUTOMOBILE ASSOCIATION 1971

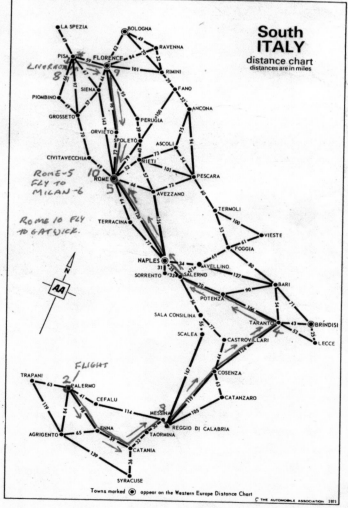

# South ITALY
## distance chart
distances are in miles

LA SPEZIA
BOLOGNA
PISA
FLORENCE
RAVENNA
LIVORNO
SIENA
RIMINI
FANO
PIOMBINO
ANCONA
GROSSETO
PERUGIA
ORVIETO
SPOLETO
ASCOLI
CIVITAVECCHIA
RIETI
PESCARA
ROME
AVEZZANO
TERMOLI
TERRACINA
VIESTE
FOGGIA
NAPLES
AVELLINO
SORRENTO
SALERNO
BARI
POTENZA
SALA CONSILINA
TARANTO
BRINDISI
SCALEA
CASTROVILLARI
LECCE
COSENZA
TRAPANI
CATANZARO
PALERMO
CEFALU
MESSINA
REGGIO DI CALABRIA
AGRIGENTO
ENNA
TAORMINA
CATANIA
SYRACUSE

LIVORNO 8
9
ROME-5 FLY TO MILAN-6
10 5
ROME 10 FLY TO GATWICK.
FLIGHT 2
3
4

N
AA

Towns marked ⊙ appear on the Western Europe Distance Chart

© THE AUTOMOBILE ASSOCIATION 1971

155

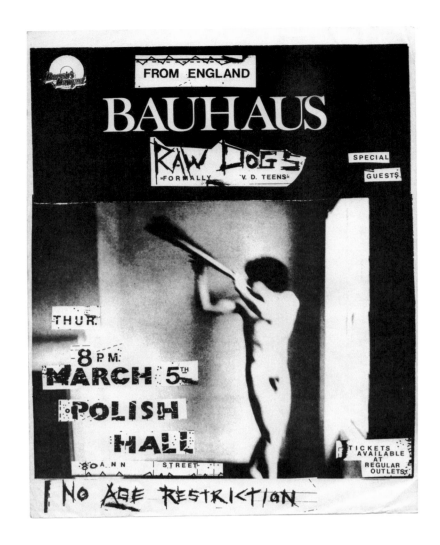

FRANCK YEZNIKIAN
21 AVENUE VILLARCEAU
25000 BESANCON
TEL. 81 81 37 47

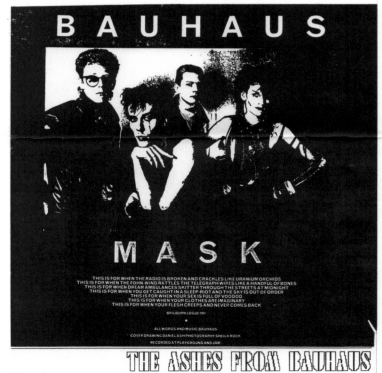

# FAC 51
## THE HAÇIENDA

**Friday August 13th**
## DELTA 5
## SECRET SEVEN
**Saturday August 14th**
## BAUHAUS
**(Group on stage at 10.00 pm)**
**Tuesday August 17th**
## RIP, RIG & PANIC
**Thursday August 19th**
## BOW WOW WOW
**Saturday August 21st**
## JAZZ DEFECTORS
**Wednesday August 25th**
## THE ASSOCIATES

### 11-13 Whitworth St. West, Manchester
**061-236 5051**

## HACIENDA August 14th 1982

Formerly a Bollywood Cinema in the 1970's, The Hacienda opened in 1982 and was owned and operated by Factory Records and the band New Order. Just two months after the opening, the paint still wet, Bauhaus played there in between sessions for our third LP, The Sky's Gone Out. While we were loading in our equipment, a couple of chaps from the club were helping out. I thought that one of them looked a bit familiar, and I suddenly realized it was the bass player from New Order, Peter Hook! Talk about hands on. I really admired him for that; mucking in with the rest of us. Apparently a stage hand wasn't his only mode of employment at the club, he was also a volunteer bouncer. It transpired that later on, Peter got into some sort of disagreement at the door with Hook because Peter didn't have a pass and Hook threw him out! He eventually managed to gain entrance and it was all water under the bridge afterwards. Our performance at The Hacienda was filmed by the venue's own Ikon Video, owned by Malcolm Whitehead, who were almost instrumental in capturing much of the surviving footage of early Joy Division. Our performance sadly remains unreleased.

# Bela Lugosi's Dead.

White on White Translucent Black capes
Back on the rack ... Bela Lugosi's dead
The bats have left the Belltower
The victims have been bled
Red velvet lines the black Box
Bela Lugosi's dead

The virginal brides file past his tomb
Strewn with times dead flowers
Bereft in deathly bloom

Alone in a darkened room ... The count

Bela Lugosi's dead

Undead
Undead .

# Boys.

① We try to fly
Is it so high
We don't think so
We don't think so
Can we fake him
Emmulate him.

② Time is breaking
Changing faking
Grind us up now
Not too hard now
Features so fine
Rouge and eyeline
Things I fancy
Just like nancy

③ Fashions alter
Often falter
Crepe soles out now
No more fights now
Make up's taking
Lots of shaping
On my eye lash
You sure it don't clash

④ Slimline trousers
Facial Powders
Flooding my mind
You sure there's no ~~lies~~ lines
Eye me up now
Pamper me now
Please don't pass by
or I shall cry.

GRAHAM

# SINGLES ACCOUNTED FOR

SINGLES SOLD AT DISCOUNT:-

1 JOANNES FATHER - £1·00.
1 " CHAUFFEUR - £1·00.
1 KENNY/JACKY - £1·00.        } £4·00p.
1 AUNT/ROSE/UNCLE JOE. - £1·00

SINGLES SOLD AT FULL PRICE:
1 AVON WORKER) = £2·00
1 DIANNA (AVON) (£2·00).
~~GRAHAM~~                        } £7·00p
1 (AVON WORKER) (STEVE £2·00p
1 " " ANNE - £2·00p
1 DIANE (AVON) - £1·00) } -£1·00 owed

( 1·00   IN   HAND.)

SINGLES
OWED: { KEVIN OWES £8·00p) - (8 singles Taken)
ON      DIANE " £1·00) -
         GRAHAM - £1·00p) -
DANNY £4·00.    £11·00 OWED (£11·00p
                                £16·00

These are doodles that I made in order to pass time whilst touring.

Peter Murphy and Harry Isles, New York 1982 / Photo: Kevin Haskins

# VISA APPLICATION FORM TO ENTER JAPAN

Name in full ___ HASKINS ___
(Surname)

KEVIN MICHAEL
(Given and middle name)

Different name used, if any ___

Sex  MALE    Marital status ___ married ___ single ✓

Nationality or citizenship  BRITISH

Former nationality, if any ___

Date and place of birth  19 - 7 - 1960 : NORTHAMPTON  NORTHANTS  ENGLAND
(Day) (Month) (Year)    (City)    (Province)    (Country)

Criminal record, if any ___ NONE ___

Home address ▓▓▓▓▓▓▓▓▓▓▓ NORTHAMPTON

Tel. ___

Profession or occupation  MUSICIAN

Name and address of firm or organization to which applicant belongs  BAUHAUS

▓▓▓▓▓▓ NEWNHAM, NORTHANTS    Tel. 03272 - 5032

Post or rank held at present  DRUMMER WITH "BAUHAUS" BAND.

Principal former positions ___

Passport    (Refugee or stateless should note the title of Travel Document) ___

No. 16366ZF  ~~Diplomatic, Official~~, Ordinary Issued at PETERBOROUGH on 21 - 1 - 1980

Issuing authority PASSPORT OFFICE    Valid until 21 - 1 - 1990.

Purpose of journey to Japan  CONCERT TOUR

Length of stay in Japan intended  ONE WEEK

✳ Route of present journey : Name of ship or airline  TO BE ADVISED

Port of entry into Japan  TOKYO    Probable date of entry  25 MAY 1983.

Address of hotels or names and addresses of persons with whom applicant intends to stay

KEIO PLAZA HOTEL, TOKYO    GRAND HOTEL, OSAKA.

Dates and duration of previous stays in Japan  NONE

Guarantor or reference in Japan : Name  UDO ARTISTS INC.

Address  2 MIYA-CHU BLDG., 3-8-37 MINAMI AOYAMA    Tel. 03 402 7281
MINATO KU  TOKYO 107

Relationship to applicant  EMPLOYER / CONCERT PROMOTER IN JAPAN

| Persons accompanying applicant and included in his passport | Name | Relationship | Birthdate |
|---|---|---|---|
| | ___ | ___ | ___ |

I hereby declare that the statement given above is true and correct. Also, I understand that immigration status and period of stay to be granted are decided by the Japanese immigration authorities upon my arrival.

Date of application 13 TH APRIL 1983.

Signature of applicant ___

(FORM No. 1-C)

**BAUHAUS**

VAT. REG. No. 336 2766 45

NEWNHAM,
NORTHANTS,   NN11 6HE
Phone: 03272-5032

To Whom it May Concern

Re: Kevin Michael Haskins

Mr. K. Haskins has been the drummer with
Bauhaus since the groups inception in 1979,
during which time the band have recorded
3 albums and many singles.  They are currently
recording their fourth album.

Prior to this Mr. Haskins was a student at
Northampton College of Art for 3 years; he
joined Bauhaus straight from college and has
not worked with any other bands or followed
any other career.

Harry Isles
Manager

CONCERT PROMOTIONS LTD. bring you

# BAUHAUS

*Live in Paris*
April 11th
£59

## YOUR WEEKEND CONCERT PRICE INCLUDES:

Return travel by luxury coach with video.*Cross channel ferry.
One nights hotel accommodation in Paris.*Ticket to the concert.
Half day excursion of Paris (optional). * Cancellation insurance.

---

DEPART NORTHAMPTON LONDON    April 10th morning

ARRIVE BACK    April 12th morning

☎ **MicheLangelo Travel Ltd**
**Northampton 24826/7**

Or write enclosing deposit(s) to
**Michaelangelo Travel Ltd., 19 Castilian St Northampton**

# CRUEL WORLD

GOLDENVOICE PRESENTS

SATURDAY MAY 2ND

LOS ANGELES

# MORRISSEY
# BAUHAUS
## BLONDIE DEVO
### ECHO & THE BUNNYMEN
### THE PSYCHEDELIC FURS
### VIOLENT FEMMES   THE CHURCH
### ENGLISH BEAT   PUBLIC IMAGE LTD.
### GARY NUMAN   MARC ALMOND

SHE WANTS REVENGE   BLAQK AUDIO   TR/ST
COLD CAVE   JAY ASTON'S GENE LOVES JEZEBEL
BERLIN   BAD MANNERS   MISSING PERSONS
LONDON AFTER MIDNIGHT   DRAB MAJESTY
45 GRAVE   CHRISTIAN DEATH   THE METEORS
BLACK MARBLE   SEXTILE   SOFTKILL   THE KVB

CRUELWORLDFEST.COM   THE GROUNDS AT DIGNITY HEALTH SPORTS PARK

CAMERA SCRIPT                                    1/LLV F232H

BBC-1 COLOUR                                     TX: 14TH APRIL 1983.


                T O P   O F   T H E   P O P S (997)

                Featuring:

                SWEET DREAMS                     (PA/BT)
                EURYTHMICS                       (PROMO VT)
                BAUHAUS                          (PA/BT)
                USA CHARTS/JONATHAN KING         (BBC/PROMO VTS)
                KISSING THE PINK                 (PA/BT)
                SUNFIRE                          (PA/BT)
                KAJAGOOGOO                       (PROMO VT)
                DAVID BOWIE                      (PROMO VT)
                NEW ORDER                        (PLAYOUT DISC/CREDITS)

                Introduced by: DAVE LEE TRAVIS
                               ANDY PEEBLES

* * * * * * * * * * * * * * * * * * * * * * * * * * * * * * * *

PROGRAMME NO:  1/LLV F232H              REC:  13TH APRIL 1983

STUDIO:  TC3                            TX:   14TH APRIL 1983

* * * * * * * * * * * * * * * * * * * * * * * * * * * * * * * *

            Executive Producer .................MICHAEL HURLL
            Director ..........................JOHN BISHOP
            Production Manager ................TONY NEWMAN
            Production Assistants .............LESLEY COULBURN
                                               ELAINE JONES
            A.F.M.s ...........................NICK FIVEASH
                                               JOHN BIRKIN
            Floor Assistants ..................SIMON SPENCER
                                               JANE PEBERDY
            Vision Mixer ......................CAROL ABBOTT
            Floor Manager .....................TONY REDSTON
            Ryley Operator ....................CYNTHIA INIONS
            T.M.1* ............................CLIVE THOMAS
            T.M.2 .............................HARRY BRADLEY
            Sound Supervisor ..................ALAN STOKES
            Gram Op ...........................KEITH MAYES
            Vision Supervisor .................BRIAN ROWE
            Designer ..........................JOHN ANDERSON
            Costume Designer ..................JOAN WADGE
            Make-Up Designer ..................CHRISTINE WHEELER
            Visual Effects ....................DAVE HAVARD
            Video Effects .....................ROBIN LOBB
            Graphic Designer ..................LINDA THOMSON
            Photographer ......................JOHN JEFFORD
            Dance Director ....................FLICK COLBY
            Crew ..............................15 (ROGER FENNA)

| | | | |
|---|---|---|---|
| 31. | (25) | you can't hide (your love from me) | david joseph |
| 32. | (39) | LAST FILM | KISSING THE PINK |
| 33. | (28) | run for your life | bucks fizz |
| 34. | (55) | OVERKILL | MEN AT WORK |
| 35. | (42) | SHE'S IN PARTIES | BAUHAUS |
| 36. | (50) | ROSANNA | TOTO |
| 37. | (NE) | **TRUE LOVE WAYS** | CLIFF RICHARD |
| 38. | (64) | **FRIDAY NIGHT** | KIDS FROM FAME |
| 39. | (43) | TWIST (ROUND AND ROUND) | CHIL FAC-TORR |
| 40. | (NE) | WE ARE DETECTIVE | THOMPSON TWINS |
| 41. | (45) | I'M NEVER GIVING UP | SWEET DREAMS |
| 42. | (59) | TELEGRAPH | ORCHESTRAL MANOEUVRES IN THE DARK |
| 43. | (NE) | TEMPTATION | HEAVEN 17 |
| 44. | (61) | HEY | JULIO IGLESIAS |
| 45. | (31) | vision in blue | ultravox |
| 46. | (36) | joy | band aka |
| 47. | (67) | DER KOMISSAR | AFTER THE FIRE |
| 48. | (52) | JOHNNY B. GOODE | PETER TOSH |
| 49. | (NE) | OUT OF SIGHT, OUT OF MIND | LEVEL 42 |
| 50. | (33) | high life | modern romance |

Camera script for our performance of "She's In Parties" on Top Of The Pops

## BOYS ON FILM

Daniel was passing through his parent's living room where his Dad was meeting with his accountant Graham Bentley. Graham was not your typical conservative accountant type. Rather, underneath all the numbers and calculators he was more the alternative anarchist hippy. He asked Daniel about our next gig and offered to video tape us. Video was in its infancy, so this offer was very exciting. On January 3rd '79, he came to see us at the Romany pub in our home town, Northampton and was quite smitten. He offered to make more videos and so a date was set up for the following month, after we had completed our first recording session. After surreptitiously gaining entrance to the newly built theater at the college where we rehearsed, we assembled our equipment. The state of the art video camera was the size of a large boombox and weighed a ton! We were excited to be able to see ourselves "on film" and Graham captured us miming to that entire session which consisted of: "Some Faces", "Bite My Hip", "Harry", "Boys" and of course "Bela Lugosi's Dead". We also performed, "Femme Fatale" by The Velvet Underground. For the latter, we raided the theatre's costume department, dressing up in various frocks and jewellery. Any excuse to don women's clothing and put on a bit of lippy! The image quality paled in comparison to today's standards, but no one had access to a video camera and we felt very privileged. Over the next few months this rudimentary black and white video would be taken to meetings at all the big labels in London with the goal of securing a recording contract. Unfortunately, most of them didn't even own a VHS player!

Graham's talents were not just confined to punching numbers and directing. He went on to become our lighting designer and, in the early years, our tour manager. Once we began to secure shows in London, we were not content to rely on the random arrangement of multi colored house lights, so we acquired half a dozen huge industrial lamps from a disused factory. We simply laid these on the stage floor and the huge white bulbs created our signature floor-lit, film noir look. In interviews David would quip, "coloured lights are for Christmas trees!" As time went on Graham would invent new techniques such as hand-held strobe and UV strip lights. This would illuminate UV sensitive paint which Peter and Daniel would daub over their skinny bodies. In another inspired display of creativity, Graham utilized the guts of an old washing machine to recreate the slow moving shadow effect, as seen in the video of "She's In Parties." Our stage production has always been of great importance to us and in our early years, Graham was instrumental in realizing our visions.

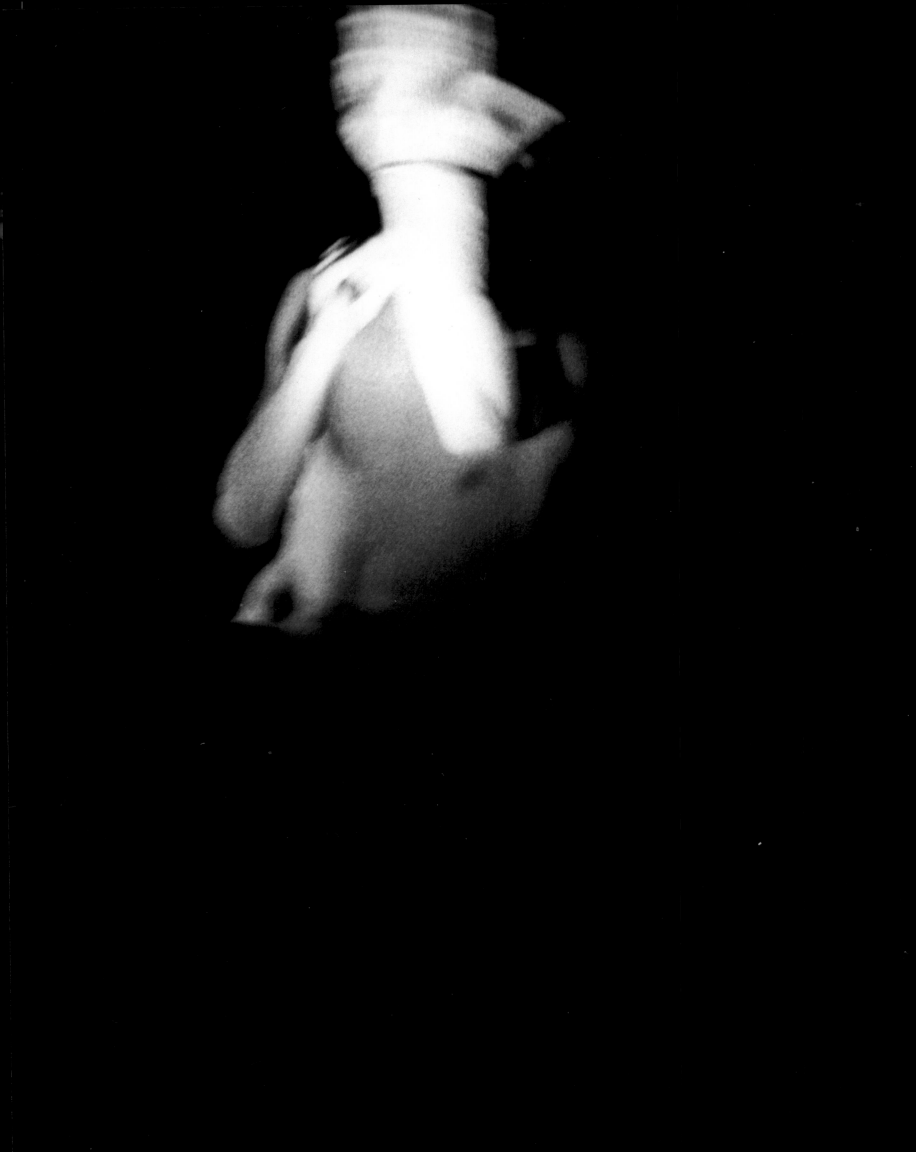

Photos: Kevin Haskins

## LUTON'S MEMOIR

The date is February 1st, 1980, I'm 14 years old and its lunchtime in a Luton high school. My friend Graham Manton approached me and asked if I was going to the gig at the Luton Tech College that night as, "There is this great band called Bow Wows or summit playing" and he's heard good things about them.

Flash forward six hours, I find myself standing at the front of the stage. There followed a moment that surely changed my life forever! The lights went out and the opening chords of "Double Dare" filled the air. Amidst the smoke and strobes a tall, skinny, bare chested and caped androgynous creature appeared. The figure stood there, then bowed, leaning his face into a beam of a single white light. His eyes and mouth opened as he unleashed his first snarl, and glared at the already fixated Luton crowd. I was hooked.

It's the 5th of July 1983 at the Hammersmith Palais in London and "Plug", their sound engineer, warned us not to miss a single moment of that night's show. It had been just over three years, and in that time I had travelled the length of the UK numerous times, as well as France, and had seen the band perform no fewer than sixty two times. Along the way I had met a superb group of twenty or so like-minded individuals from all over the country who shared my love of the electricity and energy, that was in the air at every single Bauhaus show. Why you may ask?

At each show, the level of drama and electricity never stopped. It was relentless. No gap, the mask never fell; it was pure theatre from start to finish. The physical performance from all four was sublime. They each had their own individual roles and without being contrived, they played them to perfection. The music itself was far ahead of the game too. On some nights at the early shows, the gig would start with "Double Dare" and Peter would first appear as just a stark black and white face on an old TV set balanced on some crates centre stage. Genius idea from their legendary lighting designer Graham Bentley. He was my hero and as I will explain later on; I owe him a great deal.

The timing for the likes of me and my fellow travellers could not have been more perfect either. Punk was all but over and many of us were just slightly too young to have appreciated the full impact of that explosion. We had now found our band, our sound, our scene, and we loved every single minute of it. My early ventures to such venues as Friars in Aylesbury, Northampton's Roadmender, U.L.U (London University) and the likes were normally in the company of my childhood Luton friend; Barrie Eves, but as I became more obsessed and had to be

at every show possible and on every tour, I found I was traveling alone, often hitching lifts around the country to get from venue to venue. It wasn't long before I started to notice other familiar faces in the crowd and in time we started talking.

As far as I know my record of sixty two shows was only ever eclipsed by a man who became a friend called "Milli". He was often accompanied by his younger brother Neil. These two were part of a beautiful gang of boys and girls who went under the name of "The Wicked Walton Bauhaus Crew". This moniker was spray painted on their home-made T-shirts. In fact it was my own homemade T-shirt (mentioned by Danny Cannon in the first edition of this book) that was the common ground that first broke the ice with them.

After a show, as we caught our breath and headed off into the night covered in sweat, early exchanges were along the lines of, "You going to Glasgow tomorrow?". These encounters always appeared more of a challenge to each other rather than a straightforward question. But a mutual respect was beginning to grow, as day after day we'd all appear at the next show. The numbers would vary depending on the distance from London but as the shows grew in size and the band in stature, so did the numbers in our band of merry men and women.

Once at the gigs we were all undoubtedly a band of brothers and sisters together, but travels to each show were often individual adventures for the various members of the party. We jumped trains, hitched lifts, and some travelled in an old camper van. We did whatever we needed to, to get to the next town on time. The nearest pub to the venue was our agreed meeting point. Once in town we would gather and regale our tales of our journeys from the previous night's gig. To be fair we never really went mad on drink in the pubs, and most of us were way too young to even be in a bar, but one thing that often took precedent over getting a beer was finding an electric socket to plug in our crimpers and do our hair!

It was mainly great times and good fun. We had the odd scrape here and there, such as being chased out of France after the Paris show by crazed locals. We were often given some unwanted local attention at the more dodgy venues and towns. We felt this was our band and we had found them, so sometimes it got a bit hectic as we became more territorial, protecting our space at the front of stage each night. Our playground at the shows was "down the front" and this belonged to us as far as we were concerned. We developed our own moves. Human pyramids of sorts, weird chicken dancing, and during the down tempo song "Hollow Hills" we always sat on the floor to get a breather, then back to full on whirling dervishes in a flash. There was the odd fight when this space was invaded by outside parties hell bent on starting on us, but 90% of the time it was harmless fun and there are a lot of unwritten rules in a mosh pit that must be obeyed for it to work. It's self-policed organized chaos.

Another fond memory was the show at "The Old Vic" where we were treated to a special escort by security to our place down at the front. My favourite memory was when Peter Murphy, during "Rosegarden Funeral Of Sores", climbed fifteen feet up the red velvet curtains before they tore and he fell crashing to the floor. Not missing a beat he then crawled to his microphone that was strewn centre stage, arriving just in time to hit his line. All absolute theatre and the venue could not have been a more perfect setting to stage the spectacle.

On one occasion in 1982 at the legendary Hacienda in Manchester, the bands crew helped us out. The club had just opened and there was a £5 membership that you needed to get in. We were not able to join on the day so we retreated to the nearest pub to commiserate. As we sat there working out what to do, Plug their sound engineer came in. It turned out that he'd hunted us down to tell us he had put us on the bands guest list. Hilariously he had put us down simply as Milli plus 17! This was genius and we were over the moon. The guest list was something we had never requested or expected. We always bought tickets and never hassled the band or crew for favours. We just went to the gig, had a great time and left, but Plug, Graham Bentley and Reasonable Ray always looked out for us. We'd always leave all our coats and stuff under Plug's desk during the show too. When we did that on July 5th he tipped us off that the end was nigh but we were not massively surprised.

As I walked away from the last gig at Hammersmith Palais on July 5th, 1983, I had the remnants of the homemade T-shirt in my pocket as it had been ripped from by back that night, the irony! It had been just over three years of adventures and I was still only a 17 year old kid whose eyes had been opened to the wonders and magic that can only come from seeing the band you love play live.

I wasn't to know that just three years after that in 1986 I would be on a Jumbo jet heading to the USA with Daniel, Kevin and David, who had formed a new band called "Love And Rockets". Inspired by Graham Bentley, I had taken up lighting design and here I was about to start another chapter full of even more incredible adventures and fun.

Life is but a dream….

Luton 1981

It would be rude not to give the names of the main players from those days. I'll attempt to name as many of these lovely people here as I can but I'm sure I will forget some, and for that I apologize. Remember this was nearly 40 years ago but with the help of Milli I think we have recalled the main regulars we'd meet at most of the shows. From the WWBC there was Rachael, Purce, Gareth, Debbie, Sasha, Hayley, Ricky, Nobby, Matthew, Jon Peters and last and certainly not least was the man who seemed to be Milli's main wingman and that was Bulba. From all corners of the UK we were joined by such names as Welshman, Bruce from Lowestoft, Jon and Pooh from Leatherhead, Jez, Colin and Zorch from Basildon, Mick from Middlesboro as well as Sheila and Connie from Stoke. Milli went on to join the bands crew towards the end, which was great for him, but we missed him. -Sadly whilst searching for names and pictures from these guys I have found out that both Bulba and Pooh have since passed. RIP guys.

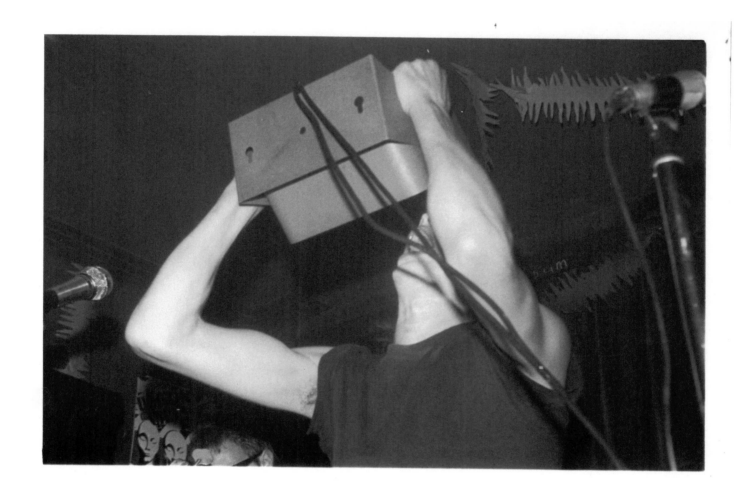

Mark Ginns,
13, The Drive,
Kettering,
Northants.

Typewritten letter from David Haskins to a Mr. Mark Ginns

Dear inquisitor,

      Thank you for writing, it is always encouraging when
interest of this nature is shown.We hope that the notes
enclosed answer your questions.
      Bela Lugosi is dead, BAUHAUS on the other hand...

love
and
dark
thoughts

BAUHAUS

BAUHAUS 1919

Northampton

OCTOBER 79

Dear Sir

1 Name of group BAUHAUS 1919

2 Formed 1.1.79

3 Drums, Kevin Haskins

4 Guitar and voice, Daniel Ash

5 Bass and voice, David J

6 Lead voice, Peter Murphy

7 Management, Graham Bentley, 21 Cotswold Avenue, Northampton
Tel: 0604 51307

8 12" single 'Bela Lugosi's Dead'  (Small Wonder).

9 Publishing contract held with Small Wonder for the above
title and 'Boys'

10 Dates played so far, 15 including The Marquee, The Nashville,
Music Machine

11 Duration of current set, one hour

12. We see Bauhaus as being synonymous with the 80's and look
forward to the coming decade

We mean to make a mark.

# BAUHAUS

# Beggars Banquet
## HOGARTH ROAD, LONDON S.W.5.

*upto alau*

### BAUHAUS

Northampton is as comfortable as last year's boots and shoes...at least, until you have lived there long enough to get a glimpse of what's hiding behind its net curtains and pebble-dashing. Per head of population it has one of the highest violent crime rates in the country, and there can be few other provincial towns whose local papers boast headlines such as "VAMPIRE KILLER GETS LIFE" and mean it. David Jay has referred to it as the "murder Mecca of the Midlands", and it should not be surprising that this is where the Bauhaus carnival of unease has pitched its black marquee.

But this is jumping the gun a little. Before Bauhaus, there was The Craze, and before that there was The Submerged Tenth. The Submerged Tenth were a punk band, formed in the crackling brain-rush of 1977. Amongst its members were David Jay and Kevin Haskins, and when the band folded after only three gigs they obviously felt that they still had something left to say. Their next venture, The Craze, was equally short-lived but significant in that it was at this point that Daniel Ash entered the picture. Exit The Craze. Enter Peter Murphy. Enter Bauhaus. The rest, as they say, is hysteria.

The principle tenet of the original Bauhaus movement had been that Art, for the sake of its own survival, must embrace the machine. It was a sentiment that their latter-day counterparts found particularly apt as, in the last months of 1978, they set about recording their first demo singles on cheap tape recorders with cheaper instruments and inadequate equipment. Oddly enough, however, the marriage worked. Within six weeks of their formation Bauhaus had their first single, "Bela Lugosi Is Dead", released on Small Wonder.

A startlingly atmospheric debut, "Bela" brought the Bauhaus sound to the attention of the audience on a wave of glittering fog. Jay's bass and Haskins' drums provided the music with its elegant and powerful metal skeleton, while Murphy's hard, haunting voice and Ash's molten glass guitar provided its white, jewel-studded flesh. The single rose to the heights of the alternative charts, and the last time I looked, some two years later, it was still there.

BEGGARS BANQUET RECORDS LTD    DIRECTORS: N.AUSTIN  M.C.MILLS
REGD.OFFICE: 8, HOGARTH ROAD, LONDON S.W.5.    BUSINESS REGISTRATION No. 1414048    VAT No. 340 1066 10

Photographs by Kevin Haskins taken during Bauhaus' first tour of Japan.

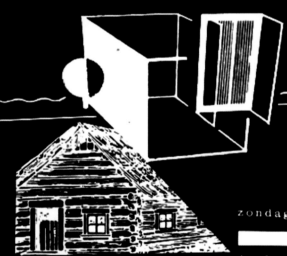

## POPPERS

We had just played our final show in Rotterdam, Holland in support of "In The Flat Field" in Europe, and were driving through the Dutch countryside in the dead of night, to make some headway for our long journey home. Seated behind me were Peter and Daniel who were giggling and conspiring like two naughty boys on a school trip. To my right was David, with Graham Bentley riding shotgun to co-owner of 4AD records, Peter Kent, who had offered his services as tour manager. Despite the racket they were causing, I was gradually lulled off to sleep by the rocking motion of our mini bus.

A little back story; Whilst in Amsterdam at the beginning of the tour, Daniel and Peter had discovered "Poppers" or Amyl Nitrate. A recreational drug that is carefully inhaled from the bottle and in seconds causes a huge rush of blood to the brain, causing dizziness, and disorientation that can last up to two minutes. Unfortunately Peter and Daniel came up with the genius idea of holding the bottle of Poppers under my nose whilst I was sleeping, just to see what would happen. As chance would have it the bus hit a pot hole and the next thing I experienced was waking up to the sensation of a cold liquid soaking my shirt and trousers, and a powerful and pungent odour that made my head feel that it was about to explode! The entire contents of the bottle had emptied on me! The toxic fumes were so intense that Peter Kent had to pull over fast, as he immediately felt the adverse effects. As soon as we came to a halt, I threw open the door and ran about 500 meters in to the middle of a farmers field, removing my sodden t shirt on the way. My thinking (which was very difficult at the time) was that I needed to get as much fresh air as possible, and the middle of a vast field seemed to be the most logical solution. I sat in the field, whilst someone played pin ball inside my throbbing brain, gulping down as much oxygen as I could. Once recovered, I returned to the bus to change out of my chemically enhanced clothing and to give Daniel and Peter a severe scolding. Their sheepish grins betrayed their ill-advised actions.

KAMIKAZI DIVE

*Bauhaus*

PEARL HARBOR DAY
DEC. 7
1982

東京帝國大
徒報國隊

special guests
FIGURES ON A BEACH

METRO

3730 N. CLARK    549-0203

TICKETS AT: WAX TRAX RECORDS
ROSE RECORDS ON BROADWAY
JUST FOR THE RECORD
RECORD EXCHANGE II

DOORS OPEN 9PM

Brian Shanley

B   A   U   H   A   U   S

# BAUHAUS

PERSONNEL:   KEVIN HASKINS:   DRUMS
             DANIEL ASH    :   GUITAR + VOICE
             DAVID JAY     :   BASS   + VOICE
             PETER MURPHY  :   LEAD VOICE


RECORDS  :   BELA LUGOSI'S DEAD 12" SINGLE (SMALL WONDER)
             C/W BOYS

              DARK ENTRIES        7" SINGLE (4 A.D.)
             C/W UNTITLED


The group formed in January 1979, recording Bela Lugosi as
a demo after only six weeks.
Bauhaus use conventional instruments in an unconventional
way to achieve an effect that is both modern and disciplined
anarchic and impassioned.


Bauhaus John Peel session broadcast 3.1.80

0604 51307

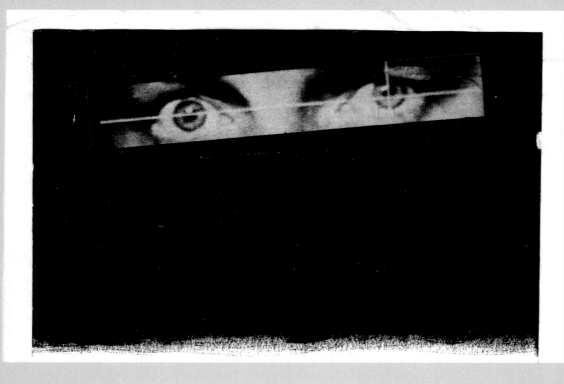

# BAVHAVS

EXPRESSION THROUGH chAncE/surrender to the UNKNOWN/plaY the DIce Man
roll YOuR oWn QUEstIonS oN anY STReEt COrNer PlaY saFE onlY wHEn It
Is DANgeROus tO dO sO rIP up YOuR ~~ANSWERS~~ all
                                    TOMORROWS     thrOW thE piecE s inTo thE

AIr
   leT them FAll fOLlow thE heArt anD the UncoNsciOUs MInd look foR thE
"BALenCe beTweEn heAVeN and Hell chAnCe anD desIgN theRE is No logIC
tO thE soUl.
   primEVal MagIc is noT plAned!

CHANCE RESULTS IN HONEST EXPRESSION
EMMEDIACY VITALITY ENERGY CHANCE INJECTS
THE SPARK THAT GIVES FEELING TO THE METHOD.
CHAOS CAN ONLY EXIST AS AN ALTERNATIVE IN
AN ORDERED WORLD. ORDER AND CHAOS
CO-EXIST TOGETHER AND ALWAYS WILL
ORDER IS MADE OF CHAOS AND CHAOS OUT OF
DISRUPTING ORDER. THE ORDER BROUGHT TO CHAOS
IS AS DISRUPTING TO THE STATE OF CHAOS AS CHAOS IS TO
ORDER, THEY CAN BE THE SAME THING. THEY ARE BOTH
VITAL, EACH TO THE OTHER. LOOK FOR THE BEAUTY
OF THE SPONTANEOUS, THE AUTOMATIC. AND APPLY THIS
TO THE METHOD

   the 1st. BAUHAUS album will be released later this year (IF ALL GOS
TO PLAN!!) 44 44 PRIOR TO THIS... A U.K. TOUR (SEE PRESS FOR DATES)
3 DATES IN NEW YORK/AND U.S.A.R U.K. TOUR (HELLOW NORTHAMPTON)
EUROPEAN TOUR (GERMANY, HOLLAND FRANCE, BELGIUM) AND POL
SOMETHING SPECIAL FOR JESUS' BIRTHDAY.
NOW RIP THIS UP AND SEE HOW THE PIECES FALL!
19.80.
                                                         David J.

KALX,KUSF,KFJC BRING YOU ALTERNATIVE RADIO NIGHT WITH

# båuhåus
## T S O L

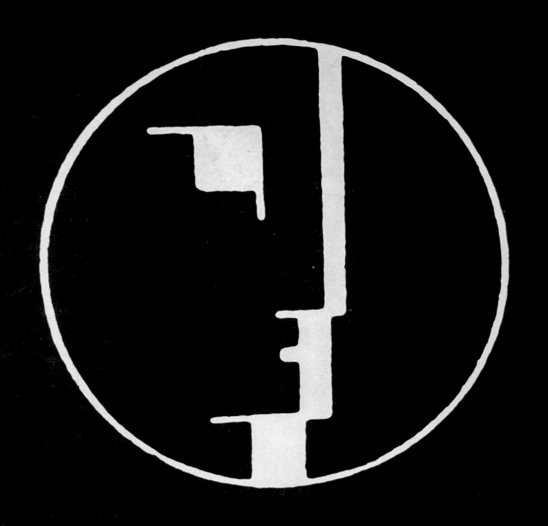

WEDNESDAY, DECEMBER 15, 9pm. OLD WALDORF,444 BATTERY

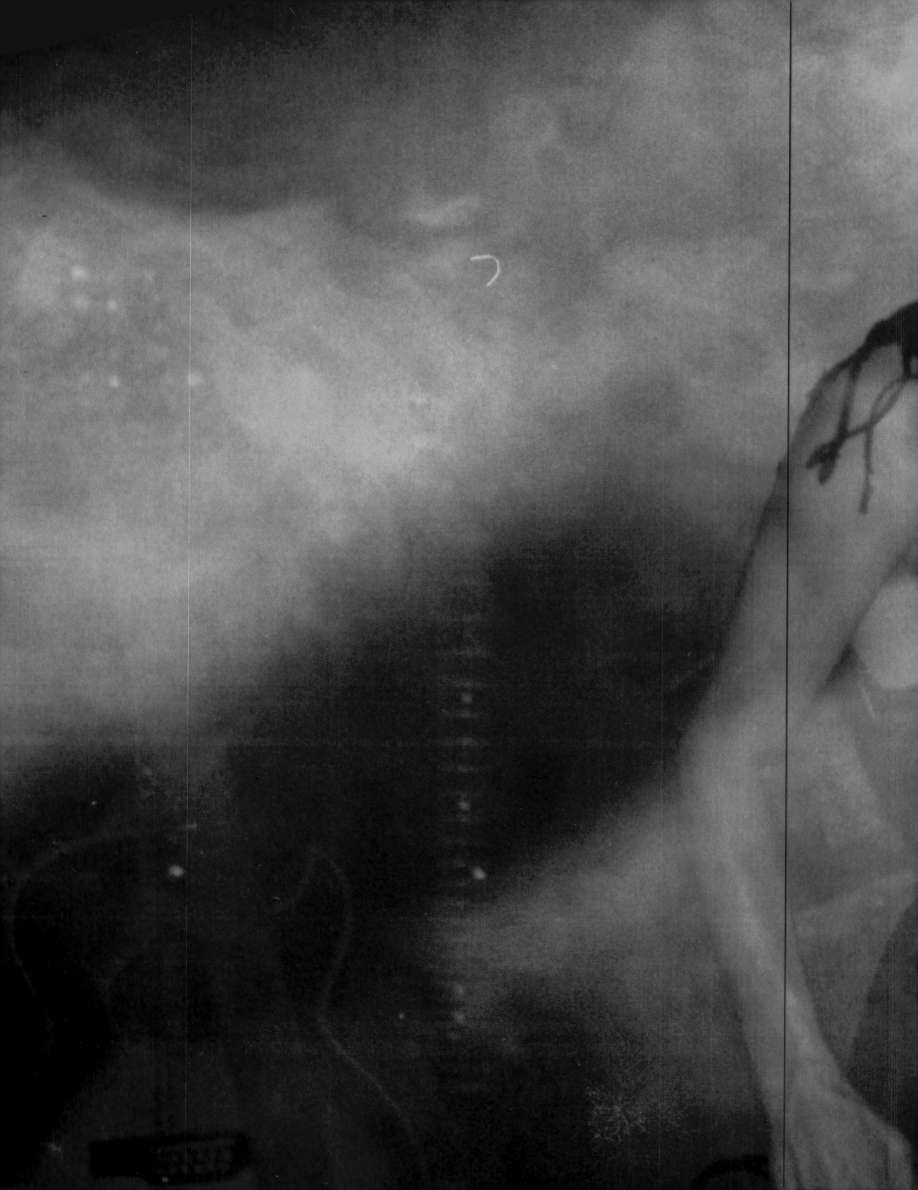

Pete Stennett owner of Small Wonder records. / Photos: The Shend

## SMALL WONDER - BELA LUGOSI'S DEAD

After recording "Bela Lugosi's Dead", we knew we had created something very, very special! Unfortunately, or fortunately, with regards to most of the record labels that we approached, the feeling wasn't mutual. Daniel visited practically every major label in London and was met with, "I really like this, it's the sort of thing that I listen to at home, but it's not commercial enough." And "We can't release this, it's way too long for a single!" Undeterred, we turned our attention to the indie labels and, at first, didn't have much joy there also. Chris Parry at Fiction (then home to The Cure) stated, "Although it has it's interesting bits, I found "Bela Lugosi's Dead" a bit too introverted and overlong."

Thankfully, there was one individual named Pete Stennett at Small Wonder Records who got it. Pete Stennett is a lovely chap, who ran his label from his small record store in Walthamstow, East London. He was a little older than us, with a mischievous smile and blond hair that protruded from under the ever present beanie.

Every spare surface in his store was festooned with 7" picture sleeves, stickers and promotional posters, complemented by homemade record bins. In the front window was hidden a large bag of weed, behind a life sized cardboard cutout of Elvis Costello. Pete figured that that would be the last place that the cops would look! The label was home to Crass, The Cravats, Patrick Fitzgerald, The Cure, Poison Girls, Angelic Upstarts and many other fine bands.

We have to thank Colin Faver, or Cos as he was known, for introducing us to Pete Stennett. Cos worked at Small Wonder on Saturdays and during the week he was DJ'ing and promoting shows under the name, "Final Solution". He went on to have a notable career

starting KissFM and four decades as a world renowned DJ. We ran into Cos at one of his events and gave him an acetate of "Bela" which he passed on to Pete the following Saturday.

Consequently, Pete invited us down to meet with him at his record store in East London and, on our arrival, put on the kettle to make a strong pot of tea. We chatted for a while and then he informed us that he needed to listen to "Bela" just one more time to make up his mind. I don't know if he was playing games and had already made his decision, or if he actually did need one more listen! He placed the needle on the acetate of "Bela" and standing amongst the record bins we listened with cautious confidence. The single, clocking in at 9 minutes 37 seconds, felt more like 9 decades! Finally the final kick drum punctuated the end of the record and we all looked at Pete with eager anticipation. There was a pause, an almost indiscernible slight nod of the head, and then Pete said, "Yes, I'd like to release it!" A rush of adrenalin coursed through my veins, and it felt like a phosphorescent display of fireworks were going off inside my head! He was going to release it!! A record label (and a fine one at that) was actually going to release one of our songs!! Being typically British, we all politely thanked him, suppressing the absolute joy and excitement we felt inside, but once outside of the store, we ran down Hoe Street whooping, hollering and leaping for joy, like little kids who just got off school for the summer holidays.

When we received the first pressing in the mail, I will never forget pulling out the twelve inches of vinyl and examining every groove. I had to keep checking the inner circle to see if our name was still there, believing that I had somehow got it all wrong, and that this was in fact a record by another band. This was another beautiful and magical benchmark moment.

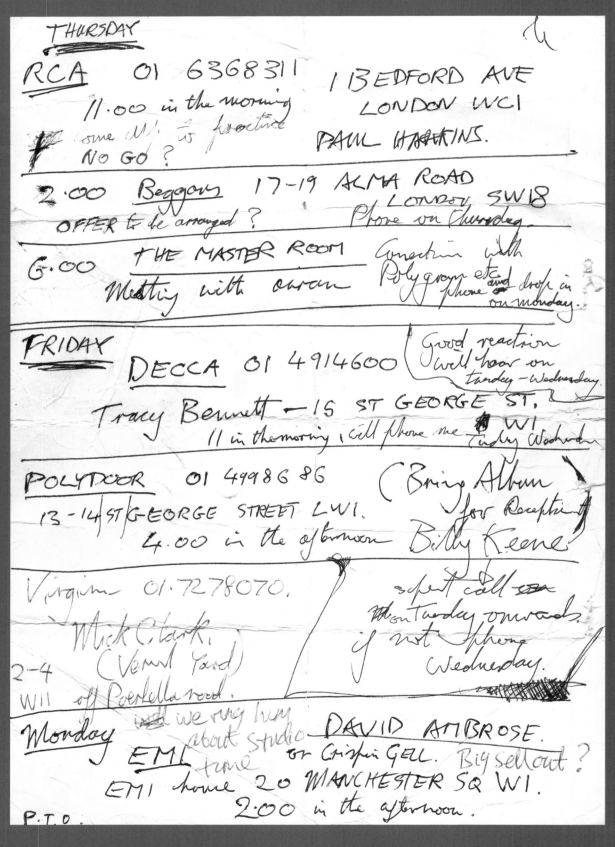

THURSDAY

**RCA** 01 6368311    1 BEDFORD AVE
11.00 in the morning    LONDON WC1
come ... to practice    PAUL HAWKINS.
NO GO ?

2.00 Beggars 17-19 ALMA ROAD
OFFER to be arranged ?    LONDON SW18
     Phone on Thursday.

6.00 THE MASTER ROOM    Connection with
Meeting with owner    Polygram etc
     phone and drop in
     on monday.

---

FRIDAY

**DECCA** 01 4914600   ( Good reaction
     will hear on
     tuesday - Wednesday
Tracy Bennett — 15 ST GEORGE ST.
11 in the morning, will phone me   WI
     Judy Woodward

**POLYDOOR** 01 4998686   ( Bring Album
13-14 ST GEORGE STREET LWI.   for Reception
     4.00 in the afternoon   Billy Keene

Virgin 01.7278070.    spent call
     then Tuesday onwards.
Mick Clark.    if not phone
( Vernal Yard )    Wednesday.
2-4
WII off Portella road.

Monday   we ring him   DAVID AMBROSE.
   about studio    or Crispin GELL. Big sellout ?
**EMI** time
EMI house 20 MANCHESTER SQ WI.
     2.00 in the afternoon.

P.T.O.

---

This is a list of major record company appointments that Daniel made and attended, in order to get a record deal for Bela Lugosi's Dead. Daniel would take an acetate of Bela to each appointment and play it during the meeting. However none of these companies were interested. Interesting that Beggars Banquet turned us down, but would later be the label we ended up on. Most of the A&R guys made comments such as, "This record is way too long for a single" and "I really like this, it's the type of record that I would play at home, but it's too uncommercial."

**Monday** Phone Simon Potts 3.00

~~Tuesday~~ 01·580·5566 3, Cavendish

(Arista Records) SQ

3, Cavendish SQ.

**CBS.** 01·734·8181 Will 17·19 Soho SQ.

(opposite Tottenham Court Tube) bring me on Friday Gordon Charlton

<u>VIRGIN</u> MICK CLARK Synthetics

Ring us Friday 4-5

26th September 4·00

Polydor 3 Cavendish SQ.

Phonogram

Polygram

Decca Arran Says.

London. Phone your self for G.B.

EMI good

~~CB~~ DECCA good,

CBS good, may loose interest

Polydor — ? Dodgy?

Virgin very Dodgy.

207 8477

re. Bauhaus 1919

Dear David,

    thanks for your cassette. Although
it had it's interesting bits I found Bela Lugosi
a bit too introverted and overlong. 'Bite my
hip' suggests your band could be interesting
live.

    Should you play near london in the future
would you let me know and I'll try to make
it.

        Kindest Regards

        Chris Parry.

**Fiction Records** 14-16 Chaplin Road, NW2 Tel: 01 459 8682

A division of 18 Age Record Co. Ltd.    Reg. Office: 7 Cavendish Court 11-15 Wigmore Street London W1    Reg. No: 1285030

Re Bauhaus 1919

Dear David

Thanks for your cassette. Although it had its interesting bits, I found  Bela Lugosi a bit too introverted and overlong.

Bite my hip suggests your band could be interesting live

Should you play near London in the near future could you let me know and ill try to make it

Kindest Regards

Chris Parry

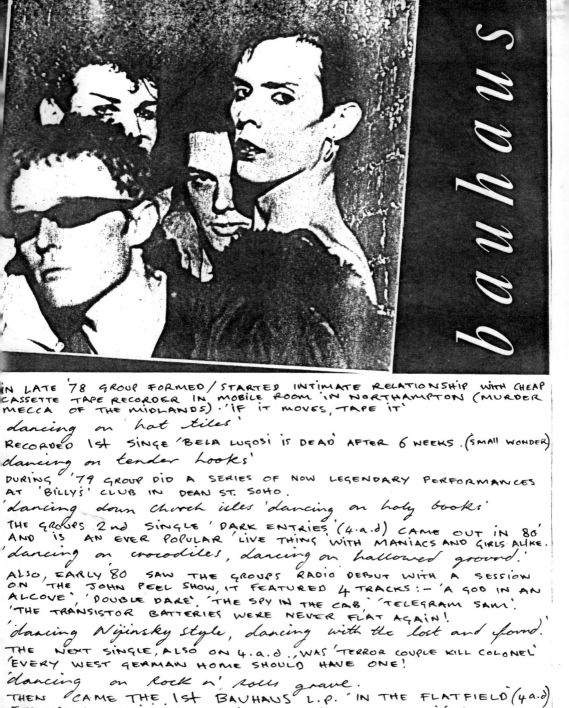

*bauhaus*

IN LATE '78 GROUP FORMED / STARTED INTIMATE RELATIONSHIP WITH CHEAP CASSETTE TAPE RECORDER IN MOBILE ROOM IN NORTHAMPTON (MURDER MECCA OF THE MIDLANDS). 'IF IT MOVES, TAPE IT'

*dancing on 'hot tiles'*

RECORDED 1st SINGE 'BELA LUGOSI IS DEAD' AFTER 6 WEEKS. (SMALL WONDER)

*dancing on tender hooks'*

DURING '79 GROUP DID A SERIES OF NOW LEGENDARY PERFORMANCES AT 'BILLY'S' CLUB IN DEAN ST. SOHO.

*'dancing down church isles 'dancing on holy books'*

THE GROUPS 2nd SINGLE 'DARK ENTRIES' (4.a.d) CAME OUT IN 80' AND IS AN EVER POPULAR 'LIVE THING WITH MANIACS AND GIRLS ALIKE.

*'dancing on crocodiles, dancing on hallowed ground'*

ALSO, EARLY 80 SAW THE GROUPS RADIO DEBUT WITH A SESSION ON 'THE JOHN PEEL SHOW, IT FEATURED 4 TRACKS :- 'A GOD IN AN ALCOVE', 'DOUBLE DARE', 'THE SPY IN THE CAB', 'TELEGRAM SAM'. 'THE TRANSISTOR BATTERIES WERE NEVER FLAT AGAIN!'

*'dancing Nijinsky style, dancing with the lost and found'.*

THE NEXT SINGLE, ALSO ON 4.a.d., WAS 'TERROR COUPLE KILL COLONEL' 'EVERY WEST GERMAN HOME SHOULD HAVE ONE!'

*'dancing on rock n' rolls grave.*

THEN CAME THE 1st BAUHAUS L.P. 'IN THE FLATFIELD'(4.a.d) FEATURING DEFINITIVE VERSIONS OF 'DOUBLE DARE, STIGMATA MARTYR, THE SPY IN THE CAB, 'ALCOVE', AND 'NERVES'.

*'dancing on burning coals, dancing on Jesus saves'*
*'dancing with old skratch soul'.*

TOURS OF ENGLAND, U.S.A, GERMANY, HOLLAND, BELGIUM ENSUED. 'THOUSANDS OF EYES SORE FROM BLINDING WHITE LIGHT. 'COLOURED LIGHTS ARE FOR CHRISTMAS TREES!''

*'dancing on flick knives, dancing a stilleto groove,*
*dancing on nine lines away, dancing in the louvre'.*

1.

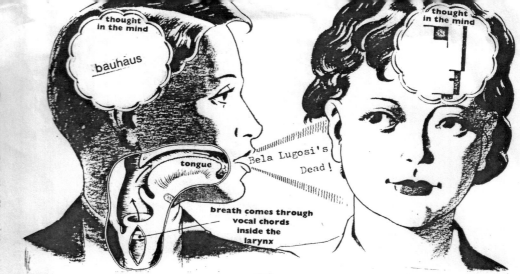

# bauhaus

THE NEXT RELEASE WAS BY POPULAR DEMAND AS A RESULT OF THE LIVE DATES, IT BEING THE GROUPS VERSION OF 'TELEGRAM SA (4 a.d.) THE T. REX HIT. FOR THIS PARTICULAR RECORD A VIDEO W MADE WITH THE HELP OF MICK CALVERT AND DON LETTS, ALTHOUGH THIS WAS NOT THE GROUPS FIRST EXPERIENCE WITH THIS MEDIUM, BAUHAUS MADE VIDEO'S BEFORE PLAYING LIVE. IT IS A FIELD WHAT THE GROUP INTEND TO EXPLORE FURTHER. IN THE LAND OF THE BLIND, THE ONE EYED MONSTER IS GOD!

'dancing in catacombs, dancing in tuxedo drag'

A CHANGE IN LIVING, A CHANGE IN STYLE. '81 IS THE YEAR OF THE DRUM. BEFORE THERE WERE ANY NOTES, THERE WAS BEAT!

'dancing in dark rooms, dancing on all your flags'

'KICK IN THE EYE' THE NEXT SINGLE (BEGGARS BANQUET) c/w SATOR ILLUSTRATES THE LAST POINT.

'dancing in the vatican, dancing on the papal, gown, dancing on the taxman, dancing on the crown.'

GROUP LINE UP:— KEVIN HASKINS - DRUMS... "I JUST LIKE, HITING THIN DAVID JAY - BASS, FELT TIPS, VOICE... "WE HAVE NOW LEFT THE UNDERGROU BUT WE DO INTEND TO GO BACK FOR LOST WEEKENDS, EVERY N AND AGAIN."

PETER MURPHY - LEAD VOICE, COW BELLS... "I TAKE RISKS ON STAGE. IT'S FAR MORE EXCITING TO HAVE UNCERTAINTY THAN TO HAVE A BORING SHOW. ALTHOUGH SOMETIMES I FREAK OUT... I THINK 'WHAT HAVE I LET MYSELF IN FOR? I HAVE TO GO OUT AND DO THAT AND I'M JUST NOT INTO IT AT ALL!"

DANIEL ASH - GUITAR, VOICE, ORANGE JUICE... "I AM FASCINATED BY THE WAY CERTAIN SOUNDS AFFECT THE HUMAN BRAIN."

dancing dancing dancing dancing dancing dancin on rock n' rolls grave.

LEARN THE STEPS!!

# bauhaus

QUESTIONS

1. Some of the newer bands seem to rely heavily on their image.
You don't seem to be part of any popular musical movement but
how important is to you the way you look ?

*It is always important for a girl to look
her best, even when doing those mundane
domestic chores around the house* DAVID JAY

*I like the excentric, the mad man the way
you dress should unease people; you've got
to wear clothes — have fun. Turn heads*
*Its my Head I'll do what I want with it.* KEVIN HASKINS

16. For some reason, you had to quit the music business altogether
what would you do ? How do you see yourself in one year from now

*In an asylum.* PETER MURPHY

Describe this picture.

DANIEL ASH

7. Would you say that pride is a quality or a shortcoming ? What
is the shortcoming you hate the most with people and what quality
do you seek more particulary ?

*pride is a short quality.
the shortcoming I hate the most is
the lack of any shortcomings.
the quality I seek most is
an aptitude for shortcomings.* DAVID JAY

## WHAT is the Bauhaus?

The Bauhaus is an answer to the question: how can the artist be trained to take
his place in the machine age?

Try and describe the room you sleep and/or live in.

*Blue, small, depictions of Rape,
love, tears, and depression.
1 womb music in one corner
1 very large mirror, one single bed.* PETER MURPHY.

AU PLAN K
SAMEDI 5 AVRIL 21 H
Soirée Vampires
BAUHAUS
BAUHAUS
films d' horreur
soirée dansante
concert rock: bauhaus
entrée: 200fb prévente:
popper 21 (tél: 5124598)
21 avenue de la toison d'or
plan K (tél: 5231834)
21 rue de manchester
b
JFO © AWP 1980

# RAFFINERIE DU PLAN K

## SOIRÉE VAMPIRES

Samedi 5 Avril
A partir de 21.00

### BAUHAUS
groupe Rock de Londres

Films d'épouvante
La fiancée du vampire
Le masque du démon
The Other (L'autre)

Films sur le Bauhaus et
les expériences d'Oskar
Schlemmer

Film et diapositives
de Michel Journiac
(Body Art, France)

Prix d'entrée : 200 F.

LE PLAN K - a.s.b.l.
21, rue de Manchester - 1070 Bruxelles - T. 523 18 34 ou 7, galerie de la Reine - 1000 Bruxelles - Belgium - T. 511 11 22

# RAFFINERIE DU PLAN K

PERSBERICHT

IN PLAN K : " BAUHAUS FILMAVOND "

DONDERDAG 10 APRIL OM 21 u. zal er in PLAN K een avond
plaatsvinden met filmvertoningen handelend over de
Duitse " BAUHAUSBEWEGING 1919 - 1933 ".

PROGRAMMA :"MENSCH UND KUNSTFIGUR"

    Bauhaus 1922 , O. Schlemmer - film 1968
    kleur / 28 min. / 16 mm/
    Regie : M.Hasting

    "DAS TRIADISCHE BALLET"

    Bauhaus 1922 , O. Schlemmer - film 1970
    kleur / 32 min. / 16 mm/

    "PAUL KLEE"

    1967 / kleur / 30 min./
    Regie : W. Grohmann - G. van der Rohe

    "REFLEKTORISCHE FARBLICHTSPIELE - KURT SCHWERDTFEGER"

    1967 / kleur / 18 min./
    Regie : R. Jüdes

In samenwerking met het Goethe Instituut , Brussel.

MET DANK VOOR DE OPNAME !

LE PLAN K - a.s.b.l.
21, rue de Manchester - 1070 Bruxelles - T. 523 18 34 ou 7, galerie de la Reine - 1000 Bruxelles - Belgium - T. 511 11 22

# RAFFINERIE DU PLAN K

PERSBERICHT

" FACTORY NIGHT "

ZATERDAG 26 APRIL om 21 u. in PLAN K " FACTORY NIGHT "
met het optreden van de Engelse groepen :
" A CERTAIN RATIO " en " SECTION 25 "

" A Certain Ratio " en " Section 25 " zijn twee nieuwe Engelse
groepen van het befaamde " Factory " label. Dit label telt
onder zijn artiesten ook de groepen " The Durutti Column " en
" Joy Division " , die reeds tweemaal optraden in Plan K .

" SECTION 25 " is een van die veelbelovende jonge groepen. Alle
vier zijn ze afkomstig van Blackpool .
Hun eerste 45 T " Girls don't count " werd geproduced door
Ian Curtis , de zanger van Joy Division.
Zij worden meestal vergeleken met Public Image Ltd.

" A CERTAIN RATIO " bestaat uit vijf muzikanten : Simon Topping
( zang ) , Peter Terrell en Martin Moscrop ( gitaar ) ,
Jeremy Kerr ( bas ) en Donald Johnson ( drum ).
De klank van de zeer ' funley ' klinkende drum geeft aan het
algemene geluid van de groep een vreemde atmosfeer .
Hun eerste 45 T die verleden zomer uitkwam " All night parties "
werd zeer goed ontvangen door de kritiek .
In plaats van het traditionele album op de markt te brengen
besloot " A Certain Ratio " een cassette op te nemen :
" The Graveyard And The Ballroom " .

MET DANK VOOR DE OPNAME !

LE PLAN K - a.s.b.l.
21, rue de Manchester - 1070 Bruxelles - T. 523 18 34 ou 7, galerie de la Reine - 1000 Bruxelles - Belgium - T. 511 11 22

# RAFFINERIE DU PLAN K

PERSBERICHT

11 APRIL VRIJDAG ITALIANA "

ZONDAG 13 APRIL OM 19 u! IN PLAN K : " GROOT ITALIAANS FEEST "

Programma :

1ste verdieping :

19.30 u. film " Nous sommes tous en liberté provisoire "
    van D. Damiani met Franco Nero , R. Cucciolla
    en G.Wilson.

21.30 u. film " Padre Padrone " van Paolo E. Taviani

23.30 u.    Dansavond

4de verdieping :

20.30 u.    Le théâtre de la Renaissance : " De avonturen van
    Pepe Cippola ".

22 u.    Optreden van de Siciliaanse zanger TONY PALERMO
    en het orkest van JUSEPPE BUONGIOVANI .

ENTREE : 100 fr. !

MET DANK VOOR DE OPNAME

LE PLAN K - a.s.b.l.
21, rue de Manchester - 1070 Bruxelles - T. 523 18 34 ou 7, galerie de la Reine - 1000 Bruxelles - Belgium - T. 511 11 22

## PLAN K BRUSSELS

Plan K is an intriguing venue. Housed in an old sugar refinery in Brussels, Belgium, at six stories high, one had to navigate a maze of floors, rooms and narrow foot bridges to explore its industrial interior. It wasn't just the building itself that was interesting; the kids who ran it were our age and took a lot of pride in making each show a real event. I recall finding this very inspiring and had the idea of doing something similar in our home town. The night that we played there on April 5th, 1980 they named it "Soirée Vampires!". Before we took to the stage, they screened several films from a 16mm projector including: La Fiancée Du Vampire", "Le Masque Du Demon" and "Mensch Und Kunstfigur", the latter being a documentary about Oskar Schlemmer, an artist and teacher associated with the Bauhaus art movement.

Bauhaus perforning live at Plan K                    Photos: Andy Marlow

# ZIGZAG
## EAST

No. 2　1981年4月
ZIGZAG誌版権独占

創刊2号

380yen

マッドネス
ストレイ・キャッツ
スピズルズ
バウハウス
トーヤ
スロッビング・グリッスル

特集
大迫力で動き始めた
**ブリティッシュ・ファンク**

# 音楽一週

## MUSIC WEEK

No.427 JUNE 10,1983 $2

PETER MURPHY
(Bauhaus)

# SFX
The Talking Magazine

SIDE ONE: 1-MARTIN RUSHENT, 2-KEVIN ROWLAND, 3-TOTO COELO, 4-CIRCUS NEWS, 5-INDEPENDENT LABELS FEATURE, 6-THE YOUNG ONES (DEMO).

SIDE TWO: 1-GREEN, MARTIN FRY, REVIEW LP'S BY STEVE WINWOOD, AND DONNA SUMMER, 2-MARTHA LADLY, 3-PETER MURPHY (BAUHAUS), 4-GARRY ROBERTS, 5-THE ALARM, 6-THE 7-HOT TRACKS.

75p
INC VAT

**Issue No 19, August 12-24, 1982**

An hour of music, news, interviews and meaningless innuendoes

**MARTHA LADLY'S**
18 Carat Love Affair

**Pete Murphy**
From Bauhaus to our House

## C'mon Kev!

**Rushent Roulette**

Back issues now available
see reverse for details.

SIDE ONE: 1-MARTIN RUSHENT, 2-KEVIN ROWLAND, 3-TOTO COELO, 4-CIRCUS NEWS, 5-INDEPENDENT LABELS FEATURE, 6-THE YOUNG ONES (DEMO).
SIDE TWO: 1-GREEN MARTIN FRY, REVIEW LP'S BY STEVE WINWOOD, AND DONNA SUMMER, 2-MARTHA LADLY, 3-PETER MURPHY (BAUHAUS), 4-GARRY ROBERTS, 5-THE ALARM, 6-THE 7-HOT TRACKS.

THE ONLY MUSIC MAGAZINE ON A C-60 CASSETTE　EVERY FORTNIGHT

# 音楽一週

## MUSIC WEEK

No.422 May 6, 1983 $2

送 O.M.D手冊
有獎遊戲

BAUHAUS
IN CONCERT

NEW YORK NEW YORK,
New World Centre,
Kowloon
24th May 1983.
Time : 9:00 p.m.
All enquiries : 5 - 281359

**Picture By Kishi Yamamoto** **Bauhaus** *Beggar's Banquet*

BAUHAUS

*Beggars Banquet*

**BAUHAUS**

Beggars Banquet

**BAUHAUS**

Beggars Banquet

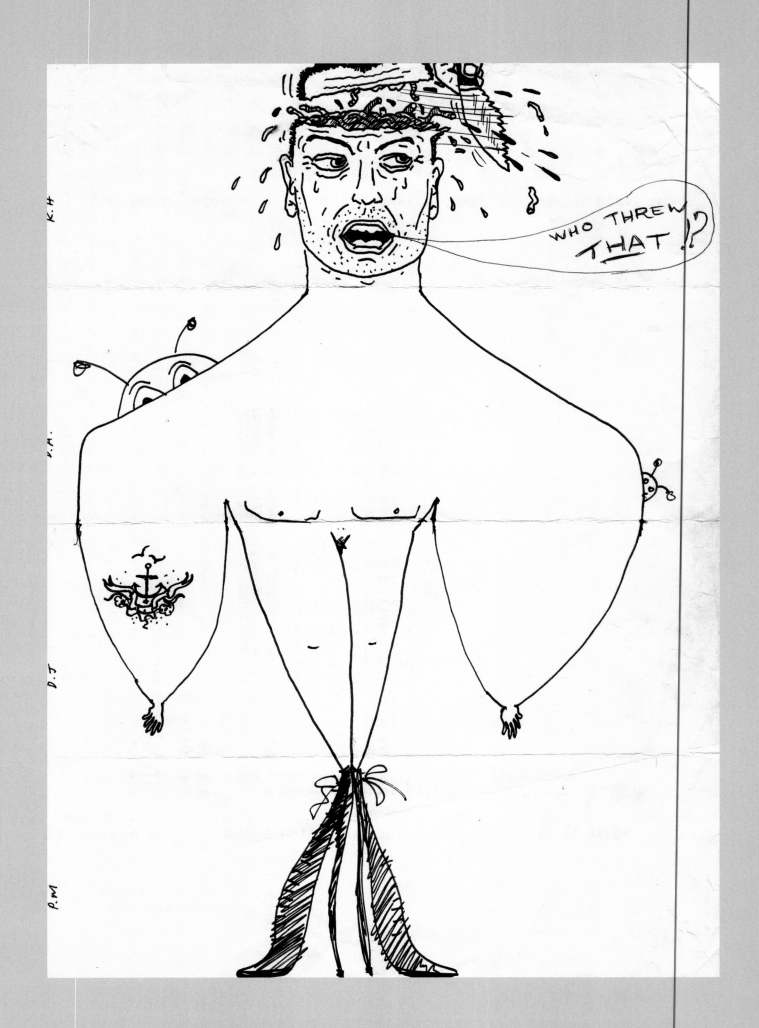

Exquisite Corpse drawings. This technique was invented by the surrealists, in which each participant draws in turn on a sheet of paper, then folds it to conceal their contribution.

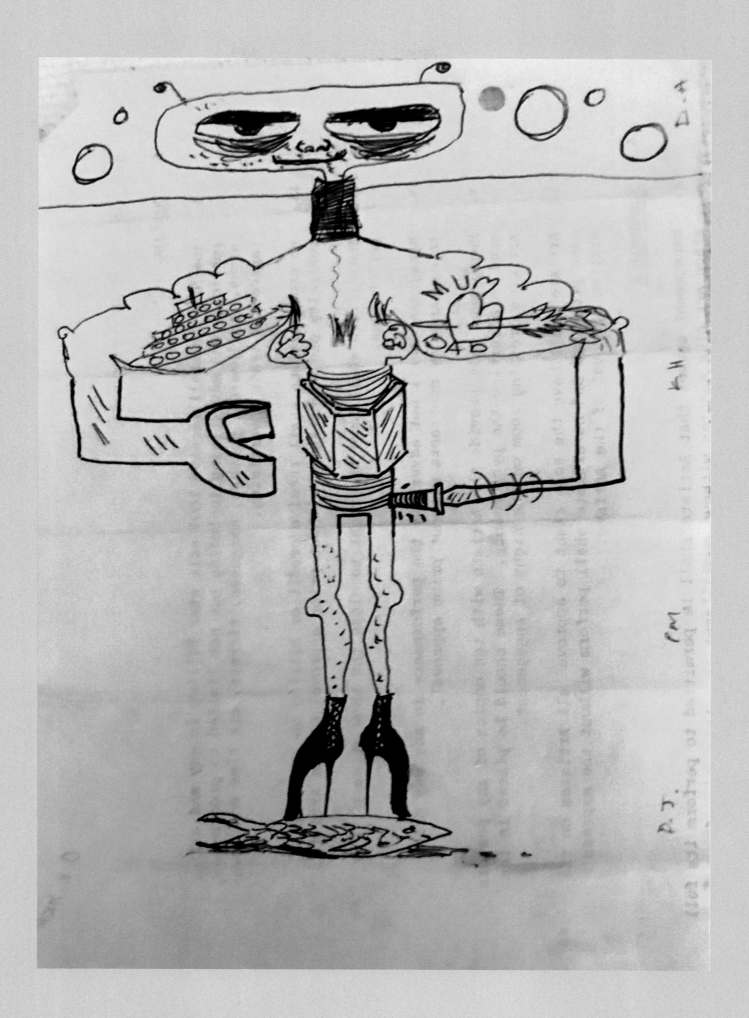

It is then passed it to the next player so that they can add to the piece. At the end the full image is revealed. We would make many of these drawings to pass the time when traveling.

0H30M22s
16.57
0H30M23s
0H30M30s
16·57
0H30M33s
0H30M33s
16·57
0H30M35s

## THE BIRTHDAY PARTY- CAMBRIDGE CORN EXCHANGE

SPLAT!! A direct hit! Nick Cave just took a custard pie, directly to his face. Well it wasn't actually custard, it was shaving foam, but it sufficed. Born out of the silent era, slapstick comedy attained great popularity as it didn't require sound to conjure up laughs. Charlie Chaplin, Mack Sennett, Laurel and Hardy, Harold Lloyd, The Three Stooges and Buster Keaton all mastered the art of the pie in the face. Now I'm not putting myself on the same level, but myself and roadie, Glenn Campling did a pretty good job of plastering each member of the band, as they played their final song, "Cry".

It  was June, 27th 1981; the last date of our British tour supported by The Birthday Party, who I must say, were on phenomenal form. It was customary on the last date of touring to play pranks on the crew, support bands and vice versa. Everybody was on heightened alert; running surveillance and checking their shoes for toothpaste and the like.

I must admit that it was with some trepidation that I took to the stage armed with two pies as The Birthday Party could appear very intimidating. The lads from down under took it on the chin, (excuse the pun), and I did garner a reluctant, "nice one!" from some unfortunate sporting a cream covered mug. However, what I didn't work into the equation was the word, "retaliation".

Mid way through our somewhat aptly named opening number, "The Passion Of Lovers", every member of the Birthday Party stormed the stage and wrestled Peter Murphy to the floor. Once they had him pinned down, and wielding a thick black marker pen, Tracy Pew drew a huge penis on his naked chest. Miraculously Peter didn't

miss a note and would spend the remainder of the set with this lewd graffiti on full display.

The final prank involved a flight case, a smoke machine, a stage lamp and Bauhaus roadie Glenn Campling. During "Bela Lugosi's Dead," we had devised a simple but effective piece of theater. During an instrumental section in the middle of the song, Peter would walk slowly and purposefully towards the flight case, (which was draped in black cloth), and slowly and very dramatically open up the lid of the casket, as it were. Upon doing so, a strong beam of light would illuminate his stark chiseled features, evoking a scene from an expressionistic horror film.

He would react to the light with a look of astonished audacity, his entire body shaking, he would dramatically, slam the lid back down. Well on this particular occasion, what none of the band were privy to, was that Glenn Campling was hiding within the case! As Peter was lifting the lid up, he couldn't see Glenn in there, due to the powerful beam of light. Just before Peter was about to slam it shut, Glenn reached out, grabbed Peter's waist, and pulled him inside the case! What transpired was this illusory casket, slowly careering across the stage, with Peters flailing legs, protruding from the lid. I did all I could to not burst out laughing and cause the song to fall apart.

Pranks aside, for the shows finale, The Birthday Party joined us onstage for a dark and moody, spine chilling version of the classic song, "Fever", most notably covered by Peggy Lee.

As for my contribution to the evening's entertainment, it may have not met everyone's haughty expectations, but there's a certain heartwarming nostalgia attached to it. And who else can say that they "custard pied" Nick Cave?

Left: At this point The Birthday Party have finished their set ('Cry' was the last number) Nick, covered in shaving foam is asking the audience to stick around for Bauhaus' last number. Which of course was a very loose take on Fever. The last frame here is just as Nick walks off stage and off camera.

Photo credit: Judy Lyon

morgan

artiste BALHAUS     date 26/1/79
client     replay NAB
engineers     speed 15IPS
studio
producer

dolby   no    frequency run    —    master

24 track   L R    matrix system

title      time

① BELA LUGOSI IS DEAD   WHITE EL/RED EL
② BOYS

MASTERS

SMALL WONDER
102 HOE ST, WALTHAMSTOWE.17

title      time

Recording Studios Limited, 169-171 High Road, Willesden, London N.W.10. Telephone: 01-459 7244. Cables: Morganmus London N.W.10. Telex: 923022

**The Sound-Suite**     **01 485 4881**

| Client | SMALL WONDER RECORDS | MASTER | ~~COPY~~ |
|--------|----------------------|--------|----------|
| Artist | RAUHAUS | STEREO | ~~MONO~~ |
| Producer | | NAB | ~~CCIR~~ / DOLBY |
| Engineer | ALVIN | ~~7½~~ / 15 / ~~30~~ |

| TITLES | duration | remarks |
|--------|----------|---------|
| | | |
| 1k, 10k, 100 hz, all @ 0vu | | |
| 1) BOYS | | |
| | | |
| | | |
| | | |
| *(ISIS STEREO PRODUCTION MASTER)* | | |
| | | |
| | | |

SOUND SUITE RECORDING STUDIOS LTD.   92 Camden Mews, London NW1      Telephone 01 485 4881

Master tape / Boys

BILL GRAHAM PRESENTS IN SAN FRANCISCO

BAUHAUS

MONDAY, AUGUST 17
& TUESDAY, AUGUST 18, 1998
THE WARFIELD
982 MARKET STREET, SAN FRANCISCO

## THE SHADOW IS CAST

When video director Christopher Collins and his Producer Ken Lawrence arrived at my doorstep with twenty car batteries, I thought they were taking no chances on their car starting the next morning! However, I soon learned that collectively they made up what one could call a poor man's generator. They were also completely silent, which is a plus when one is breaking into an old shoe factory directly adjacent to the town's police station. These rather unconventional sources of power would provide all the electricity for our guerrilla style video shoot, for the title track of our new LP, "Mask". "But why", I inquired, "have you already unloaded them?" Chris explained that he needed to charge them overnight and asked if he could do so in my flat. "Well of course that's fine" I replied, "except the only problem is that I live on the fourth floor and there's no lift!" I think it took us almost one hour including a couple of customary tea breaks. Once charging, my spare bedroom resembled Frankenstein's lab, underscored by the loud hum of all the battery chargers working diligently away.

The following day, assisted by the rest of the band, we began the arduous task of moving all the batteries downstairs, although this time, with more hands and gravity, it was far easier. After a short drive and a long slog over deserted waste ground, breaking into the disused factory wasn't too difficult. Inside, it was cold, damp and neglected. The old Victorian shoe factory had enjoyed much better days, but in all its decaying industrial splendor, it was a perfect setting for a film shoot. The opening shot of the video is the imposing presence of the old factory at night as a shroud of darkness falls upon Northampton Town. For the following shot of the full moon, we "borrowed" the image from an old Hammer Horror film, filmed off my TV screen! Did I mention that this was low budget?

Once we had our "generator" assembled, we went about decorating our set. This involved a bit of artful graffiti and vandalizing several windows. The next task was hair and makeup which we each created and applied ourselves, David drawing a realistic eye beneath his real eye to great effect. Peter lay prostrate on a makeshift sepulcher that we assembled from old wooden pallets we found lying around. We wrapped him in cling film and covered him in flour, lending a surreal mummified quality to the recumbent figure. In the main section of the video, shot in the factory, the rest of the band are seen performing some type of magic ritual that results in resurrecting the deity, played by Peter.

Once we were done in the factory and had lugged the now spent car batteries back to Chris' car, it was time to head out into the countryside. "Hey lads, it's two o'clock in the morning........who fancies finding a forest, crawling through thorny brambles and a putrid stagnant pond, in temperature approaching freezing point?" "Any takers?!" Well it wasn't presented as such, but it was exactly what we ended up doing. Around four a.m., I had lost all feeling in my toes and fingers as I beat a large bass drum illuminated by the headlights of my Morris Minor. My jeans were soaked in cold evil-smelling pond water that I had crawled through just thirty minutes before. I felt really miserable and all I could think of was a nice warm and cozy bed. Oh the glamour of being in a band!

However, I did enjoy the spontaneity and the "leaving it up to chance" approach that we employed for this and which we would also employ in the studio. In situations like this we would inspire and feed off each other, the ideas constantly flowing.

Dark and brooding and drenched in atmosphere, our vision was perfectly realized.

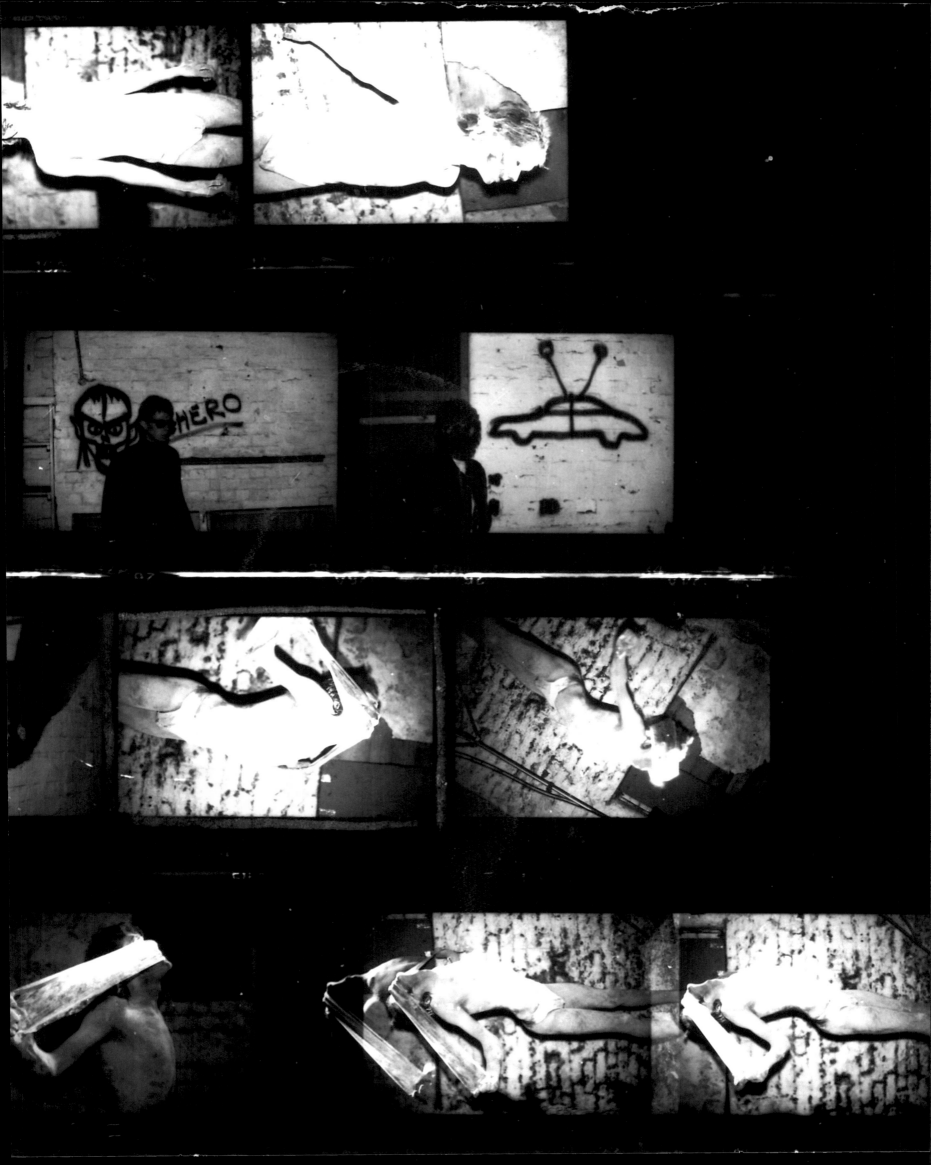

BAUH

MASK

THIS IS FOR WHEN THE RADIO IS BROKEN AND CRACKLES LIKE URANIUM ORCHIDS

NEW E.P. OUT NOW

THE TOUR

OCT 22nd   READING UNIVERSITY
OCT 23rd   SHEFFIELD LYCEUM
OCT 24th   NORWICH UNIVERSITY
                    OF EAST ANGLIA
OCT 25th   GUILDFORD CIVIC HALL
OCT 27th   BIRMINGHAM LOCARNO

# AUS

**BEGA 29**

BEGGARS BANQUET

| | | NOV | 4th | CARDIFF TOP RANK |
|---|---|---|---|---|
| 28th | MANCHESTER FAGINS | NOV | 6th | HULL TOWER BALLROOM |
| 29th | GLASGOW NIGHT MOVES | NOV | 7th | NOTTINGHAM ROCK CITY |
| 30th | LANCASTER UNIVERSITY | NOV | 9th | HAMMERSMITH PALAIS |
| 31st | LIVERPOOL | NOV | 10th | PORTSMOUTH |
| | ROYAL COURT THEATRE | | | GUILDFORD |
| 2nd | BRIGHTON TOP RANK | | | |

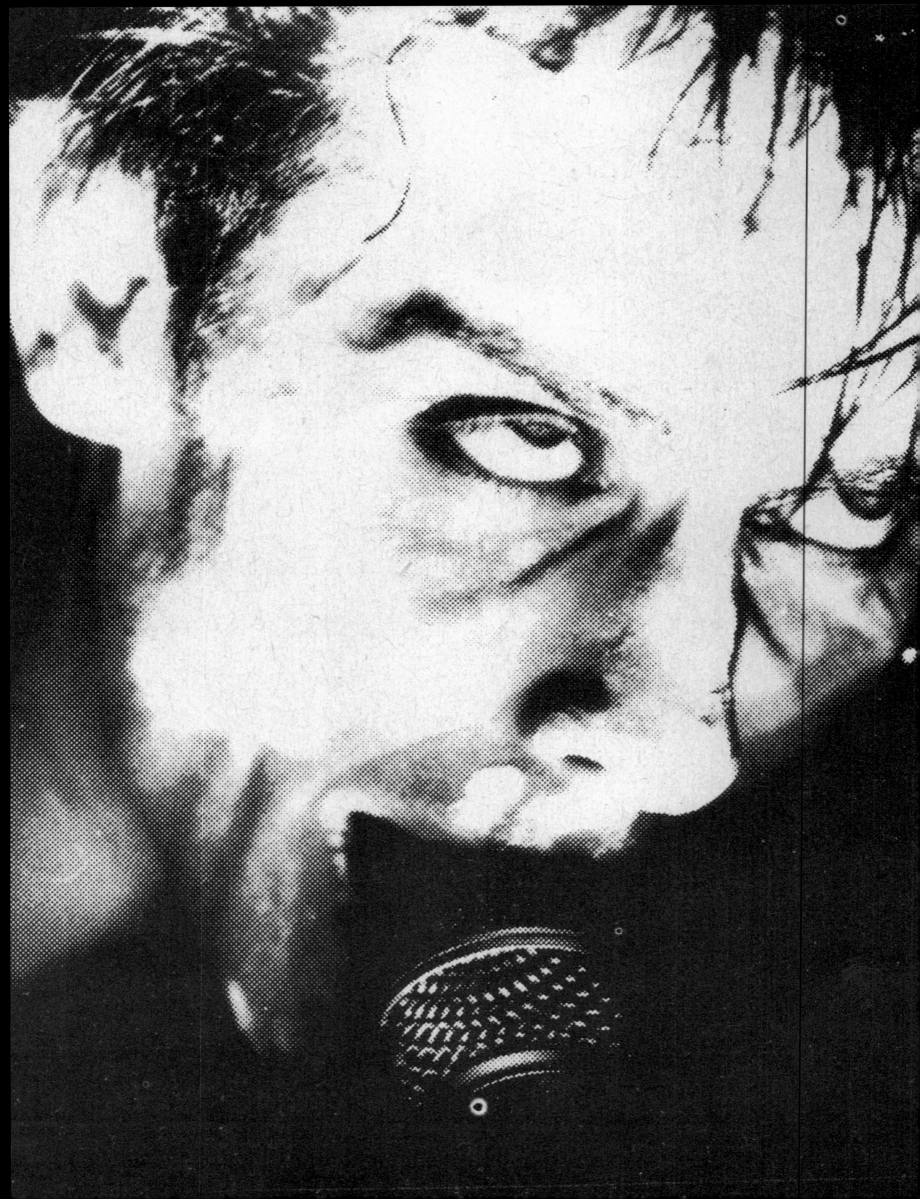

THURSDAY, APRIL 28TH 2005  8PM  AT THE GLASS HOUSE  200 W. SECOND ST.  POMONA $25

USDAselect

Poster design: Jason Walker

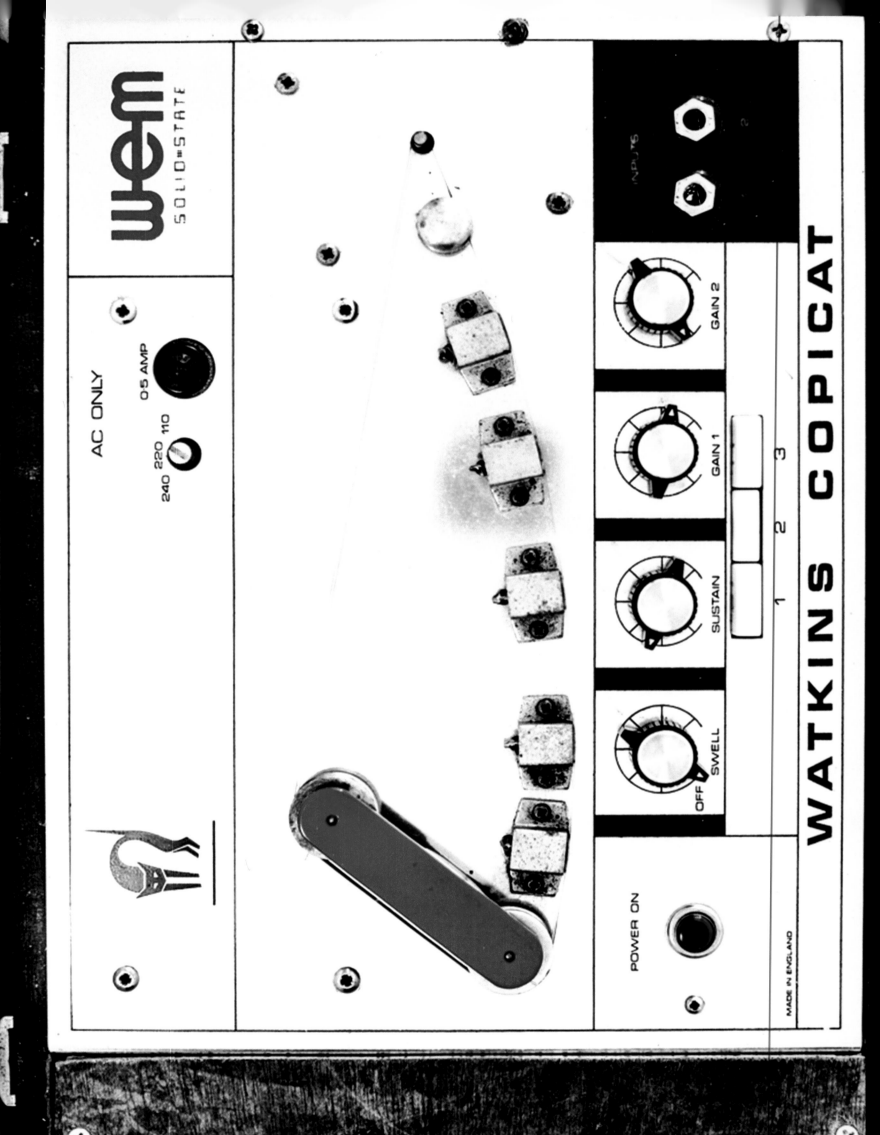

This is the Watkins Copicat that was used By Daniel Ash on early live performances and was also used by Daniel to create the delayed dub effects on Bela Lugosi's Dead.

# bauhaus

BAUHAUS 'KICK' GIANT GOLD LOGO DOWN THE SIDE AND PETERS EYES IN WHITE ON BLACK SHIRT ◀ £4·50 EACH ▶

PLEASE STATE S·M·L

BAUHAUS 'BELA' BLACK PRINT ON WHITE SHIRT CLASSIC DESIGN

+ 35p P+P

FRONT    BACK

'BURNING FROM THE INSIDE' BLACK TOUR SHIRT BAND PHOTOS IN WHITE, GOLD BORDERS + LOGO ON FRONT AND TOUR DATES+ SECTION FROM ALBUM SLEEVE IN WHITE ON THE BACK £4·50 + 35p P+P
S.M.L

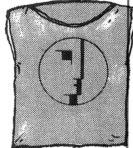

BAUHAUS 'TUBE' SWEATSHIRT ACME'S OWN BLACK SWEAT WITH LARGE 'TERROR' LOGO IN GLOSSY BLACK PRINT £8·50 + 60p + P+P

SET B

SET OF 4 'BURNING' BADGES — PETER-KEVIN DAVID + DANIEL (FACES) 1" £1·00 + 20p P+P

BLACK + SILVER BAUHAUS ENAMEL BADGE 1" £1·00 + 20p P+P

SET A

1" TERROR COUPLE BADGES BLACK + WHITE SET OF 2 — 50p + 20p P+P

FRONT    BACK

(BLACK) BAUHAUS SLEEVELESS COMBAT SHIRT. TOP QUALITY SHIRT - BREAST POCKETS, NICE + LONG - GREY BAUHAUS STRIP PATCH ABOVE POCKET + LARGE GLOSSY TERROR COUPLE LOGO ON BACK PLEASE STATE S.M.L £9·50 + 80p P+P.

FRONT    BACK

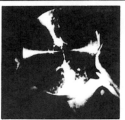

S.M.L.
BURNING FROM THE INSIDE TOUR (WHITE) LARGE PRINT IN BLACK, BLUE + BROWN FROM ALBUM SLEEVE ON FRONT (LYRIGSET) + TWO COLOUR TOUR DATES ON BACK £4·50 + 35p P+P.

PLUS
● – BAUHAUS TOUR PROGRAMME – A FULLY ILLUSTRATED PROGRAMME PACKED WITH DETAILS ON THE BAND £1·50 + 30p P+P
● – POSTERS @ BAUHAUS MASK VIDEO STILLS (COLLAGE) ⓑ LARGE COLOUR COLLAGE - LIVE PICS ETC £1·00 EACH + 30p P+P

● – POSTCARDS – SET OF 4 COLOUR CARDS £1·00 + P+P
● – BAND PHOTO (BLACK + WHITE) 50p + 20p P+P

PLEASE SEND CHEQUES OR P.O's WITH CLEAR ORDER, SIZE etc + FULL NAME AND ADDRESS TO:

## Acme Tour Products Ltd
## 26–40 St Andrews St Northampton Tel 0604 36888, 20411/2/3.

## "SUPPORTING" THE PRETENDERS

Feeling and behaving like mischievous schoolboys, we lugged our equipment as fast as we could up a snowy grass embankment between our porta cabin rehearsal room and the unguarded doors to The Student Union Hall. It was December 1978, and we got word that evening The Pretenders were playing a mere twenty yards from where we were rehearsing. We had about five songs and couldn't wait to play them live. We came up with the idea of just setting up our gear in the corner of the hall and playing as support band, guerrilla style! We were greatly assisted in this endeavor, due to the conveniently placed sliding glass doors of the hall and its close proximity to where we rehearsed. Timing it just so, forty five minutes before The Pretenders were to take to the stage, we snuck our equipment in, set up faster than the speed of light, and proceeded to play! As our first song came to an end, a very puzzled young chap representing the student union inquired as to what we were doing. We simply responded with, "we're the support band". He further inquired as to why we weren't on the stage and we responded with something along the lines of, "We prefer it here". Now looking even more mystified, he slowly sauntered away, with the occasional skeptical glance over his shoulder. We continued on and

began to draw quite a sizable audience. We had just managed to finish our short set, when the puzzled one returned with the rest of the student union guys, now wise to our ruse and intent to shut us down. This was technically our first live show. However we were not actually booked to play!

Our first official show was a few weeks later in the back room of The Cromwell Pub in Peter's home town of Wellingborough. It was New Year's Eve, but only about three people had bothered to show up. We were engaged to play two sets but we only had about five songs. To overcome this considerable lack of material, we decided to learn "Raw Power" by Iggy Pop and The Stooges, beginning and ending each set with it, (incidentally, David and I had also played this number during an early punk band we were in, The Submerged Tenth). Consequently, the poor New Year's Eve revelers had to endure it four times. During one song entitled "Bite My Hip" (we re-worked and resurrected this number three years later, it became "Lagartija Nick"), one of our friends, Leo Casey, decided to take the lyrics literally. Sliding down from her bar stool, she crawled along the floor in a feline fashion and suddenly pounced on to the stage! Grabbing Peter by the leg, she proceeded to actually bite his hip!

Small Wonder Records

April 1987

To:   Bauhaus

Teeny 2 - Bela Lugosi's Dead/Boys

Number pressed                                15380


Amount received for 15380 pressings          £17687.00

Less pressing costs                           £9290.67

                                              £8396.33

To band - £4198.17

To 3 members = £3148.62 ÷ 3 = £1049.54

**SMALL WONDER RECORDS**

VAT No. 249 4479 21

GREAT WALDINGFIELD, Nr. Sudbury, Suffolk, CO10 ORN.
Telephone: Sudbury ▮▮▮▮▮▮▮▮

*Exquisite Corpse* drawn by (from top)
19.82   David J / Daniel ash / Kevin Haskins / Peter Murphy.

The original "She's In Parties" video footage reel.

// BAUHAUS // "SHE'S IN PARTYS" // TL...

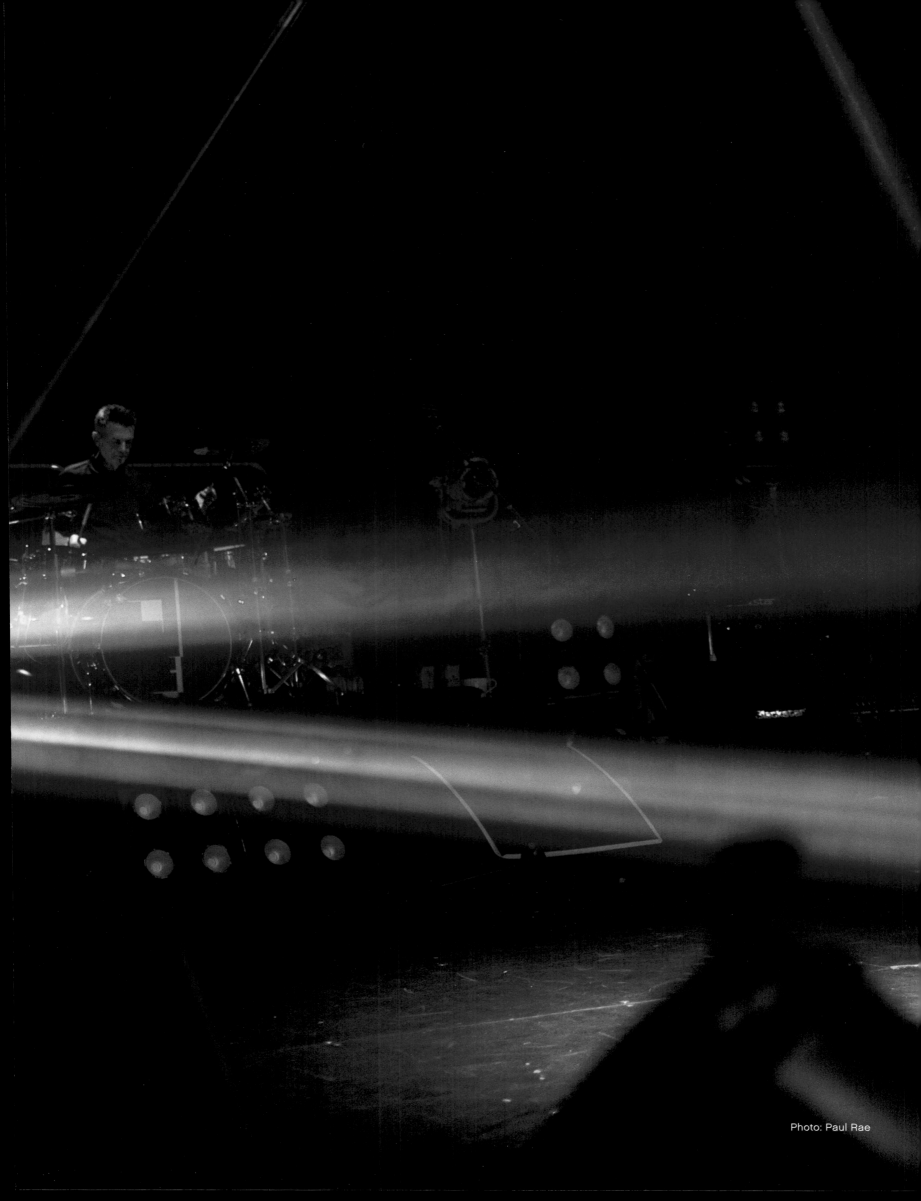

Photo: Paul Rae

## IT'S IN THE CAN

In 1982, the highly acclaimed TV commercial director Howard Guard chose Peter Murphy for the starring role in the Maxell cassette tape advert. Suited and booted in his artist's loft apartment, Peter was seated in a "Bauhaus" leather chair, listening to Mussorgsky's "Night On Bare Mountain". Peter appeared to be relatively calm as the exceptional ability of the Maxell Cassette tape caused all hell to break loose around him. Potted plants and duck ornaments took flight as a mini tornado emitted from the speakers.

Howard Guard:
"The shoot was quick and dirty through lack of money and the script called for the actor to sit in the chair for 30 seconds and do nothing. This called for someone really different and charismatic, and Peter was. He was a kind of Bowie, not a lookalike, but more a feel-a-like, and the ad was all about how things felt."

Stylized and sophisticated, the campaign was a huge success in Britain which helped raise the profile of Peter and the band. Following this, when it came time to choose a director for the "She's In Parties" video, Peter approached Howard and he agreed to direct. He must have really liked Peter and our song, as in the entirety of his career he only made one other music video for Roxy Music's, Avalon.

Shot on 16mm, predominantly in black and white, it has a beautiful, sensual cinematic quality with a subtle touch of film noir thrown in for good measure. Whilst the footage looks very sophisticated and glamorous, the actual location on Dean street in Soho, London, was not. As with most of our video locations, we were as usual freezing to death in a dank and cold, derelict building. But one has to suffer for one's art, and art indeed was created. I recall one conversation that I had with Howard during the filming. In order for the female chauffeur's outfit to fit well, the stylist had employed about six large bulldog clips, hidden from view, to create the necessary makeshift alterations. I thought that in the context of the song, it would be a great idea for there to be a reveal of the clips, to illustrate the fake nature of the femme fatale; the realism within the charade. Well basically Howard deemed it to be a somewhat corny idea and quickly ushered me away! In contrast to our previous videos, this one was slick and very cinematic, Howard capturing the essence of the song implicitly.

In a turn of good fortune, at this time Howard was partners with Tony and Ridley Scott, the acclaimed movie directors at RSA2. Tony was in pre-production for his independent vampire film, "The Hunger". During the edit of "She's In Parties", Tony would occasionally wander along the corridor and pop his head into the edit bay to view Howard's rushes. Impressed with what he saw, this was when the initial spark of hiring Bauhaus to play in the opening night club scene came to him.

Photo: Jean Ramsey

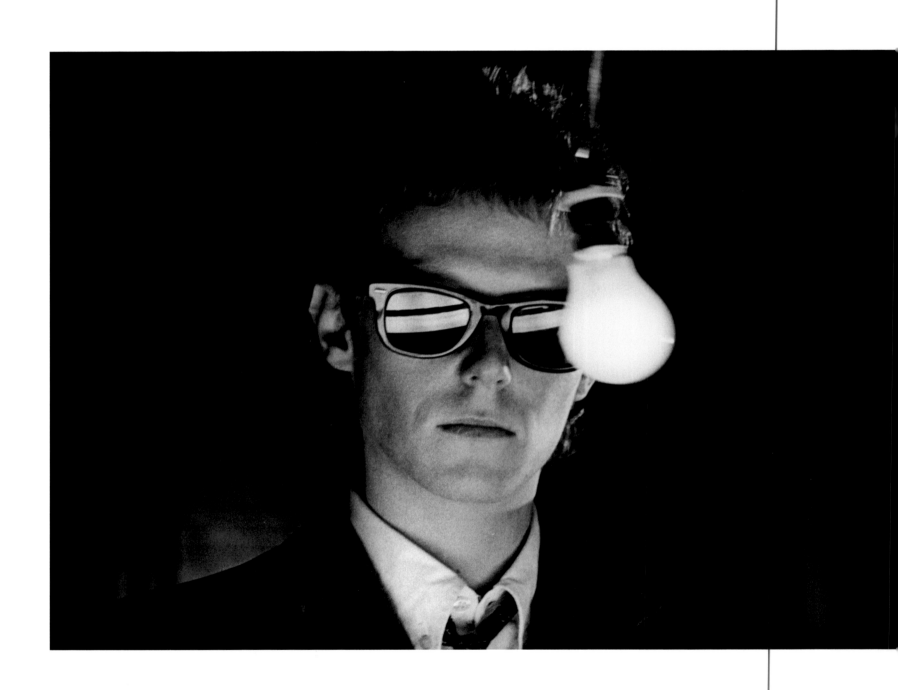

BAUHAUS: schedule for 'Riverside' T.V. recording, Tues.2nd.Feb.

8.30  Equipment arrival at Riverside Studios, Crisp Road, Hammersmith W6
                    (phone-Admin-741 2251, Box Office-748 3354)
9.00  Band arrival
10.00-12.00 noon, Rehearsals
4.00 -5.30  Run through
6.45 <u>sharp</u>  Recording of show with live audience.

<u>Format of show</u>
Opening sequence - Bauhaus - 'Kick in the eye'
Link
6 minute film on hairstyles
5 or 6 people from audience featured with outrageous hairstyles
Chat sequence with people from N.M.E. and Stiff Little Fingers
2 minute promo video of Graham Dean
Graham Dean live
Video? 3 mins 19secs.
Spinooch
Closing sequence - Bauhaus -Bela Lugosi -credits

<u>B.B.C. Personnel</u>
Programme director - Roy Chapman
Lighting        - John Wilson
Sound          - John Caulfield
Designer        - Paul Allen

<u>Band Hotel</u>
Nayland Hotel, 134 Sussex Gardens, W.2.
            (phone: ~~723 7380~~/258 3877)

WED 27 JAN. - LOAD UP GEAR AT ROADMENDER
- RIVERSIDE PRODUCTION MEETING IN FOYER OF RIVERSIDE STUDIO
CRISP ROAD, HAMMERSMITH AT 3 P.M.
- LOAD GEAR INTO MORGAN STUDIOS DURING EVENING
167-171, WILLESDEN HIGH RD. N.W.10.   459-7244.
- DAVE & KEVIN STAYING AT NAYLAND HOTEL
134, SUSSEX GDNS. W.2. - 723 3380/258 3877.
_____

THURS 28 JAN. - KEVIN & PETER TO MORGAN STUDIO 10. A.M.
- DAVE & DANNY 12 NOON - SESSION OPEN ENDED.

FRI 29 JAN - START AT MORGAN 2 P.M.
BACKING TRACKS FOR RIVERSIDE TO BE DONE IF NEEDED.

SAT 29 JAN - START MORGAN 2 P.M.
_____

MON FEB 1ST. TRAVEL TO LONDON DURING EVENING CHECK INTO HOTEL
HOTEL & MEANS OF TRAVEL T.B.A.

TUES 2ND GEAR AT RIVERSIDE STUDIOS AT 8.30
CALL TIMES FOR BAND T.B.A.
RETURN TO NORTHAMPTON AFTER
_____

WED 17 FEB - REHEARSAL AT ROADMENDER 12 NOON - 6 P.M.

THURS 18 FEB - GIG AT WHITE ELEPHANT - PLAY APPROX 9 P.M.

FRIDAY 19 FEB - REHEARSAL AT ROADMENDER 12 NOON - 6 P.M.

SAT 20 FEB - GIG AT LINGS FORUM, DOORS OPEN 7 P.M/ON STAGE 8.45


WED 24 FEB - GIG AT OLD VIC THEATRE WATERLOO.

2ND SHOW POSSIBLE ON 23RD, REHEARSAL POSSIBLE 22ND IF
REQUIRED.

Peter attempting to enter The Red Cube by the artist Isamu Noguchi, in downtown Manhattan. Although ably assisted by Daniel and David, I recall that unfortunately this particular en-devour was not successful.

Departing Heathrow Airport in London to the USA for our 1982 Winter tour. It appears that Glenn Campling has decided to wrap Daniel up in Gaffer tape, and Peter is assisting him in this playful caper. Im either pretending not to notice or have spotted something very interesting on the floor, whilst our tour manager Harry Isles is checking that his bag hasn't been pilfered.

## BAUHAUS SCHEDULE - Sunday 21st.-Monday 29th. March 1982.

**Sun.21st.** - Backline into 'Heaven' 10.30am
Band to London afternoon/evening, check into:
Charing Cross Hotel, Strand, London WC 2.
(above Charing Cross B.R. Station) phone 8397282
N.B. Everybody must stay at hotel Sunday night because you are
needed on the film set very early next morning.

**Mon. 22nd.** - Filming all day at 'Heaven'(under Charing Cross Station)
phone 839 3852
YOU MUST ARRIVE ON FILM SET BY 7.30 A.M.
Staying at Charing Cross Hotel again Monday night.

**Tue.23rd.** - 10am. notification re T.O.T.P.
If required for TOTP - into studio for backing tracks.
(times and location TBA.)
Filming may continue today but if so it should befinished in
time to do backing tracks in theafternoon or evening.
Check out of Charing Cross Hotel and check into Nayland Hotel
134, Sussex Gdns. W2. - 723 8275
Dinner with Martin - details to be advised.

**Wed. 24th.-** Mixing at Morgan Studios with Mike Hedges. 12 noon, open ended.
169, Willesden High Road, N.W.10. - 459 7244
( OR TOTP recording at BBC TV Centre, Wood Lane, W.12.)

**Thur. 25th.-** Mixing at Morgan with Mike Hedges.

**Fri. 26th.** - Check out of Nayland Hotel.
1.30 - Peter - Photo session with Sheila Rock  221 5189
6.00 - Whole band - Photo session with Finn Costello
18, Cloudesley Rd. Islington N.1. - 837 1484

**Sat. 27th.** - Phil drives PA Hollingbourne to Manchester collecting drum
riser from Plugs en route.
Back line and lights loaded out of Roadmender, afternoon/evening.

**Sun. 28th.** - Gig at 'Rotters' Oxford St.Manchester - 061 236 934(opposite Fagins)
approximate times: load-in, PA 12 noon, other stuff 12.30.
gig, 7 - 11 pm.
Fulldetails to follow.
Hotel : The Sandpiper Inn, 5-7,Wilbraham Road, Manchester.
061 224 3107 / 225 5483

**Mon. 29th.** - Home

Danny on holiday until April 5th.
Next gigs - April 23,24,25,
Suggest rehearsals - 7&8, 14&15, 21&22.

## THE HUNGER

One of the most anticipated days in my career was our part in the filming of "The Hunger" starring David Bowie and Catherine Deneuve. The film was based on Whitley Strieber's novel of immortal beings and vampirism set in modern day America.

Although we had the unnatural set time of 07:30 AM on March 22, 1982, couldn't arrive soon enough. Bauhaus were contracted to perform "Bela Lugosi's Dead" in the nightclub scene where Bowie and Deneuve's vampire characters were hunting for young blood.

Tony Scott:
"I love rock 'n' roll and impact at the beginning of movies and Peter Murphy had this sort of ethereal, vampire quality to him and I thought that would make an interesting opening title sequence in the movie".

Although the scene was set in New York, it was filmed at the London night club Heaven, a club where we had previously played. We were all very big fans of Bowie and, like many musicians of the post punk era, Bowie's performance of "Starman" on Top Of The Pops, was a significant and profound turning point in our lives. So to say that we were excited was somewhat of an understatement.

Prior to the filming, Tony Scott wanted to re-record "Bela Lugosi's Dead" so that he would have his own designated version. We were booked in to Morgan Studios in January '82 with the musical supervisor on the film, Howard Blake. Classically trained, Howard had attempted to transcribe our recording, which was a formidable and almost impossible task. Unfortunately he couldn't achieve what he wanted due to the experimental and spontaneous nature of the dub delays and Daniel's experimental guitar work on the original version. As we had already captured a good live version the previous November at The Hammersmith Palais, frustrated and defeated, Howard and Tony eventually agreed to use that recording.

Radiating with charisma, and walking with a confident swagger, Bowie arrived on set in green designer army fatigues, appearing a tad shorter than I had imagined him to be. After surveying the set he disappeared in to hair and makeup, later to emerge, magnificently transformed, sporting a very resplendent black silk suit and jet black pompadour wig....he looked amazing!
We were then ushered on stage to play our part, Peter delivering an electrifying performance, I'm sure spurred on by the knowledge that Bowie was watching from the wings.

After Tony was satisfied with our part, the crew had to set up the next shot and I watched as David Bowie's stand in took his place. It was then that I noticed the real Bowie gravitating towards an old Wurlitzer juke box, housed in

an adjacent room of the club. I, along with about twenty extras, regulars of the club and who, one could tell, were also big fans, followed him at a respectful distance. David proceeded to begin selecting records, and so we all moved closer, and eventually, on his invitation, sat down before him. It was from that point on, for the next two blissful hours, that we were treated to a private audience with the legendary musician! Many of the songs he played were from his LP, "Pin Ups" and he regaled us with wonderful stories about when he originally saw the bands at the Marquee Club and Eel Pie Island, and why he chose to record each one; bands such as The Yardbirds, The Who, The Kinks and The Pretty Things, etc.

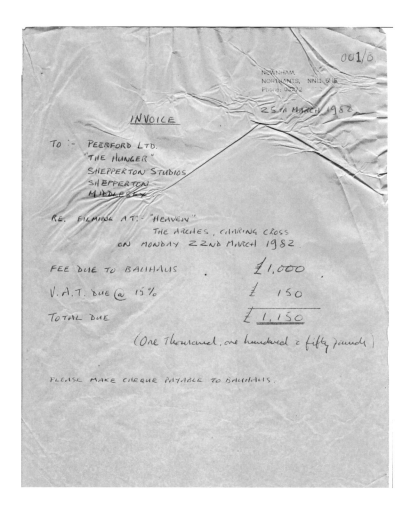

As this remarkable day was coming to a close, I was looking for a light for my cigarette and asked David's assistant Coco for one. Unbeknown to me, Bowie was only one foot away from me, hidden from view, just the other side of a doorway. She said words to the effect of "Sorry, I don't, but I think that David has one". It was at this moment that he magically appeared before me, presenting a lit lighter! It was all I could do to manage to bring the cigarette to the flame, as my star struck hand was shaking so uncontrollably! He had a devil of a time actually getting it lit, but eventually succeeded, and so, yes, David Bowie lit my cigarette!

## THE NIGHT OF THE LIVING DEAD

It was September 7th, 1979 and we were supporting Gloria Mundi at the legendary Marquee Club in Soho, London. This being only our second London show, it was a relatively big deal for us and we wanted to reach as many people as possible. As there were only five people and one dog in attendance, we played over our allotted time in the hope that more people would suddenly fill the room. This didn't happen and we were fined ten pounds, which happened to be exactly how much we were going to be paid for the gig! Well, we were in Soho. One of the five attendees was a young chap by the name of Michael Mason who came backstage offering his services as our manager. Being hungry for success and still wet behind the ears, we thought that he might be able to catapult us up to the next level.

A week later and we were now en route in David's Ford Cortina to where he lived, in his parents house in Hertfordshire. It was mid-winter and several degrees below freezing point, which will become significant later on in this story.

The gravel crunched underneath David's bald tyres as we maneuvered up the driveway of MIchael's parents swanky home. Michael invited us in and quickly proceeded to go over the terms of the contract which had the name of some previous band crossed out with a crayon, and Bauhaus scribbled in underneath it! We questioned the validity of this but he assured us that it was common practice. Without taking it to a lawyer, we scanned over the contract and signed our lives away! Once signed, Michael set about revealing his master plan which required us all to move to London and live in the same flat. He went on to provide us with some tips for a harmonious co-existence. Namely, "if Daniel wants to wear Peter's trousers, then let him, and Kevin, if David wants to wear one of your shirts, so be it." He also offered up an idea he had for a change of image. Peter and Daniel were to dye their hair black and wear white clothing and David and I were to dye our hair white and wear black clothing. This rather incongruous suggestion manifested exchanges of puzzled, squinty eyed looks, but he appealed to us to give it some thought.

By this time, without conferring, we were all beginning to feel a bit unsure about this new arrangement, However he was of a very different opinion and announced that we were all to repair to the local village pub to celebrate our new union. We all felt like we needed a strong drink so we complied and off we all went. As we sat down with our drinks I noticed an artist who was seated right next to us drawing portraits of the clientele. Michael immediately secured his services to capture this auspicious occasion in graphite on paper. In a bout of paranoia, I recall thinking that he had set this up, so that there would be concrete evidence that we had in fact signed his contract on that very night.

After imbibing a pint or two, we announced that it was time to return to Northampton and duly set off. About half way home, David's usually trusty steed began to show signs of reluctance to complete our journey. As clouds of steam erupted from under the bonnet, David pulled over to the side of the road just outside of a village. A quick inspection revealed a gaping hole in a water hose, and we all knew that at midnight, on a frigid winter's night, that this was not very good news. Fortunately though, Daniel belonged to The AA, an organization that would come and rescue stranded motorists day or night. Ok, we thought, this is not all bad. We will make the call, get towed back to Northampton, and be warm and snug in bed in a couple of hours. Two of us set off to the nearby village to find a phone box and called the AA, who showed up half an hour later. Once the car was hooked up, we found sanctuary in the warm cab of the tow truck and were happily on our way. After about twenty minutes, to our surprise, the driver pulled over on to a garage forecourt in the town of Towcester about ten miles from home. "Ok lads, jump out now, this is as far as I can take you". The puzzled squinty eyed expression, just expressed not a few hours before, returned to our unfortunate faces. Upon enquiring, it was explained that Daniel's coverage only extended thus far, and that the garage would be open for business in about three hours. Of course we protested vigorously, but to no avail, and as our traitor drove away we quickly retreated to the interior of the car. However, once inside we couldn't decide if it was colder inside or out. Although there were beautiful icicle patterns on all the windows, we decided that there was less of a wind chill factor inside. We couldn't run the engine to use the heater, and were basically sitting inside a very large ice box. We decided to strike up conversation to lift our spirits, however, we soon found it difficult to talk because of our trembling lips. A little while later, when all sensation disappeared from our fingers and toes, someone hit upon the idea of utilizing David's faux sheepskin seat covers as improvised sleeping bags. Unfortunately, this didn't hold muster, as they were not of the deluxe variety and barely protected a third of our bodies. However, taking on the appearance of malnourished sheep, we did get a good laugh out of it. An hour or so later, Peter remembered that he had one cigarette left. Once lit, we all cupped our hands around it, in a vain attempt to extract some heat.

07:00 AM finally approached and so I wiped away the icicles from the windows to keep watch for the garage mechanics. This action revealed the prying eyes of curious by-passers on their way to work who probably thought that we were zombies.

For the record, we didn't follow any of Michael's suggestions and were able to wiggle out from the contract. He did however return a few years later in an attempt to reconcile, suddenly appearing, as if by magic, backstage at The Hammersmith Palais, ironically minutes after we had just played our "last show".

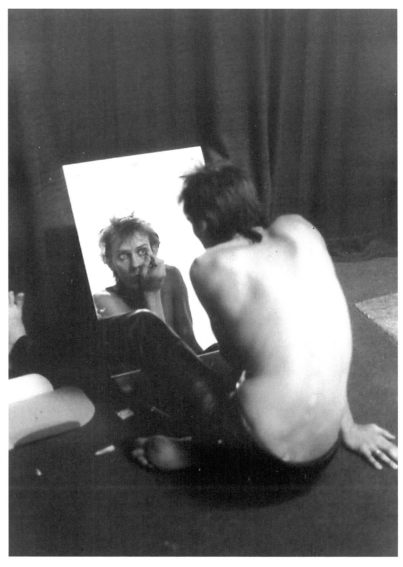

THIS IS FOR WHEN THE RADIO IS BROKEN
AND CRACKLES LIKE URANIUM ORCHIDS
THIS IS FOR WHEN THE FOEHN-WIND
RATTLES THE TELEGRAPH WIRES LIKE A
HANDFUL OF BONES THIS IS FOR WHEN
DREAM AMBULANCES SKITTER THROUGH
THE STREETS AT MIDNIGHT THIS IS FOR
WHEN YOU GET CAUGHT IN A SLEEP-RIOT
AND THE SKY IS OUT OF ORDER THIS IS
FOR WHEN YOUR SEX IS FULL OF VOODOO
THIS IS FOR WHEN YOUR CLOTHES ARE
IMAGINARY THIS IS FOR WHEN YOUR
FLESH CREEPS AND NEVER COMES BACK

Photo: Brian Shanley

## THRIFT STORE JACKET

Everybody noticed him at the sound check. He was around our age, early twenties, skinny and dressed in black. He didn't look out of place but there was something strange about him. He was leery. He had a bad vibe. It was only later in retrospect that I realized my gut feelings were spot on. I was curious as to why he was attending the sound check. I thought he must have known someone who worked at the club.

It was our second tour of Europe promoting In The Flat Field. We were playing a small club called Vera in Groningen, Holland. After sound check we walked back to our hotel as it was only three blocks away; a pleasant alternative to the usual oppressive dressing room. On our return I noticed the kid again and he was still on his own. I figured him for a loner and didn't give him any more thought. The gig was a good one, the audience very receptive. We had just completed our second headlining tour in the UK and as a band, were beginning to hit our stride.

After the show we helped our crew pack up the gear as we had arranged to leave it in the venue overnight. Daniel and David left first with our crew of three and Peter and I left about one minute later. As we set off I could see the rest of the band about one block away. Peter and I were chatting away and I soon became aware of footsteps following behind us. Something didn't feel right and as I glanced at Peter he gave me a look that he was feeling exactly the same. The fight or flight adrenalin started to kick in and we stepped up our pace. The trailing footsteps followed suit and then all of a sudden Peter nudged me and took off running! I guess that I didn't react fast enough and

before I could take flight I felt a hand grasp my left arm and something cold and sharp on my neck. I froze for a second and then the penny dropped. It was a flick knife. I had a flick knife to my throat! My assailant was yelling something in Dutch. I didn't even know how to say, "good morning" or "can you pass the sugar please" in Dutch, let alone understand what he was saying. Adrenalin was pumping so hard and I was really scared, but it was all happening too fast to really process. I decided that I needed to make eye contact to communicate with my assailant. Somehow, I swiveled around in a circle really fast and managed to remove my neck from the knife. I thought I was almost home free when the kid grabbed the sleeve of my leather jacket. I looked him in the eye and it was the shifty kid I had been so wary of in the club. Now he was yelling much louder and yanking on my sleeve. "He wants my jacket.....Really?" I thought. So I began slipping out of it, but just as the sleeve was about to fly off my hand and be gone forever, I involuntarily grabbed hold of it. This was my favorite jacket that I had recently bought in a thrift store on the Bowery in New York. I loved that jacket and wasn't going to let this punk ass kid steal it! So we began this funny tug of war, me yelling expletives in English and he the same, I imagine, in Dutch. He started to lose grip and I thought that I was going to win, until he suddenly lunged at me with the knife. It took me a split second to make the decision to let the jacket go. It just wasn't worth a knife in the gut. Then in a moment he was gone. As I stood there in shock, I heard Peter and the rest of the cavalry arriving just a little too late. My dear old friend and sound engineer Plug insisted that we go searching in our van for him, and described in graphic detail, what would become of the kid when we found him. Luckily for him our quest was to no avail.

BAUHAUS in...

RAISING VENOM

Art by MATT HOWARTH
Script by BAUHAUS

LUNCH WITH THE BOMB.

RAISING VENOM

We met Matt Howarth backstage at one of our early shows in New York. Matt asked us if we would be interested in collaborating on a comic strip. We responded with enthusiasm and gave Matt our contact information. A few months later we received photocopies of his beautiful artwork with the word balloons left blank for us to fill in. We decided to employ the cut up technique championed by William Burroughs and Brion Gysin. We set about creating a storyline and after being distracted by something or other, completed all but one page. The comic strip was put on the back burner and then sadly all but forgotten. Thankfully I came across this little gem when sorting through my collection and managed to track down Matt. On contacting him he told me that after not hearing back from us, he put the strip in a drawer where it remained for a few decades until I reached out to him.

I decided to complete the text on the unfinished page by employing the same cut up technique and after three decades the comic strip was finally finished! Matt added the final cherry to the cake by coloring it, which really bought it to life.

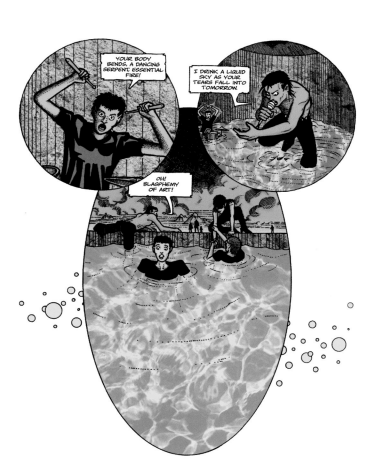

# Bauhaus

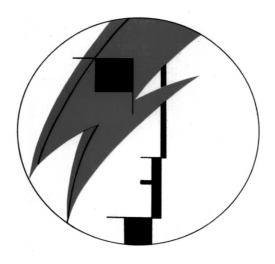

# ziggy Stardust

## ZIGGY STARDUST

The familiar chords rang out to the intro of "Ziggy Stardust" as I anticipated my entrance on the drums. It was May 7th, 1981, and we were recording our second LP entitled *Mask* at Playground Studios in Camden, North London. We had chosen to play "Ziggy Stardust", a song that we would use to warm up with at the beginning of our sessions. As the final chord died out, our engineer/producer, Mike Hedges', voice came loud and clear over the intercom. "Let's record it! This is a hit single!!" We all looked at each other and burst out laughing. "We can't do that!" we exclaimed in unison. Mike inquired as to why and we explained that, for a start, the press would have a field day. They hated us enough already. If we had the nerve to release "Ziggy Stardust" then their accusations that we were Bowie copyists would be affirmed. Mike suggested that would be even more of a good reason to do it! We all traded looks whilst Mike continued to try and convince us. Well why not?, we thought. We played that song because we loved it. Are we going to let a bunch of failed old music hacks make our decisions? In fact it would be the last thing they would expect. So that sealed it.

We set about committing it to tape with Daniel adding the bass as David was absent. I think that it was done and dusted within one hour. On David's arrival we played a prank on him. We pretended that in some dusty corner of the studio, we had a found an extremely rare lost demo recording of Bowie doing "Ziggy Stardust". It didn't take David all that long to realize he was being punked and, although a little bemused, was very taken with our recording. However, we ultimately shelved the whole idea as the song didn't fit in with the vibe of the LP, but this was the genesis of the eventual single.

"Ziggy" was laid to rest only to resurface a year later during our first major tour of Italy (we had played two open air events the year previous). As with most things Bauhaus, it was a spur of the moment idea to play it as an encore and the reaction was startling. It was fun to play and it went down a storm! This gave us the incentive to play it live in the UK at the ill-fated Adelphi Theatre gig in London on June 11th. Although our fans ripped up the first six rows of seats of the hallowed theatre causing the cancellation of the second night, we did receive the golden seal of approval from them and it remained in our set for some months to come as well as the "Resurrection" and all subsequent tours thereafter.

The version that was eventually released as a single was recorded for a BBC Radio 1 Kid Jensen session on July 1st in Maida Vale, London. Following the airing of the session, Martin Mills at our Label, Beggars Banquet contacted us suggesting, with great enthusiasm, that we should release it to coincide with our UK tour in October. I think that some of us still had slight reservations but eventually agreed. For the video we commissioned Standard Pictures and came up with a predominantly live gig concept, with the addition of placing Peter into an animal cage, quite blatantly "borrowing" the idea from The Hunger. For the setting, we chose the basement of legendary venue The Roundhouse in Camden Town London. It was comprised of tunnels and catacombs, originally the home for the horses that would shunt railway wagons on to the nearby tracks.

To add a degree of authenticity, on Wednesday 25th of August our entire back line was loaded into the Camden Catacombs. Lights, camera, action! Now all we needed was an audience. We thought it only fitting to invite our hardcore following of about forty kids who would literally show up to every show on our UK tours. But how would we get in touch with them? Social media didn't exist in those dark ages. So we came up with the somewhat risky idea to announce it on the radio the day before the shoot and it worked out perfectly.

"Ziggy Stardust" was released on October 1st 1982 and reached number 15 on the UK charts. Just one week later we performed it on Top Of The Pops. We had come full circle. On July 6th, 1972, when I was a mere eleven years old, David Bowie performed "Starman" on Top Of The Pops in a performance that influenced every punk and post punk band and beyond, and here we were on the same show, paying homage to the great man himself.

Filming the video for Ziggy Stardust in the catacombs of The Roundhouse, London. / Photo: Fin Costello

TELEGRAM SAM
AND
DOUBLE DARE.

# BAUHAUS

# AMPEX PRECISION MAGNETIC

RECORDING SPEED _____ 15, ps _____     RECORDING TIME ____ TAIL

TRACK 1 TELEGRAM SAM.

TRACK 2 * TELEGRAM SAM (SINGLE) *     STEREO

TRACK 3 DOUBLE DARE.                  NOT D

TRACK 4 DOUBLE DARE.

TRACK 5 DOUBLE DARE.

TRACK 6 * DOUBLE DARE. *
(Alternative Album Track).          TONES A

Engineered by                         1K  10K
~~scribbled out~~
~~scribbled out~~                     100Hz
~~Studio~~
                                      To Peak

Bauhaus with Peter Kent at O'Hare International Airport, Chicago, USA.

Photos: Kevin Haskins

276

Photos: Joseph Brookes and Henry Peck

## THE CITY OF ANGELS

Before Peter Kent formed 4AD records with Ivo Watts - Russell, he managed the Beggars Banquet record store on the Kings Road in London. It was 1978, and Peter was watching with suspicious curiosity as two American guys were stacking up several piles of records, pulled from all the bins in the store. "Are you actually going to buy all these?!" Peter said in a rather skeptical and inquisitive tone. "You bet!" exclaimed Joseph Brooks. Joseph and Henry Peck had just flown in from Los Angeles and from Heathrow Airport and had taken a cab directly to the record store. They went on to explain that they had traveled to England purely to buy records and see bands. Peter was impressed and over their mutual love of music, these comrades in arms soon became very good friends. Their transatlantic friendship continued and on a subsequent visit in November 1981, Peter Kent took them to see Bauhaus for the first time at the Brighton Top Rank, on The Mask Tour. They were very impressed by both the band and the audience. On their walk to the venue, they were witness to separate packs of our followers converging from various streets until they were eventually swallowed up by this post punk army. Their feeling was that this was not a random collection of people simply going out to check out a band, this was a tribe whose allegiance was displayed with white paint and metal spikes on leather jackets, and whose presence and passion at every gig would lift the band to the top of their game. I recall the evolution of our audience, who grew as the band grew and even influenced us, with a hairstyle here and a fishnet there. These devotees came from far and wide: Millie, Bulber, Basildon John, Bruce from Lowestoft, Middlesbrough Mick, Sheila, Connie and Peter "Luton" Hosier, who eventually became our lighting director for Love And Rockets.

After our show, Peter brought Henry and Joseph backstage to meet us and we hit it off right away. The second time we crossed paths was in their home town of Los Angeles, for a record signing appearance at Vinyl Fetish. However, Joseph and Henry were not there as fans, they owned the record store!

After a smooth landing at LAX I looked out of the window of the plane and saw palm trees. I motioned to the band, "Look, there's palm trees!" We were all surprised at seeing such exotic vegetation and more so when we felt the warm Californian sun kiss our skinny pale white arms. It was mid winter and we had just flown in from a frigid Minneapolis, naively expecting the same miserable climate to greet us on the West Coast. This was the moment that my love affair with LA began. Our sound engineer, Plug, lost no time acclimating to our new surroundings and duly rented a huge convertible Cadillac. The next day, he drove us in style down the palm lined boulevards to Vinyl Fetish for our in store record signing appearance. The store was on Melrose Ave. Similar to The Kings Road in London, it was the street to shop for vintage clothing, English imports, vintage furniture, etc. The enterprising duo of Joseph and Henry also had their own radio show called The Import Show, hosted by Dusty Street on KROQ. After the conclusion of each weekly show, they would leave several singles behind. On one particular occasion, Dusty took a

big liking to our latest single, "Kick In The Eye". From that point on, KROQ became our biggest supporter in Los Angeles.

The queue seemed to stretch all the way down Melrose Avenue as we were ushered in the front door of Vinyl Fetish. Joseph had hand painted a huge version of the front cover to our current LP, titled The Sky's Gone Out, which served as our backdrop for the record signing. I felt a bit overwhelmed, as kid after kid handed over their records to be signed. I used to find fan adoration a bit embarrassing, as I didn't feel in any way different to them, but I could relate when I thought about how much it meant to me to meet Joe Strummer. After the signing we repaired to The Hyatt Hotel with excited anticipation of the first show of three to be held at The Roxy Club on Sunset Blvd that night.

The Roxy's parking lot resembled a German car dealership as the BMW's and Mercedes pulled in to park, the drivers of which were not middle aged as one would expect, but the kids coming to our show! This sort of affluence was very alien to us coming from a small factory town. Not every attendee was born with a silver spoon though, as

BAUHAUS BASH—Peter Murphy of the British group Bauhaus greets fans at the Vinyl Fetish record store in Hollywood. His visit coincided with their shows at the Roxy in Los Angeles, where they performed tunes from their A&M LP, "The Sky's Gone Out."

was illustrated by a knock knock on our dressing room window. This was odd because we were two flights up! On opening the window I discovered about ten kids who had climbed the fire escape. They explained that they couldn't afford to buy tickets and could they come in? I felt a strong pang of compassion and so I pulled a "Joe Strummer" and let them all in. On exiting our dressing room the security guard shot me a confused look, so I lied that they were our friends who had shown up before he did. I guess that word got around as we ended up repeating this favour the following two nights.

The LA audiences were very attentive and I remember us firing on all fours. We tapped into "The Spirit" and delivered a very intense performance. It was a marvelous introduction to the city that I would eventually call my home.

PLUG - NOSE CITY '88

THIRD UNCLE'S NOSE

~~FEAR (SEA)~~ OF NOSES

BOYS NOSES

T.C.K. NOSES

SHE'S IN NOSES

ARTAUD BIG NOSE

NOSE SHADOWS

NOSE GARDEN

NOSE IN ALCOVE

HOLLOW NOSE

KICK IN THE NOSE

NOSE ENTRIES

ZIGGY BIG NOSE?

BELA LUGOSI'S NOSE

# RAFFINERIE DU PLAN K

Brussels march 3rd

Dear Graham,

My last hours in London were a little bit disturbed. But now it's ok. Well the gig is planned for saturday april 5th. I enclose an advertisement we'll do. I know, it looks a little bit artificial, but I hope it's a good way to bring more people.

The fee that will be paid is

400 £
or 350 £ + television show (which brings ±150 £)

The hotel is paid by Plan K. We provide also the P.A.
(Hotel van Belle - Chaussée de Mons)

So I hope hearing some news from you -
By the way, we intend to record a single (an E.P live at the Plan K) which eventually would be distributed in Belgium. Would you agree with this?

Hope I'll see you soon

michel Duval

210 rue de la Victoire
Bruxelles 1060

Please write
to this address. ——→
it will avoid some complications

LE PLAN K - a.s.b.l.
21, rue de Manchester - 1070 Bruxelles - T. 523 18 34 ou 7, galerie de la Reine - 1000 Bruxelles - Belgium - T. 511 11 22

Plan K 21 rue de Manchester (1070 Brussels

Raffinerie du **PLAN K**
Rue de Manchester, 21
1070 Bruxelles
—

**40.-**

Bauhaus c/o Graham
21 Costwold Avenue
Duston Northampton
England

Abr. Arming c/o Plan Kaan
23 Belgica St.
1000/62
Germany

Graham Bentley
21, Cotswold Avenue
GB — Duston/Northampton
England

# BAUHAUS

| MOERS W. GERMANY | 27 March |
| BERLIN - (so 36) | 28 March |
| BRAUNCHWEIG | 29 March |
| TO BE CONFIRMED | 30 March |
| TO BE CONFIRMED | 31 March |
| TO BE CONFIRMED | 1 April |
| TO BE CONFIRMED | 2 April |
| DUSSELDORF - (Okidoki Club) | 3 April |
| TO BE CONFIRMED | 4 April |
| BRUSSELS (Plan K) | 5 April |

Dear Sounds,

"All angst and no play" was the title of the totaly
inaccurate review of the Bauhaus album 'In the flat field'
which appeared in sounds last week, and after reading it
I can only assume that the writer, D.McCullough, is a very
dull boy indeed.
A lot of care, passion and commitment went into
making that record and we are proud of the end result.
Contrary to McCulloughs supposition we do not like, want
or need his 'review', nor do we adhere to rules, "bogus
underground" or otherwise.
Perhaps it is McCullough who has strayed over "the
line?"

David Jay
(Bauhaus)

p.s. I am responsible for fifty percent of the "bad
    poetry" along with Murphy.
p.p.s. Edgar Broughton???

# bauhaus

21 Cotterell Avenue
Weston Northampton
Phone Number 51307

AN AGREEMENT made the............7th............day of....MARCH....1980....

between BAUHAUS and .........ARMIN ANDERSCH (SO 36)....

WITNESS that.....ARMIN ANDERSCH.....hereby engages BAUHAUS

and BAUHAUS accept the engagement to appear at

..............SO 36    WEST BERLIN..............

SCHEDULE Date of engagement.....28th...MARCH...1980.......

Fee.....£500.......... payable in advance by the

following method..£250 payable by 14th MARCH 1980 BALANCE
PAYABLE 1 HOUR BEFORE PERFOR

CLAUSES The Venue of the engagement to be made available to

BAUHAUS by..1600 Hrs (4pm) on the date of the engagement

for sound checks and rehearsal.

ARMIN ANDERSCH SO 36.......... shall provide a suitable

P.A., consisting of at least eight channel mixing deck,

eight microphones, echo facilities, mike stands, adequate

amplifiers, monitors and speakers for the Venue, and

a proficient person to assist with the sound control.

An English / German / French speaking person to be

available for any linguistic problems.

Accommodation shall be provided for BAUHAUS (five persons)

if required by BAUHAUS.

Signed on behalf of:-

ARMIN ANDERSCH SO 36 / ~~BAUHAUS~~

Address.

~~1000 Berlin 62~~
Berger Str. 23

PLEASE RETURN THIS TO
ADDRESS AT TOP ↗.

# bauhaus

21 Cotswold Avenue
Duston Northampton
Phone Napton 51307

**AN AGREEMENT** made the........6th........day of...March....19.80.
between BAUHAUS and ...Propaganda Music Services.......
............................................

**WITNESS** that...Propaganda Music Services.....hereby engages BAUHAUS

and BAUHAUS accept the engagement to appear at

....Oki Poki......Dusseldorf......................

**SCHEDULE** Date of engagement....3rd April 1980.

Fee...£200............. payable in advance by the

following method......In Full By March 16th 1980

**CLAUSES** The Venue of the engagement to be made available to

BAUHAUS by..16.00 hrs. (4pm.). on the date of the engagement

for sound checks and rehearsal.

..Oki Poki.................. shall provide a suitable

P.A., consisting of at least eight channel mixing deck,

eight microphones, echo facilities, mike stands, adequate

amplifiers, monitors and speakers for the Venue, and

a proficient person to assist with the sound control.

An English / German / French speaking person to be

available for any linguistic problems.

Accommodation shall be provided for BAUHAUS (five persons)

if required by BAUHAUS.

Please send Address +
map of club

LB

Return This Copy

Signed on behalf of:-

Propaganda Music Services BAUHAUS
.....PROPAGANDA·music
Address V. deFries
Moerser Str. 278
D-4132 Kamp-Lintfor
W. Germany

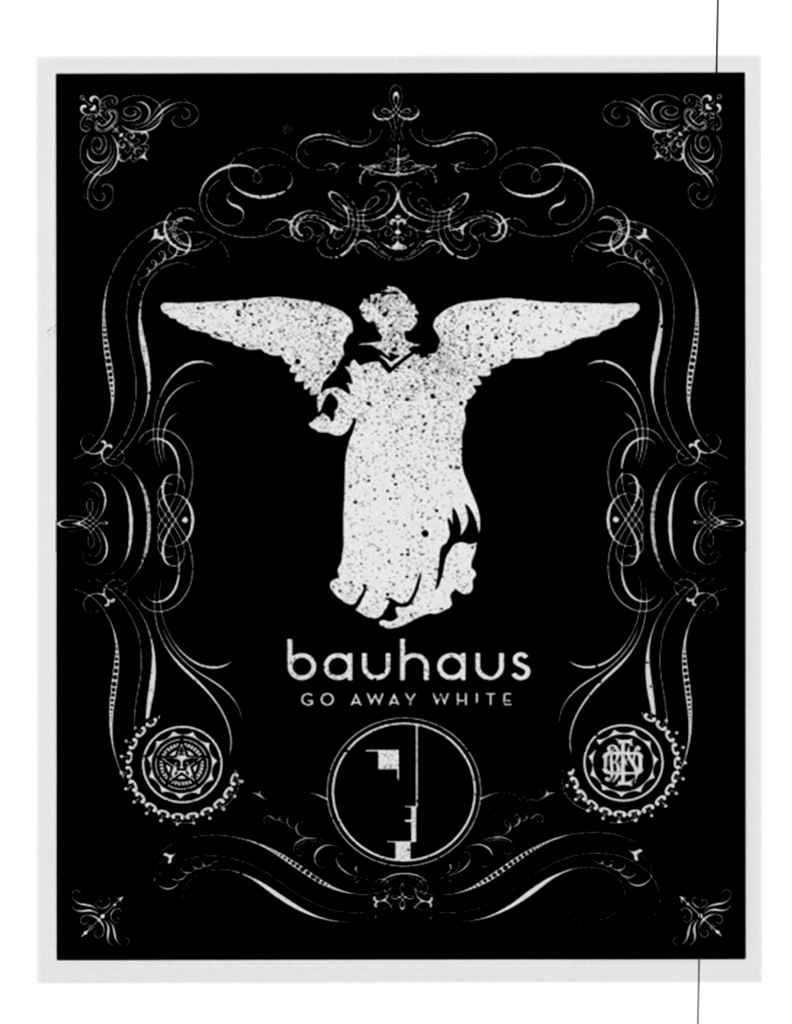

Promotional poster by Shepard Fairey for the LP *Go Away White*

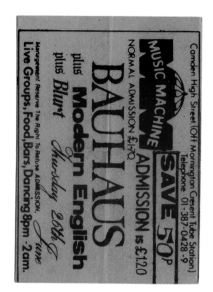

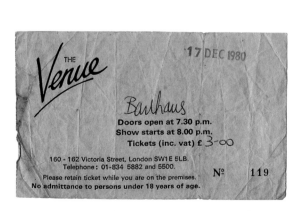

The Royal Theatre and Opera House
Northampton

**BAUHAUS IN CONCERT**
Sunday, 26th October, at 8.00 p.m.

| STALLS | £4 | £1.50 | inc.VAT |
|---|---|---|---|
| Seat No. | | Price | |

Photo: Graham Trott

Photo: Brian Shanley

**TIFFANY'S**
MERRION CENTRE LEEDS
Leeds (0532) 663252 or 31668/9

# BAUHAUS

SUNDAY **25**th APRIL

Videos AND

**SPECIAL GUESTS**

TICKETS £3

ACE 15 IDWARDS
NO DRESS RESTRICTIONS
GROUPS ON STAGE
OPENING 7.30pm & 22pm

TIFFANY'S
Merrion Centre Leeds
Leeds (0532) 663252 or 31668/9

# BAUHAUS

UEASU   LCR
13 OCT   £2·75 ADV.

Friars Aylesbury is a Club and therefore it is essential that Membership Cards are produced on the night even if an advance ticket has been purchased. If you are not a member, membership must be obtained on the night. Minimum age for membership is 16 years. Life Membership is 25p (including VAT). Thank you.

**FRIARS**
PRESENTS

# BAUHAUS

Saturday, October 16th   7.30 p.m.

MAXWELL HALL, MARKET SQ., AYLESBURY

This Ticket value 350p. (including VAT)

AYLESBURY IS GOOD FOR YOU

---

DE MONTFORT HALL, LEICESTER

M.C.P. presents

# BAUHAUS

*Wednesday 27th October*
at 7.30 p.m.

**STANDING   £3.50**   INC. V.A.T.

Tickets not transferable or money refunded

**1124**

*To be retained*

---

THE DOME, BRIGHTON

**SATURDAY**
9th OCTOBER, 1982
at 7.30 p.m.
Derek Block Concert Promotions
presents

# BAUHAUS

ROW

## A 74

**STALLS CIRCLE**
including VAT   **£3.50**

Tickets cannot be accepted for exchange
or refund. Latecomers will not have access
to their seats until a suitable interval.
**TO BE RETAINED**

---

ODEON THEATRE, Birmingham

M.C.P. presents—

# Bauhaus + Special Guests

Saturday, 23rd October 1982

Evening 7.30

**REAR STALLS**

£3.50

**BB   18**

NO TICKET EXCHANGED NOR MONEY REFUNDED
THIS PORTION TO BE RETAINED          (P.T.O.)

A. B. Cooper (Printers) Ltd. Manchester

---

OLD VIC
Theatre

EVENING

Stalls
£4·50
Incl. VAT

**Q 8**

OLD VIC THEATRE
WATERLOO ROAD

EVENING

presents

FOR TIME OF PERFORMANCE
SEE DAILY PRESS

**STALLS**
£4·50
Incl. VAT

£3.50

BAUHAUS
FEB 24

**Q 8**

THIS PORTION TO BE RETAINED

---

HAMMERSMITH PALAIS
DEREK BLOCK PRESENTS

# BAUHAUS

PLUS GUESTS

Monday 1st November 7.30pm
ALL TICKETS £3.50

GAUMONT THEATRE
SOUTHAMPTON
DEREK BLOCK presents
**BAUHAUS**
plus SUPPORT
DOORS OPEN 6.45 p.m.
EVENING 7.30
THURSDAY
JUNE **16**
STALLS
£3.50
**G 22**

No Tickets exchanged nor
money refunded.
TO BE RETAINED   P.T.O.

ROYAL COURT THEATRE, Liverpool
M.C.P. presents—
**Bauhaus** plus Support
Wednesday, 22nd June 1983
Evening 7.30
STALLS – STANDING
£3.50
**№ 1067**

A B Cooper (Printers) Ltd., Manchester

Retain this portion

No Ticket Exchanged nor Money Refunded
No Cameras or Recording Equipment
Official Programmes sold only in the Theatre

HAMMERSMITH PALAIS
DEREK BLOCK PRESENTS
**BAUHAUS**
**PLUS GUESTS**
Tuesday 5th July 7.30pm
**ALL TICKETS £3.50**
INVALID IF DETATCHED FROM COUNTERFOIL
**№ 0993**

DE MONTFORT HALL, LEICESTER
M.C.P. Presents
**BAUHAUS**
plus SPECIAL GUESTS
TUESDAY 21st JUNE
at 7.30 p.m.
**STANDING £3.50** INC. V.A.T.
Tickets not transferable or money refunded
**955**
To be retained

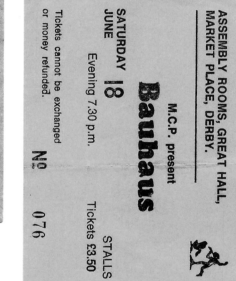

ASSEMBLY ROOMS, GREAT HALL,
MARKET PLACE, DERBY.
M.C.P. present
**Bauhaus**
SATURDAY
JUNE **18**
Evening 7.30 p.m.
STALLS
Tickets £3.50
Tickets cannot be exchanged
or money refunded.
**№ 076**

AN UDO ARTISTS, INC. PRESENTATION 1983 DOCUMENTATION '83 第11巻
主催●文化放送 ワンダー音楽事務所
協力●ワーナー・パイオニア
協賛●ブリチストンタイヤ株式会社
パウハウス
**BAUHAUS**
5月28日(土)渋谷公会堂 3:00pm
S ¥3,900
1階 ち列 44番

GAUMONT THEATRE
IPSWICH
Telephone 53641
Stalls        Seat No.
**A        15**
**BAUHAUS**
7.30 p.m.
SATURDAY, 2nd JULY
Admission £3.50
This portion to be given up on
entrance to theatre
Printed by The Halesworth Press Limited

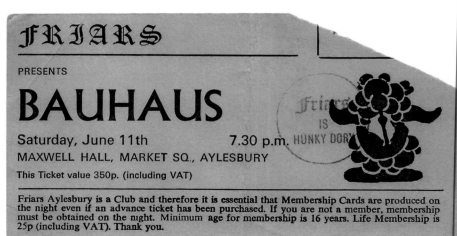

**FRIARS**
PRESENTS
**BAUHAUS**
Saturday, June 11th        7.30 p.m.
MAXWELL HALL, MARKET SQ., AYLESBURY
This Ticket value 350p. (including VAT)

Friars IS HUNKY DORY

Friars Aylesbury is a Club and therefore it is essential that Membership Cards are produced on
the night even if an advance ticket has been purchased. If you are not a member, membership
must be obtained on the night. Minimum age for membership is 16 years. Life Membership is
25p (including VAT). Thank you.

294

# M. C. Edwards (Insurance Brokers) Ltd.

Registered Office

82 Wellingborough Road
Abington Square
Northampton NN1 4DP
Telephone: 0604/38349

Registered in England
No. 1232753

---

Our Ref. 8003518/CFC                24th October 1980

Your Ref.

G.J. Bentley, Esq.,
21 Cotswold Avenue
Duston
Northampton.

Dear Mr. Bentley,

<u>Theft of Musical Items</u>

Your claim form has now been returned to us by
your Insurers. They require the back of the claim form
to be completed with the items stolen and their insured
values.

Also, they require to know why they were not
notified of the loss until 29.9.80 when the theft
occurred on 28.3.80 and also the date on which the
matter was reported to the Berlin Police.

Your receipts are returned herewith.

Yours faithfully,

C.F. Craddock (Mrs)

---

DIRECTORS:   M. C. EDWARDS   J. D. RAFTER   N. D. PRITCHARD   G. L. NEWBROOK

ENTERTAINMENT
& LEISURE
[Insurance]
SERVICES.

P. O. BOX 64 HARROGATE.
NORTH YORKS. HG2 9ND
TEL HARROGATE (0423) 870741

3518.

# CLAIM FORM

| | |
|---|---|
| ASSURED: G. J. BENTLEY | POLICY No.: S 8099 |
| ADDRESS: | TEL. No.: |

| | |
|---|---|
| Date and time of loss &/or damage | BETWEEN 1am + 3am (a.m./p.m.) |
| Date loss &/or damage discovered | 28th MARCH 1980 |
| Place where loss or damage occurred | SO.36 WEST BERLIN |
| STATE FULLY HOW LOSS OR DAMAGE OCCURRED<br><br>Please give a detailed list of all items claimed for on reverse of this form.<br><br>An estimate should be enclosed for repairs in respect of damaged items.<br><br>- 2 OCT 1980 | WHILST LOADING OUR VAN SOMEONE RAN OFF WITH SOME OF OUR EQUIPMENT |
| In the event of a theft from a vehicle, how was the vehicle protected ? | N/A. |
| HAVE THE POLICE BEEN INFORMED ?<br>State date police advised and name of station<br>If your claim is for an article lost, stolen or maliciously damaged or destroyed the police must be advised promptly | YES/NO<br>THE PROMOTER OF THE GIG -ARMIN ANDENSCHT NOTIFIED THE WEST BERLIN POLICE |
| IF THE LOSS IS OCCASIONED BY THEFT PLEASE GIVE FULL DETAILS OF :—<br>(a) Protections in operation at time of loss<br>(b) How was entry to the premises gained ? | 5 MEMBERS OF BAUHAUS WERE LOADING THE VAN BUT SOMEHOW THE THIEVES MANAGED TO GET AWAY UNSEEN. |
| HAS ANY OTHER PERSON AN INTEREST IN THE PROPERTY CLAIMED FOR ? | NO |
| Is there any other insurance covering the property concerned ? | No |

I/We hereby declare that all the details given by me/us on this form are to the best of my/our knowledge true and complete.

DATE: 20/10/80          SIGNED: Graham Bentley.

Photo: Brian Shanley

Photograph taken by Kevin Haskins from behind his drum kit, just prior to the curtain opening for Bauhaus'
"Final" concert at The Hammersmith Palais, July 5th, 1983.

## THE "LAST" SHOW

The day had arrived, July 5th, 1983, and what we believed to be, at the time, our final concert. We had made the decision to disband and to avoid sentimentality, we chose not to tell anyone, not even our crew. In retrospect, I feel that this was disrespectful, and I wish now that we had announced it beforehand. However as it happened, it wasn't the end but just the beginning of a fifteen year hiatus!

Minutes before the show, I remember sitting down on my drum stool and observing the rest of the band plugging in their instruments behind the closed curtain at the front of the stage. It was a very odd feeling, knowing that in just over one hour, it would all be over! I took a photograph of Daniel for posterity and thought it odd that he was laughing as I felt quite sad. Then in a moment the curtain opened and the chords to "Burning From The Inside" rang out. When it was time to join in on the drums, with my first hit of the snare, I broke my drumstick in half! This was in fact an odd occurrence, as I'm not known for being a hard hitting, demonstrative drummer. I quickly reached for another stick and again, the bloody thing broke in half! It then dawned on me that someone was playing a prank, and on close inspection of my sticks, I observed that most of them had saw marks on them. It's customary at the end of a tour to play pranks on the band, the crew, the support band, etc, so I realized what was going on. Thankfully and with a certain degree of responsibility, the crew had left me with a few good pairs. The next surprise came when I took my first hit on the floor tom...a billowing cloud of flour exploded into the air! I wondered what was coming next and I didn't have to wait for long as I suddenly felt something wrap around my ankle. I looked down to see our lighting designer, Graham Bentley, chaining my left leg to my drum stool!

It was by all accounts a great show, ignited with the emotion that we were all feeling, including David's chanting of "we're so pretty, pretty vacant" as "Dark Entries" reached its furious climax. This was to be our final stand and we were determined to making it really count.

And all too soon, in a blink of an eye, the final chords rang out into a feedback swell and, fired up with emotion, I found myself trashing my drum kit! Well, I wasn't going to need it anymore! First of all the Kick Drum went flying off the drum riser followed by cymbals, hi hats, stands, and anything I could lay my hands on. Eventually the only one thing remaining was the floor tom. In a rush of adrenalin I picked it up and irresponsibly threw up into the air. I honestly didn't notice that Graham had took to the stage, and, unfortunately for him, it came crashing down on to his unsuspecting cranium! In the chaos of the moment, I wasn't even aware of this regrettable occurrence until about ten minutes later,

when I happened upon a bucket of bloody water backstage! I inquired to our tour manager Harry as to who's blood it was and was duly informed that it was Graham's. He went on to explain his close encounter with my floor tom, and that he had been rushed off to the local ER! I felt so, so awful, but was reassured that it appeared far worse than it actually was. After contemplating my stupidity, I then turned my attention to the drum stool that I was forced to carry around, it still being firmly chained to my leg. I asked Harry if he had the key and he informed me that it was still in Graham's pocket, at the emergency room.

I spent the next karmic hour or so carrying the annoying accessory around with me until the very welcomed return of Graham, sporting a cartoon sized bandage around his poor old noggin.

Original set list for the "final" concert that was taped to David Haskins' bass guitar.

# SIDE ONE [8pt Med.]

▲ THIRD UNCLE (BRIAN ENO & EG MUSIC)

— 2 line space.

## SILENT HEDGES

FOLLOWING THE SILENT HEDGES
~~NEEDING~~ NEEDING SOME OTHER KIND OF MADNESS
LOOKING INTO PURPLE EYES
SADNESS AT ~~THE~~ CORNERS
WORKS OF ART WITH A MINIMUM OF STEEL

~~SELF CONFIDENCE LEAKS~~
PURE SENSATION
THE ~~BEAUTIFUL~~ DOWN GRADE
GOING TO HELL AGAIN
GOING TO HELL AGAIN

SELF CONFIDENCE LEAKS ~~FROM A THOUSAND WOUNDS~~
FROM A THOUSAND WOUNDS
FAULTS OF CIVILISATION
BURNING THE PRIVATE PARADISE OF DREAMS
MINUS HANDS OF THE ELECTRIC CLOCK.
CLOCK
CLOCK
CLOCK.
PURE SENSATION

THE ~~BEAUTIFUL~~ DOWN GRADE
**BEAUTIFUL**
GOING TO HELL AGAIN
GOING TO HELL AGAIN.
AGAIN
AGAIN
AGAIN.

## IN THE NIGHT

IN THE NIGHT, IN THE CHAIR
HE SITS THERE, HE SITS TIGHT
NO MORE CANS, NO MORE CRIME
SEE THE PLACE, SEE THE TIME
YOU NEVER KNOW, ~~YOU NEVER KNOW~~

HE WALKS LIGHT, DON'T KNOW HOW
MAYBE NOW, IN ~~THAT~~ THE NIGHT
OH, I KNOW, YES I KNOW
THERE'S NO ~~CHAT~~ CHAT
HE'S FOR SHOW
YOU NEVER KNOW.

SEES THE PLACE AND TRIES TO GET THE TIME
HE'S SLOWLY SLIPPING INTO ~~THAT~~ THE SLIME
CAN'T INJECT INTO ~~THAT~~ HIS VEINS
BLOOD AND GUFF OOZE OUT AND STAIN
CARES NOT THAT HE REALLY BLEEDS
DEATH, NOT HELL IS WHAT HE NEEDS
SEES THE PLACE, CHECKS THE TIME

---

IN THE NIGHT, CONTINUED,

~~YOU NEVER KNOW.~~

SLIPPING UP AND DOWN HIS WRITHING SIDE
HIS EYES BEGIN TO PONDER PRIDE
~~SUBJECTIVE~~ SUBJECTIVE PICS OF MISLEAD YOUTH
BEFORE HIM LIES THE DREADFUL TRUTH
~~UNDIGNIFIED~~ INSIGNIFIED — HIS WRIST ON ~~TO THE~~
?? RAZOR SLIDES.
~~OH LOOK AT HIS WIFE.~~

YOU NEVER KNOW

## ✶ SWING THE HEARTACHE

OUT OF HER MOUTH IT CAME AS NO
SURPRISE
LIPSTICK STAINED ON **WHIPCREAM** LIES
I FEEL THAT IF I HAD BEEN UGLIER
IT WOULD HAVE BEEN EASIER

THERE IT SAT, BLINKED AND SPAT
IN A BLACK FEATHER HAT
AND SAID 'THE RAT'
(I NOW POSSESS QUASI SUCCESS)
~~BUT~~

BUT SHE WANTS TO BE A BETTER SINGER
~~SWING THE HEARTACHE~~
JUST FOR HER SAKE
~~BUT SHE WANTS TO BE A BETTER SINGER~~
SWING THE HEARTACHE
JUST FOR HER SAKE.

## SPIRIT

TONIGHT I COULD BE WITH YOU
OR WAITING IN THE WINGS
LIFT YOUR HEART WITH SOARING SONG
CUT DOWN THE PUPPET STRINGS,
CUT DOWN THE PUPPET STRINGS

I WEAR A COAT OF DRUMS
AND DANCE UPON YOUR EYES
TURN THE TABLES UPSIDE DOWN
CHANGE THE LOWS TO HIGHS
CHANGE THE LOWS TO HIGHS.

I FILL YOU UP WITH BUTTERFLIES
CROWN THE HEADS OF KINGS
BE GLAD OF FIRST NIGHT NERVES
FOR FEAR GIVES COURAGE WINGS
FEAR GIVES COURAGE WINGS.

IF I AM ON THE SIDELINES
CHANCES ARE YOU'LL MISS
WAIT ALONE AND SPOTLIT
FOR DOCTOR ~~THEATRES~~ THEATRE'S KISS.
THE STAGE BECOMES A SHIP IN FLAMES
I TIE YOU TO THE MAST
THROW YOUR BODY OVERBOARD
THE SPOTLIGHT DOESN'T LAST
THE SPOTLIGHT DOESN'T LAST.
COULD BE WITH YOU
OR WAITING IN THE WINGS
LIFT YOUR HEART WITH SOARING SONG
CUT DOWN THE PUPPET STRINGS
CUT DOWN THE PUPPET STRINGS
(continued above)

SOME OTHER PLACE, SOME OTHER TIME
YOU NEVER KNOW

I MAY TAP ~~YOU ON~~
THE SHOULDER
AND WHISPER 'GO' IN ~~RED~~ LEAD
STRIP YOUR FEET OF ~~LEAD~~
MY FRIEND
STRIP YOUR FEET OF LEAD.

CALL THE CURTAIN
RAISE THE ROOF
SPIRITS ON TONIGHT
CALL THE CURTAIN
RAISE THE ROOF
SPIRITS ON TONIGHT.
CALL THE CURTAIN
RAISE THE ROOF
SPIRITS ON TONIGHT.

WE LOVE OUR AUDIENCE
REPEAT

SIDE TWO (CONT'D)

## THE THREE SHADOWS (PART III)

O GENTLEMEN
SWALLOW YOUR PRAYERS
BECAUSE THE WIND MAKES A MOCKERY OF MEN
YOUR SOUL BECOMES A FISH
YOU SWIM IN IDLE WATERS AND DRINK **OTHER** FISHES PISS
YOUR SOUL FEEDS ON FISH
ON PISS, PISS AND MEN
WHO IN TURN BECOME, AS YOU HAVE BECOME,.
A FISH.
NO, NOT EVEN THAT, BUT A SYMBOL OF FISH
HOOKED BY THE BABY FLESH OF MAGGOTS
A RIPPLE OF LIFE IN TIN
THIS TIN COULD BECOME YOUR WORLD TOO
SO CHOOSE BETWEEN THIS AND WATER
CHOOSE BETWEEN ~~A~~ TIN AND PISS
DO YOU STILL FEEL THIRSTY NOW
ARE YOU THIRSTY NOW
ARE YOU THIRSTY NOW
DO YOU STILL FEEL
THIRSTY
THIRSTY NOW ....ETC....
~~ARE YOU~~

SIDE 2 (CONT'D) ALL WE ② ❸ EVER WANTED WAS EVERYTHING

ALL WE EVER WANTED WAS EVERYTHING
ALL WE EVER GOT WAS COLD
GET UP, EAT JELLY
~~SANDWICH~~ BARS, AND BARBED WIRE
**SANDWICH**
SQUASH EVERY WEEK INTO A DAY

THE SOUND OF THE ~~DREA~~ DRUM IS CALLING
THE SOUND OF THE DRUM HAS CALLED
**FLASH** OF YOUTH SHOOT OUT OF DARKNESS.......
~~FACTORY TOWN~~. FACTORYTOWN.

OH TO BE THE CREAM (~~REPEAT TO END~~)

# EXQUISITE CORPSE

SMALL LETTERING →   # — line space.

( 1 DAVID JAY )
( 2 PETER MURPHY )   64 pt Med
( 3 DANIEL ASH )     CAPS.
( 4 KEVIN HASKINS )

~~8~~ ~~CULMINATION~~
5 COMBINATION.   # ——— line space.

⑤ THE SKY'S GONE OUT
~~(REPEAT TO END)~~
REPEAT.

① LIFE IS BUT A DREAM
LIFE IS BUT A DREAM
LIFE IS BUT A DREAM
LIFE IS BUT A DREAM
LIFE IS BUT A DREAM
LIFE IS BUT A DREAM
LIFE IS BUT A DREAM
LIFE IS BUT A DREAM
LIFE IS BUT A DREAM
#

② I MAKE THE AIR FALL APART
AROUND ME
NOW AS THE PETALS ARE ~~NOMORE~~ NO MORE
A CORRODING, ~~SHRIVELED~~ SHRINKING STALK REMAINS
BEREFT OF HIS BLOOMS
AND ~~THE~~ ULTIMATE ~~CRUELTY~~ OF LOVES ~~TALONS~~ PINIONS
BESET HIS APPEARANCE
BESET HIS APPEARANCE

NO KING COULD REPLENISH HIS STATE
NOW BROWNING, SINKING, DYING, A ~~THOUSAND DEATH~~
A THOUSAND DEATHS
A THOUSAND DEATHS
A THOUSAND DEATHS

③ TERRY SAT UP    #
AND HUGGED THE ARMY SURPLUS BAG
AROUND HIS ~~THIN~~ SKINNY WAIST
IT WAS COLD,
AND THE PERSON BESIDE HIM HAD FADED ~~RATH~~ BADLY
LEGS APART HIS EYES LIT UP
THE SKY'S GONE OUT — THE SKY, THE SKY — THE SKY'S GONE OUT

④ ~~THE SKY~~ ZZZZZZZZZZZZZ !

THE SKY'S GONE OUT ] 12pt med.   ▲ TITLE (LARGE LETTERING) ⑤

CREATED AND PRODUCED BY BAUHAUS.
ENGINEERED BY DEREK THOMPKINS AND TED SHARP.
EXCEPT 'THIRD UNCLE', ~~AND~~ ENGINEERED BY MIKE ROBINSON.
RECORDED AT ROCKFIELD STUDIOS ~~EXCEPT SWING THE~~
~~HEARTACHE EXCEPT~~ ✻ BECK STUDIOS, ▲ BBC STUDIOS,
EXCEPT ✻ BECK STUDIOS, **WELLINGBOROUGH**
        ▲ BBC STUDIOS, ~~MAIDA~~ VALE, LONDON
'THIRD UNCLE' WRITTEN BY BRIAN ENO
~~RELEASED~~ BY ARRANGMENT WITH THE BBC.
COVER PAINTING DANIEL ASH.
INNER SLEEVE PHOTOGRAPHS - FIN COSTELLO.

ZZZZZZZ — DERICK.

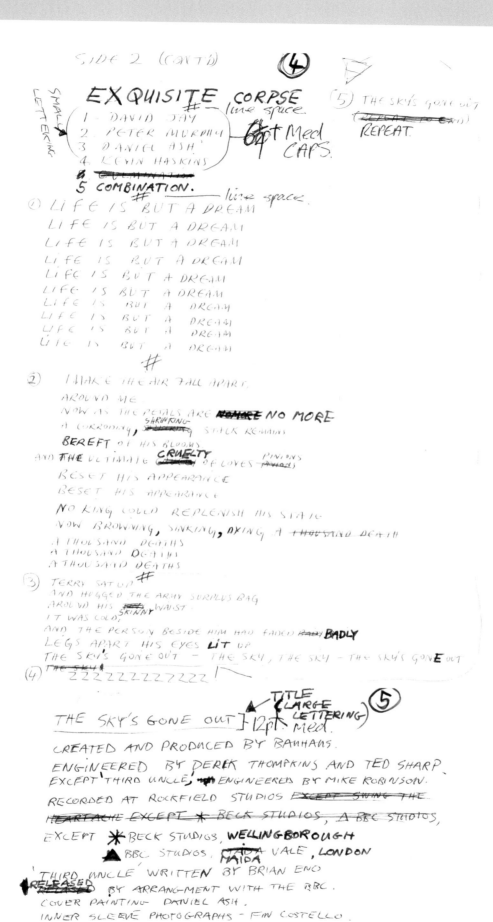

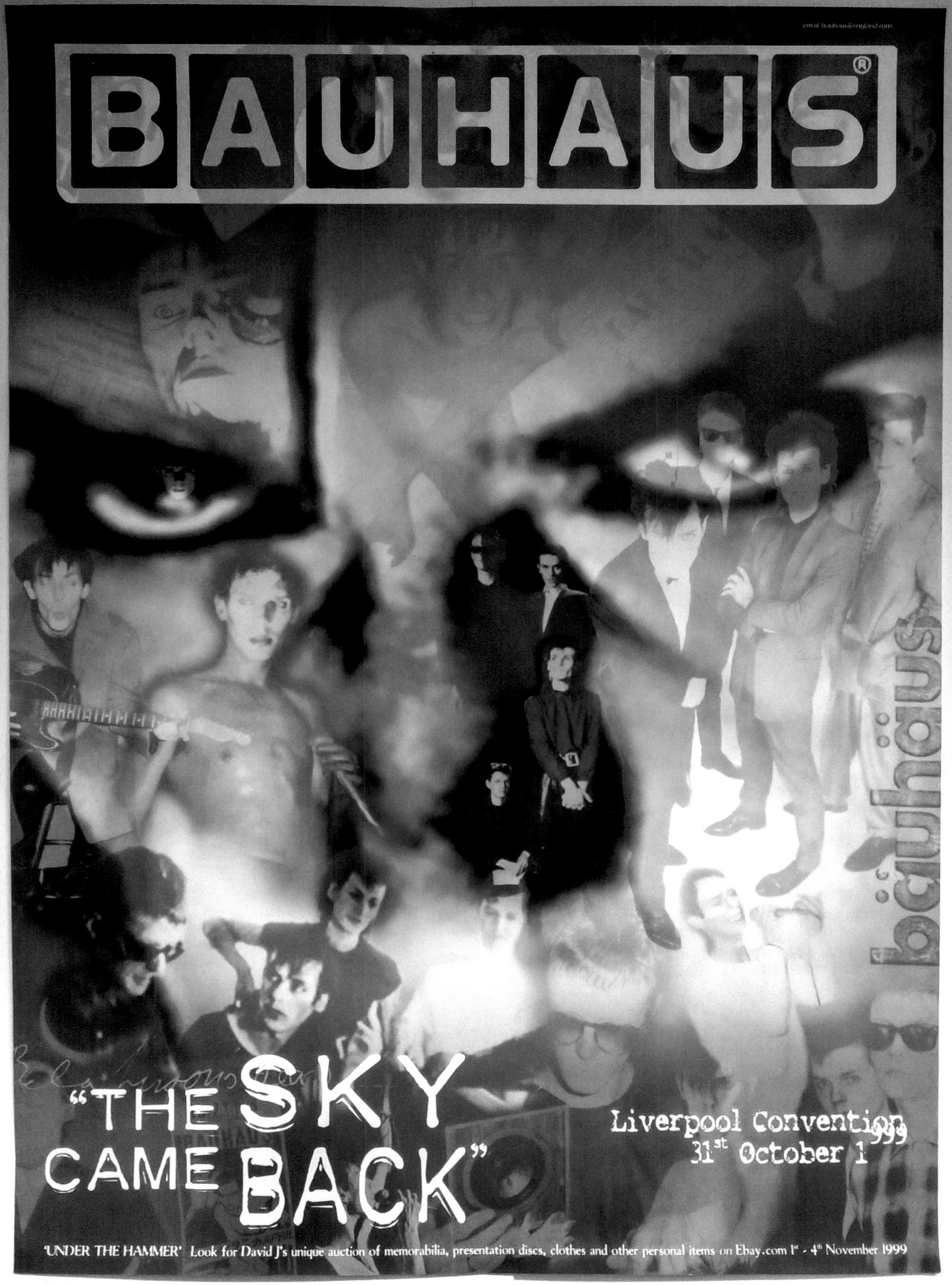

email bauhaus@england.com
BAUHAUS®
bauhaus
"THE SKY CAME BACK"
Liverpool Convention
31st October 1999
'UNDER THE HAMMER' Look for David J's unique auction of memorabilia, presentation discs, clothes and other personal items on Ebay.com 1st - 4th November 1999

308

FINAL SOLUTION PRESENT
**BAUHAUS, CLOCK DVA & TORSO** in Heaven

9.00 PM~3.00 AM, MON, MARCH 30TH

OVER 18's ONLY. HEAVEN IS UNDER THE ARCHES AT CHARING CROSS, WC2. TICKETS £3.00 FROM BEGGARS BANQUET, SMALLWONDER, ROUGH TRADE, HONKY TONK, BONAPARTE (KINGS X) & PREMIER BOX OFFICE OR ON THE NIGHT

notre dame hall

leicester square

friday 29th august

bàuhàus
Terror Couple Kill Colonel
Single on 4AD Records

Advance tickets £1.75 from Rough Trade & 4 AD 8 Hogarth Road SW5 or £2.00 on the night when the doors open at 8.00 p m

# BAUHAUS

**TOUR PACK**

THIS SPECIALLY COMPILED "ACME TOUR PACK" GIVES FANS A SECOND CHANCE TO OBTAIN A SET OF OFFICIAL TOUR MERCHANDISE AS SOLD ON TOUR. BY PURCHASING ALL THESE ITEMS TOGETHER IN THIS TOUR PACK YOU CAN SAVE POUNDS OFF THE "ON THE ROAD" PRICE

**THIS PACK CONTAINS:**

1. TOUR TEE SHIRT  2. TOUR PROGRAMME
3. SET OF FOUR BUTTON BADGES
4. ENAMEL BADGE  5. STRIP PATCH

# BAU

## VIC GODARD &
## SUBWAY SEC

### LYCEUM
STRAND, WC2

### THU

TICKETS £3·00 (INC. VAT) ADVANCE LYCEUM BOX O
LONDON THEATRE BOOKINGS, SHAFTESBURY AVE.,
OR ROCK ON RECORDS, 3 KENTISH TOWN RD., NW

STRAIGHT MUSIC PRESENTS

# HAUS

THE

# BIRTHDAY PARTY

SDAY 25th JUNE at 7·30

E, TEL: 836 3715,
439 3371; PREMIER BOX OFFICE, TEL: 240 2245,
.: 485 5088

# BAUHAUS

FLAT 25, HAMILTON COURT, HAMILTON ROAD, LONDON W 5

The BAUHAUS Information Club is designed to keep a close
link between you and BAUHAUS.  This club is a positive
move towards retaining the general, unique and interesting
approach that the group: Peter Murphy, Daniel Ash, Kevin
Haskins, David J and myself will be working together
compiling ideas.

The following are some of the items available to members
throughout the year:-

* Official badge
* Merchandise sheet
* 4 posters exclusive to the club (for sale)
* consequence cartoons by the group
* cartoon booklet from the U.S. tour
* Newsletters whenever news and plans occur
* Biography
* Interviews, reviews, lyric sheets

Please fill in the application form
if you'd like to join

To join it will cost £3.00
(overseas members £4.00) for one year.

NAME: ...............................................

ADDRESS: ).........................................

...........................................

AGE: ................ TELEPHONE NO: ..................

SUGGESTIONS TO THE CLUB: ...........................

I WOULD LIKE TO JOIN THE "BAUHAUS INFORMATION CLUB".  I
enclose a fee of three pounds, made payable to: STELLA WATTS

(BAUHAUS INFORMATION CLUB)  Cheques and postal orders made
payable to the above.

Dance

Hot Tubes
Tender Hooks
Church Isles
Holy Books

on Crocodiles
~~Dan~~

on Hallowed ground
— nijinski style

— with the lost a found

Dance on Rock a Roll a group
— on Burny coals

— on Tenements

with the taxmen     with old man at the sail
in tuxedo Drag    in catacombs
                  a sixties groove
the Papal Gown    ~~to be booked~~

D on all your flags   Dark moons
Dance on the crown   Its lovme

on the vatican

## BAUHAUS INDIVIDUAL PLANS
****************************

Over the next two months, BAUHAUS are for the first time embarking
on their own individual projects.
As they all have a certain amount of spare time on their hands,
in between work on the live video and live album, the move is a
natural one.
The group feel that their projects can only add new ideas to collective
BAUHAUS creativity.
A 12" single featuring four songs is being released in March, on 4AD
Records by Daniel Ash.  As yet no titles have been decided on  but Danny
is working very hard and feels this is something he needs to get out of
his system.  At the very least its something to look forward to.
Although he's being pretty cagey about its content, he says that he's
very pleased with the results.  He is working with a Northampton based
musician called Glen Campling, who features on bass on some of the tracks
and comments from Ivo Russell Watts of 4AD Records promise that the songs
are 'good enough!'
Although Dave J has no definite release plans, amongst other projects he
plans to 'conduct' (ha  ha) a local gig, on a local bus, to "whoever
happens to be on the damn thing at the time".  He's doing it with his
spare time superstars called the "SINISTER DUCKS" who feature a
stunning sinister prose vocalist who goes by the delightful name of
Brilburnlogue(see MASK sleeve notes).  Who is this you may ask?
Little do we know, except for anonymous breathtaking phone calls received
from the above,reciting "old gangsters never die" to which the sinister
quadruplets back up.  This being a possible single on release on 4AD.

Peter Murphy is now working on a film that he and an artist friend
called Joanne Woodward are releasing around May 1982.
The release will be in a video form, alongside a film called 'The Grid'
which was shown on the BAUHAUS British tour in 1980.
The new film is texturing the sculptures and ideas of otherwise obscured
work of Joanna Woodward with the ideas of Peter Murphy - through the
more accessible form of film.
It's theme is basically idealistic in that it deals with the basic
search for that ideal spark of creativity within us all, which the
character in the story finally achieves, or finds.
The Grid is different.  It associates an underworld elf, played by
Peter Murphy surfacing from his underground abode, to an open, more
wordly environment.  Something is in the air, the elf's intuition tells
him he must look for something - what he doesn't know.  His search begins.
He finds a grid holding magical properties. The film takes off.
This video will be made available exclusively to Information Club
members as soon as the release is complete.

# Beggars Banquet

**17-19 ALMA ROAD, LONDON S.W.18.**
**Tel. 01 870 9912   Telex 915733**

## B A U H A U S

It is with considerable sadness that we learnt at the end of last week that Bauhaus have decided to disband as a unit and go their separate ways. Over the last three years, with your support we have brought Bauhaus very much to the top of their particular musical tree and we had great hopes of bringing this across to a far wider audience. However, in the final analysis, we have to agree with the band when they say that they feel that they had reached the end of their particular road and that the creative impulses between the four members are not what they once were. The band feel that they have grown apart both personally and musically and I think that a listen to "Burning From The Inside" reveals the different directions the different members are going in.

The individual members of the band all feel very positive about their individual projects, as do we. As far as they have emerged so far they are.

Peter Murphy will continue as a solo performer but the extent to which he might assemble a group behind him is as yet in doubt. Peter will definitely inherit substantially the Bauhaus mantle and Beggars Banquet will definitely be continuing to work with him. Peter needs a couple of months to sort out his plans but we hope to have a single this side of Christmas. There is a distinct possibility that this might involve a collaboration with Alan Rankine, the musical / Instrumental half of the Associates. This could be a very exciting collaboration.

Daniel Ash and Kevin Haskins propose to devote their full time energies to Tones On Tail, the unit which has already released three singles on our assorted labels and also contains the bassist Glenn Campling, Bauhaus' (ex) roadie. Although Kevin only played on the B side of the last Tones On Tail single, it appears that he will now be a full time member of the band. Whether or not this will be a touring unit is unclear as is the timing of their next release.

David J. already has solo projects in the pipeline so the next few months will see the fulfilment of these. On 26 August Situation Two release the Sinister Ducks single, a project which is basically David J. under the pseudonym of Jose Da Silva. On 16 September, David releases a solo single entitled "Joe Orton's Wedding" followed by an album in October.

We will keep you advised of developments in these three areas. Whilst it is obviously sad to pull down the curtain on Bauhaus, the old saying that every cloud has a silver lining is certainly true in this case and it could even be a golden one!!!

MARTIN MILLS

BEGGARS BANQUET MUSIC LTD.  DIRECTORS: N. AUSTIN M. G. MILLS
REGD OFFICE: 17 - 19 ALMA ROAD, LONDON S.W.18
BUSINESS REGISTRATION No. 1414047  VAT No. 240 1066 10

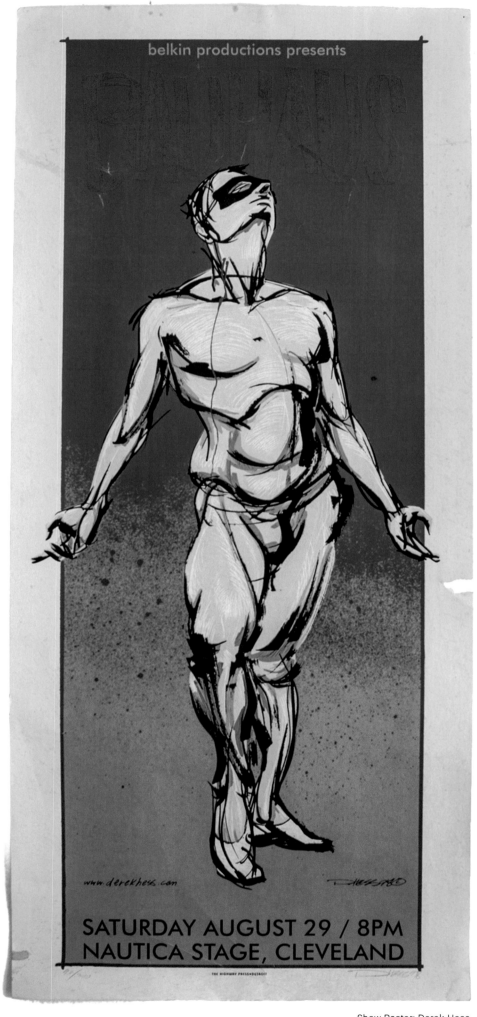

Show Poster: Derek Hess

Show Poster: Rex Ray, Tom Scott, Great Impressions

Crowds.

What do you want of me
What do you long from me
A slim piece thin and forlorn
A count, white and drawn
What do you make of me
What can you take from me
Pallid landscapes off my frown
Let me rip you up and down.

For you I came to forsake
Lay wide, despise and hate
I sing you my lamented songs
for you and your stimulations

Take what you can off me
Rip what you can off me
And this i'll say to you
And hope that it gets through
You worthless bits, you fickle shits.
You will spit on me, you will make me spit
And when the Judas hour arrives
And like the Jesus Jews you epitomise
I'll still be here as strong as you
And i'll walk away, in spite of you

And i'll walk away
        Walk away.
            . . . . . away

Terror Couple Kill Colonel.

His eyes were heavy, they carried a card
One couple were questioned, the others discharged
Terror Couple Kill colonel in his west German Home
Three shots from three feet, dragged himself to the phone.

Terror Couple Kill colonel
Terror Couple Kill colonel

And as he laid there, playing games with his pain
He felt his choice of Job was such a mistake.
He could have been a doctor in a soft easy chair
Instead he chose three stars,
A territorial affair.

Terror Couple Kill colonel
Terror Couple Kill colonel

. . . . . . in his West German Home.
            in his West German Home.
            in his West German Home.

She had painted arms,
That were hers to keep
They were also her cultural arms,
Creating the presence of divinity
and her need for real life,
Impassion and society, was her
fear.
  A Myth as a sacred story of profain
eyes and ears.
  The real passion of lovers is for
death! Said she — The pyramid is
chaos, and the primeval hill too
ever hereby became an orthodoxy
and sanctuary possessed its
original Holyness. ——(BOO) Pullmary Leethswatts.

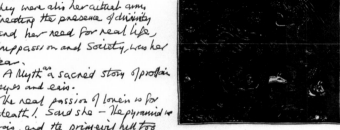

Kick in the eye.
_____

And he spoke of Pastures Green
But I was never told why
Each Journey lasts an age
And my throat feels dry.

It must be the Lesson
Hidden deep inside
It must be the Lesson
So roll the tide.

So I begin the crossing
My throat burned dry
Searching for Satori
The Kick in the eye.

I am the end of reproduction
Given no direction
Every care is taken
In my rejection
Kick in the eye.
Kick in the eye.

Every care is taken
In my rejection
And my abduction
From my addiction

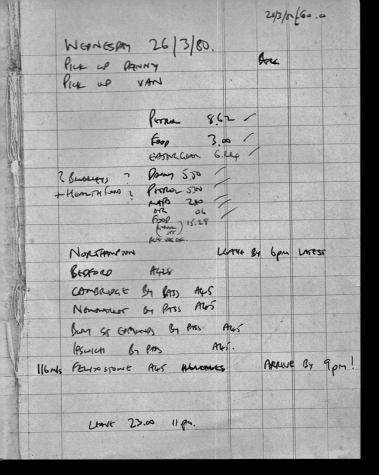

Our rehearsal room above the vacant shop at 57 Horseshoe Street, Northampton

## AWOL

After numerous knocks on Daniel's front door followed by increasing shouts of "Danny, Danny…..DANNY!" Graham Bentley, our trustworthy lighting engineer and tour manager couldn't raise a response. Daniel had gone AWOL. It wouldn't have normally mattered too much had we not been embarking on our first European tour, with the ferry due to leave later that evening.

Undeterred, Graham set off to pick up the Parcel Van from Bugbrooke, on the west side of town, and then on to collect Peter, David and myself from our rehearsal room above a shop at 57 Horseshoe Street. Graham had hoped that Daniel would have shown up there, but alas, there was no sign of him. We loaded up our equipment and various pillows and cushions which would serve as makeshift bedding, laid on top of the drums and amplifiers.

Suddenly, out of the blue a very polite but nervous individual named Volker appeared. He was the German promoter for our first show at "Aratta" in Moers, Germany. He had written to Graham and mentioned that he would be in London around this time, and would maybe pay us a visit in Northampton. It later transpired that this was not a casual visit at all, but that he was so nervous that "the English could not organize themselves", that he had come all the way from Germany to make sure that we made the ferry crossing on time! Well, with Daniel still missing, his concerns were right on the money. With no cell phones in those archaic days, we had no idea where our guitarist was!

Our next port of call was the health food shop, to stock up on vegan

fair and homeopathic medicine. Aside from Graham, none of us were vegans however we trusted that it would keep us healthy. On the way there we luckily spotted the absent guitarist at the top of Gold Street accompanied by Glenn Campling, and carrying a keyboard. He appeared surprised to learn that we had a European tour to go on and explained that he had promised Glenn that he would fix his keyboard. Glenn took the keyboard and said he would take a bus so that we could get a move on. At this point Volker, with beads of sweat running down his forehead, appeared to be a little relieved. That was until Daniel exclaimed, "I have to go to my Mum and Dads house to get my lucky socks!" Volker immediately disappeared behind the back of the van to try to contain himself, but subsequently our introduction to Germanic swear words could be heard emanating from his hiding place. Graham managed to calm him down by explaining that he had built in a two hour buffer to the schedule. A by now beaming Volker congratulated Graham and praised him as having, "ein wunderbares Deutches gehrin" which roughly translates as "a wonderful German brain!"

After said socks were retrieved from Daniels parents house we were finally on our way, and just made the ferry to Zeebrugge by 11PM.

PROPAGANDA musical services
Volker de Fries
Moerser Str.278
D-4132 Kamp-Lintfort
Phone 2843/4348

21/3/80

Dear Graham,
please find enclosed here the second contract,a copy of
a map:the money's on the way to you.
I will be in London from Monday until Wednesday and perhaps
I will have time enuogh for a quick trip to Northampton.
Anyway,bring lots of records with you (also T-shirts etc.)
when you come to Germany.If you need adapters for electricity,
I think it's better to buy them in GB,because it's very hard
to get hold of them here.

Yours

Graham Bentley standing outside parcel van as we were getting situated inside. Im not sure why he's holding a plastic dump truck toy?

(AN ACOUNT OF THE BAUHAUS LAST AMERICAN TOUR)
## BAUHAUS IN THE LAND OF SILK AND MONEY

On approaching american territory, the mood in the bauhaus outfit,
for a second visit in one year, was one of apprehension, regarding
our capability in sustaining the important feeling for the live gig,
which is so difficult on a non-stop tour situation such as this was.
Daniel didn't enjoy the first tour, owing to post flight physical
attacks on his ears, amusing for us, not for him.  But upon setting
foot in the land of silk and money, settled like a duck to heroin.

The tour promotion team were generous in the allowance of one full
day for us to recover from jet lag.  Until we finally reached our
first venue, which was the 'Blitz' club on Lond Island, New York.

The first gig on any tour is harrowing, bringing pags of paranoia,
as to the possibility of falling flat.  The gig turned out very well
with the 'paranoid' elements acting as more of a booster than a
suppressant, it forced a strong feeling on stage.

The depressing 'Spandau' single was heard in all the preceding club
date pre-gig disco's and gave one that sick, outraged pissed off
feeling for those pathetic bands who spew out of DJ's like Peter Powe
soft soap support.  Then to see the audience spattered with the
'Visage' - 'Ballet'  fashion sheep produced many comments from my
stage 'Persona' speaking words of detestation and mockery.

The second impression one got from the american audience was of great
eagerness to accept us as a class band, enjoying their usual pain-
staking observations of all things, from the bulge in my tights to
the very deepest interpretation of a particular lyric.  I can never
honestly admit to seriously feeling the animosity that I tell of,
when referring to the average American, realising that generalisation
on any mass body is naive and foolish, but I can never resist the
urge to giggle when I am either being interviewed or just chatting
to an American.  It's because they seem to have cultivated this
extraordinary craft of coming across as super natured intellectuals,
which is a good weapon for approaching any person of importance, and
could act, in many instances as a disarming prospecting interviewee.

Cont'd...

It was becoming a long tour, but it was not the strain of so much
work that was reaching through, it was the strain of being in cities
like Detroit, and Chicago .  At times I was feeling very negative
impressions of the characteristics of the USA that I actually believed
I was in danger of being shot dead on stage, very over the top, but
real nevertheless.

Back to the hotel and twenty four hour non-stop media punch out -
television - "If you need a job,a car,a lover, a fortune, ring New York
New York 38195 4657, that New York,New York 38195 4657 on and on and on
................. Television dummy men with deep average man voices,most
men burying any evidence of femininity deep inside their patriotic
souls.  Guns have become another bulge in the trouser of MR AMERICA
and the city that killed John Lennon carries on .. on the notice board
hangs the direction to the nearest fallout shelter, and the string
that Theseus laid awaited us at Kennedy airport.

PM.

HOTEL TAFT - NEW YORK
7th AVENUE AT 50th STREET

Then began the rush, the round of hotel, gig, sleep, drive, hotel,
gig, sleep, drive, meal, interview, drive, gig, sound check, handshake,
captured glances, gulped back gin, offers of drugs ranging from
'horse sedatives to cigarettes, annoying rapps on hotel doors,
signalling time to move onto whatever appointment came next, automitan
ant like pedestrians taking you with their flow, the second you hit
the New York avenue.  Blazoned 'des rues' of neon, hooting car horns,
yellow taxi cabs, street level comments, black and white femme fatales
offering me yet another 'dark entry'...where was the string that
Theseus laid!

Time for a telephone radio interview scheduled for 4pm in David and
Kevin's hotel room.  Danny and I relax in room 3710, a thirty seventh
floor cubicle designed for comfort and maximum efficiency.  A rush to
the other room to witness a unique telecommunication/banter
Radio Interviewer: David the album, it seems.... ...sophisticated.
David: Oh yes?
RI: Yes.
David: Oh.
RI: Can you elaborate more about the seemingly sophisticated nature
    of the album.
David: What exactly do you mean by sophisticated?
RI: It's just that it seems complex and well put together, looking at
    the use of sound.
David: I suppose you could say that, but we don't agree we are
    necessarily sophisticated in our technique, we prefer to take
    a basic approach to what we do, not needing to rely on the
    studio tricks/sophistication.
RI: Eh- huh!!!..and how are your songs constructed musically, you
    seem very competent musicians, are your musical backgrounds very
    comprehensive?
David: No they are not, I would say that our music comes about out
    of a musical illiteracy. Would you like to talk to Kevin?...
RI: Yes, sure...
Kevin:(reluctant to take over) ....hello?...
RI:(intense approach, very)..Kevin your album seems sophisticated!....
    (long pause)
    (Highly amused by his strange line and style of questioning, Kevin
    finds it extremely difficult to reciprocate, and succeeds in
    collapsing with hysterics, and in vain, stammers out an indeci-
    pherable answer.)
RI: I beg your pardon, ...I didn't catch that. (with slight agitation
    in his voice)
    Meanwhile in utter panic Kevin hands back the telephone to a
    reluctant David.

                                                        Cont'd.....

David:  Hello this is David here again, I'll be carrying on the
        interview.
RI:  (By now very jumpy and confused)What's happened to Kevin?,where's
     Kevin?
David:Kevin has just collapsed on the bed...carry on....
RI:  (raised voice) What do you mean, can you tell me what has happened
     to Kevin? Will you please explain the situation.
David: It's OK, I'm carrying on with the interview, just ask me your
     questions.
RI:  (crazed voice) BUT WHAT'S HAPPENED TO KEVIN, I DON'T UNDERSTAND?
     CAN YOU PLEASE EXPLAIN THE SITUATION. WHERE IS HE?
David:  Kevin has collapsed on the bed, carry on,will you...
At this point the interviewer hangs up.........Such Fun!

New York can be a little taxing on the brain, it's life style being
100 mph., but after being exposed to it for long periods, it becomes
easier to move with.  When ordering coffee or anything a New Yorker
will rarely exercise common politeness, which I don't think is meant
as a rebuke in any way, but when a couple of "punky looking" people
(us) sit down to order breakfast or whatever it was, it was often as
if they regarded us as some inexplicable obscure breed of alien and
I really got into the game of english politeness, delivering a"thank
you"or a"please"whereever possible, as perfect manners are a good weapon
against that kind of aggression.

At the moment the american music scene is monopolised to saturation
point by the middle of the road bands, supported heavily by the
majority of both public and 'churn it out' DJ's and record company
pinheads.  Yet with so many radio stations to choose from, it was
impossible to find one that wasn't riddled with 'smuck' save one cute
station which was one of those  outback hillbilly stations with
incredible old hillbilly weeping and wailing their wonky tunes.

New wave, if you want to call it that is on the pick up, with a slow
building change in interest towards most of what's going on in Britain,
and as any outlet is rare, most gigs are independantly organised by
those people, who are keen to get bands over there and the atmosphere
is good.

In America,bands like us find it difficult to reach the wide audience
simply because of the scale of the place, and gone are the bad old days
of six month non stop tours, we believe that the video medium will cover
that loss eventually.

                                                        Cont'd......

Photos: Tony Mottram

The guard who accused us of breaking in to The Colosseum

## STORMING THE COLOSSEUM

We had played in Italy, albeit briefly, the previous year as Beggars Banquet (our label) had secured a licensing deal with Italy's Expanded Music. This time we were scheduled to play eight shows with the first two in Sicily on the 29th and 30th of April 1982. The tour was received really well and we appreciated the intense passion of our Italian fans. The final show was in Rome on the 7th of May and as we had a couple of free days before our flight home, we decided to do some, lets say, alternative sight seeing!

The full moon threw film noir shadows along the ancient walls of The Colosseum as we, the denizens of the night, ascended its perimeter in order to break in. Our trusty lighting designer, Graham Bentley, had tagged along with the four of us to enjoy our midnight lark.

Once inside its cavernous belly we all split up and ran around to explore. As our yells and hollers echoed around the ancient amphitheater, I made my way down to the lowest level which was originally below ground. It was made up of a network of corridors, rooms and cages. This is where the Gladiators, animals and the poor unfortunate souls who were sentenced to death, had to wait until they were summoned for their various contests.

As I ventured through the rooms and corridors I was imagining all the noise, hustle and bustle of the goings on, hundreds and hundreds of years ago. How terrified must those sentenced to death have felt, and in turn the poor animals, some of which were facing a similar fate. As the prisoners were escorted up from the depths, and as their eyes adjusted to the light, they were met with

a deafening roar from the 70,000 or so spectators. They were no match for the well-armed and well trained Gladiators who would quickly make mincemeat of them.

There were various barbaric forms of "entertainment" and one in particular was called "Execution Ad Bestias". This involved the condemned prisoners being sent out completely naked and unarmed, with only elaborately constructed props consisting of buildings and trees to hide behind. Hunting them down were various wild animals imported from Africa such as Lions and Rhinos, who would eventually find them and tear them apart. And they called this entertainment!

I could still feel the dark energy of those times hanging heavy in the air, which was accentuated by exploring the ruins in the dead of night. All of a sudden a distant yell of "Kevin!" shook me from my reverie and I looked up to see everyone racing for the exit. I naturally headed the same way as fast as my legs would carry me. Apparently some of the lads had heard strange moans and groans and had become rattled.

Graham and I returned very early the next morning as we wanted to witness this ancient, iconic monument in the daylight and this time, pay our way. Maybe this was our way to appease the groaning ghosts of the poor executed souls?! Graham brought his VHS camera along to record our visit and we happened upon a guard who accused us of breaking in the previous evening. He may have been the night watchman, and it could have been he who had scared us off with his fake moans and groans. We feigned innocence, but I think he knew it was us as he gave us a wry smile and a friendly wink.

Photos: Kevin Haskins

## Consequencial differences

Here is a series of "Consequencies" cartoons, done by us, during our last American tour. They were drawn up, in the periods of traveling times, which were very long and boring in the true, (by now well established) "Bauhaus" game, called Consequences.

The rules are basic, and can be applied to any form or idea. Depending on the amount of people taking part, a piece of paper, (in this case) was used, and this time we decided to use a cartoon format. Each piece of paper was folded into four sections, each participant doing a three block cartoon of whatever subject took his fancy, without seeing what the other three members had done, and the result being unveiled only when all four sections have been completed.

On one hand, it can be taken as just a fun past-time, with some interesting stories emerging, and on the other, some fascinating extraordinary links emerge as far a similarities between not only visual use, but characters, subject and sublime connections can be seen.

For Instance: In cartoon Number one:— The connection of a man at the end of his tether, with building re-occuring.

And in cartoon No 2. The Theme of aliens, and interplanitary travel figure strongly,

Number three and four were drawn totally blind, and in a pitch black limo en route to Canada. No 5 and 6, amazing connections, and 7, — strange. Have fun — and look out for the BAUHAUS "Consequences" Film too.

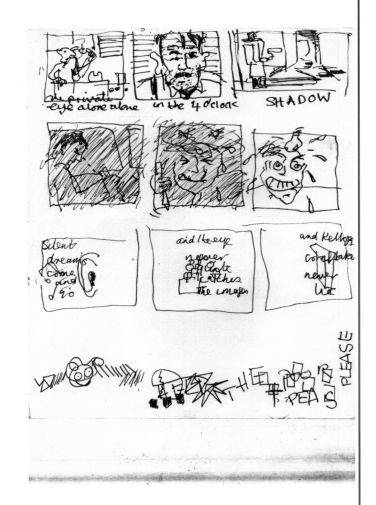

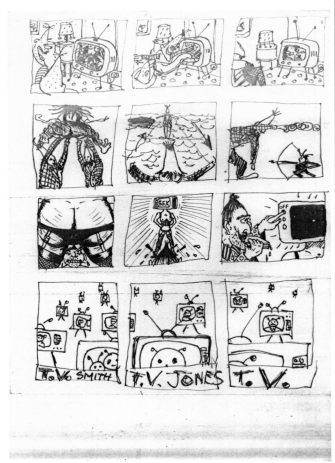

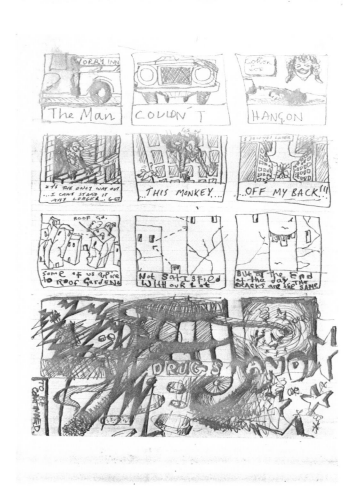

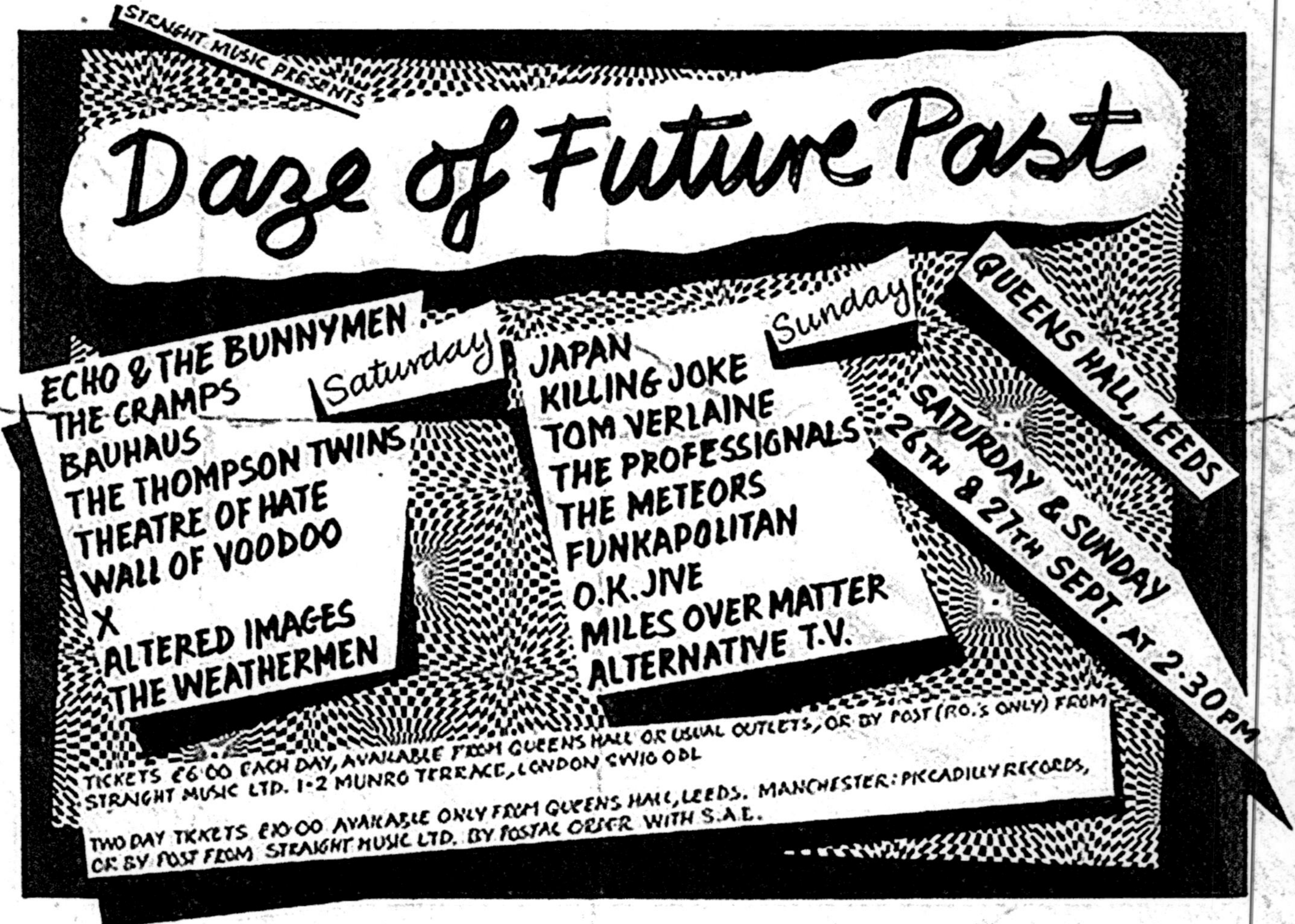

STRAIGHT MUSIC PRESENTS

# Daze of Future Past

QUEENS HALL, LEEDS

SATURDAY & SUNDAY 26th & 27th SEPT. AT 2:30 PM

**Saturday**

ECHO & THE BUNNYMEN
THE CRAMPS
BAUHAUS
THE THOMPSON TWINS
THEATRE OF HATE
WALL OF VOODOO
X
ALTERED IMAGES
THE WEATHERMEN

**Sunday**

JAPAN
KILLING JOKE
TOM VERLAINE
THE PROFESSIONALS
THE METEORS
FUNKAPOLITAN
O.K. JIVE
MILES OVER MATTER
ALTERNATIVE T.V.

TICKETS £6:00 EACH DAY, AVAILABLE FROM QUEENS HALL OR USUAL OUTLETS, OR BY POST (P.O.'S ONLY) FROM
STRAIGHT MUSIC LTD. 1-2 MUNRO TERRACE, LONDON SW10 0DL

TWO DAY TICKETS £10:00 AVAILABLE ONLY FROM QUEENS HALL, LEEDS. MANCHESTER: PICCADILLY RECORDS,
OR BY POST FROM STRAIGHT MUSIC LTD. BY POSTAL ORDER WITH S.A.E.

STRAIGHT MUSIC LTD

1-2 MUNRO TERRACE

LONDON SW10 0DL

TELEPHONE: ██████████

TELEX 8964921 SHOBIZ G

"DAZE OF FUTURE PAST" : SATURDAY & SUNDAY 26 & 27TH SEPTEMBER.

QUEENS HALL, SOVEREIGN STREET, LEEDS.    TELEPHONE ████████

PLAYING TIMES:

SATURDAY: 2.30 - 3.00  NAKED LUNCH.
          3.15 - 3.45  WAY OF THE WEST.
          4.00 - 4.30  WALL OF VOODOO.
          4.45 - 5.15  ALTERED IMAGES.
          5.30 - 6.15  THEATRE OF HATE.
          6.30 - 7.15  THE THOMPSON TWINS.
          7.30 - 8.30  BAUHAUS.
          8.45 - 9.45  THE CRAMPS.
         10.00 - 11.00 ECHO & THE BUNNYMEN.

SUNDAY:   2.30 - 3.00  MILES OVER MATTER.
          3.15 - 3.45  PAST SEVEN DAYS.
          4.00 - 4.30  INNER CITY UNIT.
          4.45 - 5.15  THE BOLLOCK BROS.
          5.30 - 6.15  B MOVIE.
          6.30 - 7.15  THE REVILLOS.
          7.30 - 8.15  THE PROFESSIONALS.
          8.30 - 9.30  CLASSIX NOUVEAUX.
          9.45 - 11.00 GANG OF FOUR.

ONLY THE HEADLINING ACTS WILL BE ALLOCATED SOUNDCHECKS AS FOLLOWS:

    SATURDAY 26TH:  10.00 - 11.00 AM  ECHO & THE BUNNYMEN.
    SUNDAY 27TH:    10.00 - 11.00 AM  GANG OF FOUR.

OTHER ARTISTES WILL BE ALLOWED TO SOUNDCHECK IF TIME PERMITS.

DOORS OPEN EACH DAY AT 12.30.

SOUND COMPANY : AUDIOLEASE  - STEVE SUNDERLAND
LIGHTS COMPANY : SUPERMICK   - ROBBIE JOHNSON
STAGE MANAGER : MIKE HEANLY - (STRAIGHT MUSIC
HALL MANAGER  : RICHARD JOHNSON.

REGISTERED NUMBER: 963428 ENGLAND.   REGISTERED OFFICE: 26 BOLTON STREET, LONDON W.
DIRECTORS: JOHN A.T. CURD, KIERAN O'SULLIV

QUEENS HALL
Box office open 9-5.30 Mon-Thurs
(9-12 Fri. and Sat.)
TEL: Leeds 31961

SUNDAY
SEPTEMBER 27
at 2.30p.m.

Straight Music presents

DAZE OF FUTURE PAST

No 1830

This portion to be retained
(P.T.O.)

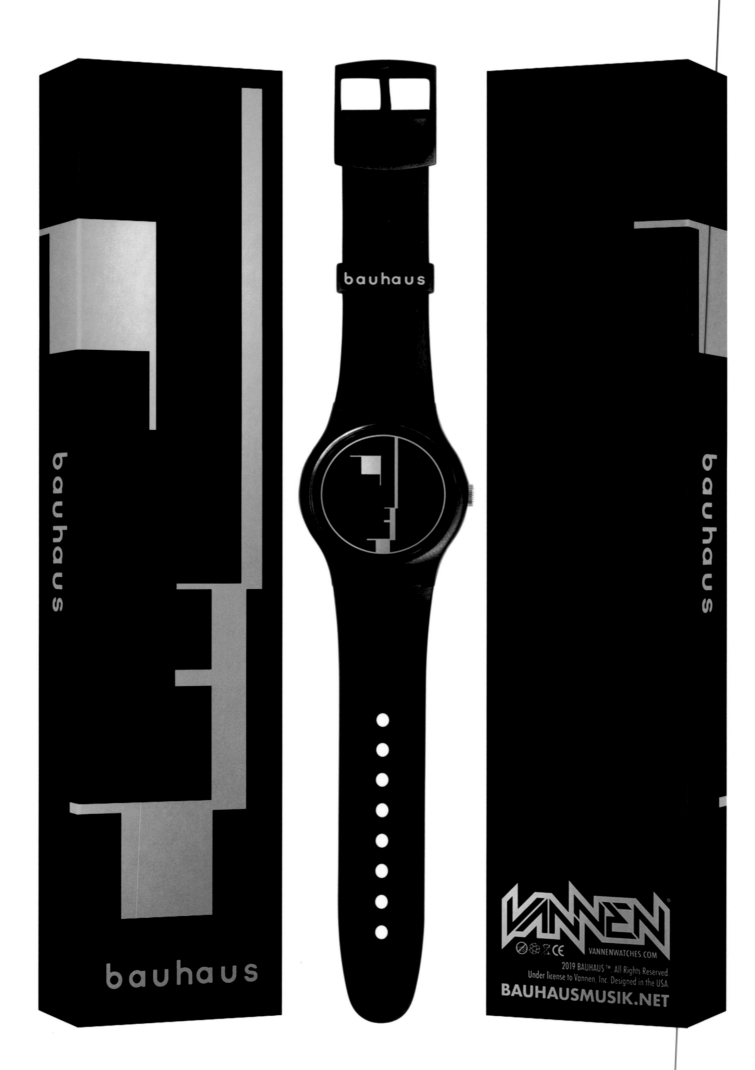

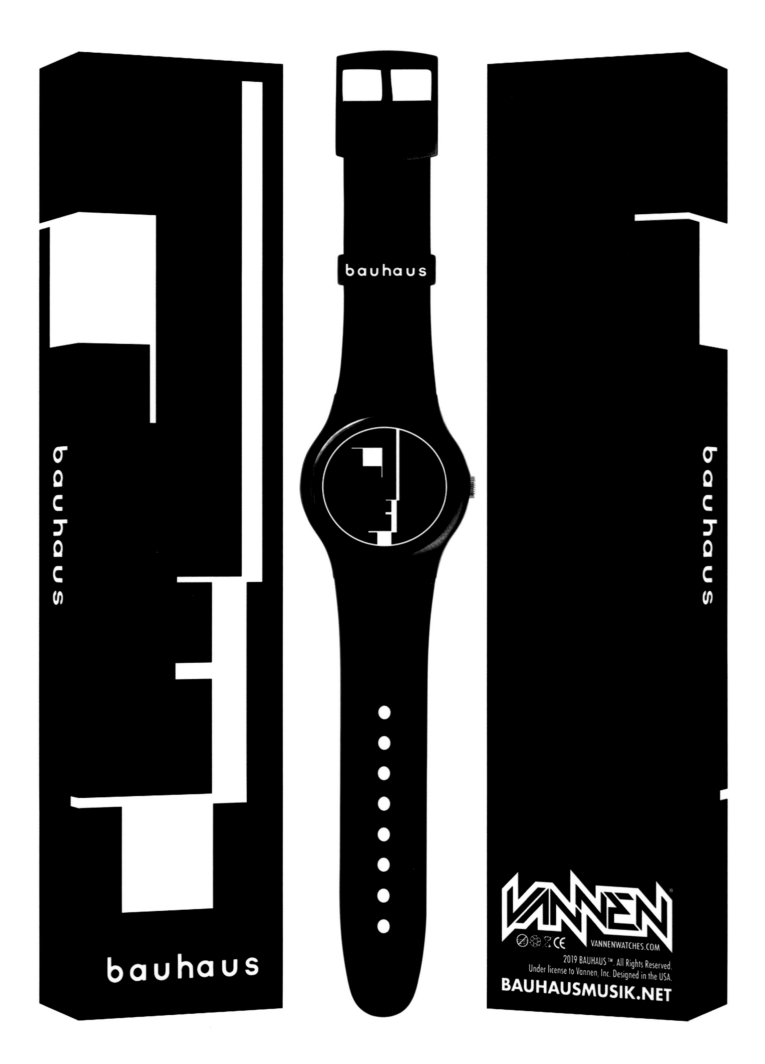

bauhaus

bauhaus

bauhaus

bauhaus

VANNEN

VANNENWATCHES.COM

2019 BAUHAUS™, All Rights Reserved.
Under license to Vannen, Inc. Designed in the USA.

BAUHAUSMUSIK.NET

FINAL SOLUTION PRESENT

# BAUHAUS
## ZEITUNG·DA!
## BLAZING AFFAIR
### PLUS SPECIAL GUESTS
### & NIGHTVISION VIDEO

7.30PM·FRIDAY·DEC 11TH
WALTHAMSTOW ASSEMBLY HALL
FOREST ROAD·E17
(WALTHAMSTOW CENTRAL TUBE/B.R.)

ADVANCE TICKETS £3.50 FROM
SMALL WONDER · HONKY TONK · ROUGH TRADE
BONAPARTE (KINGS X) & PREMIER BOX OFFICE

## HAMMERSMITH PALAIS

EXTRA SHOW

DEREK BLOCK PRESENTS

# BAUHAUS

PLUS GUESTS

## MONDAY
## 1st NOVEMBER
### 7·30pm

TICKETS 3.50

FROM BOX OFFICE (01-748 2812) KEITH PROWSE · PREMIER BOX OFFICE,
LONDON THEATRE BOOKINGS & USUAL AGENTS

Publicity & Display Ltd, Godalming, Surrey.

BAUHAUS
+
the
MYSTERY
GUESTS
£1·50
SEPTEMBER 8th
AT THE PADDOCK 7·30
TICKETS ACME PINAR'S

344

Photo: Fin Costello

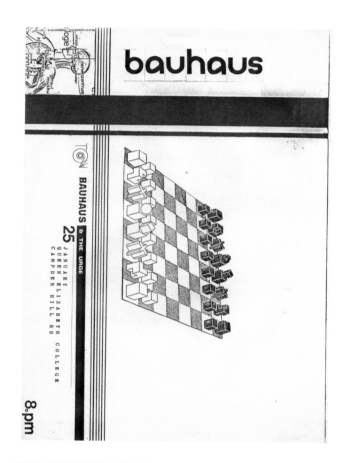

**bauhaus**

TON
BAUHAUS & THE URGE
25 JANUARY
QUEEN ELIZABETH COLLEGE
CAMPDEN HILL RD
8.pm

**bauhaus**
FRIDAY DEC 7TH - THE 101 CLUB,
ST. JOHN'S HILL, LONDON.

MONDAY DEC 10TH -
THE ROCK GARDEN,
LONDON.

MORE DATES
TO FOLLOW...

FINAL SOLUTION PRESENT
**CLASSIX NOUVEAUX**
**BAUHAUS**
**PLAIN CHARACTERS**
**PLUS GUESTS**

7.30, THURS, 20TH MARCH
**ELECTRIC BALLROOM**
184 CAMDEN HIGH ST. NW1

ADVANCE TICKETS £2.00 FROM THE ELECTRIC BALLROOM, ROUGH TRADE, SMALL WONDER, HONKY TONK, LUIGI & THE BOYS, ACE RECORDS (ISLINGTON) AND BEGGARS BANQUET (EARLS COURT) RECORD SHOPS OR LONDON THEATRE BOOKINGS TEL.439 3371 OR PREMIER BOX OFFICE TEL. 240 2245

FROM ENGLAND
**BAUHAUS**
RAW DOGS
"FORMALLY" "V.D. TEENS"
SPECIAL GUESTS

THUR.
8 P.M.
MARCH 5TH
POLISH HALL
90 A NN STREET

TICKETS AVAILABLE AT REGULAR OUTLETS

NO AGE RESTRICTION

# SHOCKING

"Snare Drum!" the words sounded more of an order than a request, this came from the clubs sound engineer. Delivered in a rather stern and mono-tone German accent, he was actually asking me to play beats on the snare drum so that he could balance the sound. He would then call out each of the other drums in order to check the levels. Seated behind my trusty Ludwig drum kit, I was engaged in our first soundcheck, on our first ever European tour! The venue, in Moers, Germany was called "Aratta" and it's still going strong today. It lives in a pleasant location close to the Haferbruchsee lake, which was a nudist hangout around the time that we played, although we didn't have the time or inclination to go skinny dipping.

Whilst I was banging away on the snare drum, David was getting ready for his part of the soundcheck. Specifically, plugging in his bass guitar and adjusting the control knobs on his amplifier. I happened to notice that when David approached his microphone he received a small electric shock from it. This suggested that the PA was on the same electrical circuit as the amplifiers, and that something was not grounded or earthed. This was

potentially fatal! As David was communicating to the stage manager that he had just received a shock, the sound engineer blurted out, "Floor Tom!" So I duly began hitting said drum. All of a sudden my attention was diverted to a blood curdling yell! I glanced to my right to witness David now receiving a massive electric shock! Shaking uncontrollably, with his eyes almost popping out of his head, he was trying to throw his guitar to the ground, but both of his hands were locked rigid on the strings. It was extremely alarming! After what seemed like an eternity, and with the aid of gravity, he finally managed to break free from the grip of death! David and his guitar hit the ground. As we all rushed to his aid, and to my upmost surprise, I heard the sound engineer call out……..."Bass Drum!"

Maybe this was a nightly occurrence as I couldn't imagine why he was so unconcerned about David's condition? Thankfully, David was able to recover in time for the show, which was somewhat, ahem……electrifying!

David (far right) resting backstage after receiving the electric shock.

## Letter to members

## BAUHAUS
## Information Club

Hello,

Firstly, apologies etc. etc. for the delay. Hope you're not all dying of impatience but things have been done as speedily as is humanly possible from the morbid depths of Wandsworth!! . . . believe it or not!!

However, your numerous enquiries and letters have been quite overwhelming and hopefully most of what you want to know is included. If there is anything else you desperately desire, suggestions or criticisms would be pleasantly appreciated. Any complaints can go straight to the band as they designed it . . .

So during the course of the year, as each session comes upon us, you will be sent all the relevant Bauhaus dates, lyrics and events and in the meantime, have a good time during the forthcoming tour which should mainly consist of the new album material.

Unfortunately, the release date for *"Burning From The Inside"* has been delayed until 15 July but once again, it is a progressive and radical piece of diverse musical innovation!!! Hope you like it anyway.

With love,

*KAREN & SUE*

---

### BAND

PETER MURPHY . . . . . . . . . . . Born July 11th, 1957 — Northampton
DAVID JAY . . . . . . . . . . . . . . Born April 24th, 1957 — Northampton
KEVIN HASKINS . . . . . . . . . . Born July 19th, 1960 — Northampton
DANIEL ASH . . . . . . . . . . . . . Born July 31st, 1957 — Northampton

### MANAGEMENT

HARRY ISLES, 4 Badby Road, Newnham, Daventry, Northants.
Tel. No: 03272 5032

### RECORD COMPANY

BEGGARS BANQUET, 17-19 Alma Road, Wandsworth, London, SW18
Tel. No: 01-870-9912
Telex No: 915733
Contact: Martin Mills

### BOOKING AGENT

WASTED TALENT, 28 Alexander Street, London, W2
Tel. No: 01-221-6136
Telex No: 895591
Contact: Ian Wilson

### TOUR MERCHANDISING

ACME CLOTHING CO, 26-40 St Andrew's Street, Northampton
Tel. No: 0604-36888/0604-20411/2
Contact: Mick Wright

### RETAIL MERCHANDISING

ACME CLOTHING CO, as above
MOBILE MERCHANDISING CO, No 1 Wharf, Shad Thames, London, SE1
Tel. No: 01-407-5116/9
Telex No: 883217
Contact: Lance Yeats

---

## *playing* Live!

**MAY**

| | | |
|---|---|---|
| 12 | PARIS | Le Palace |
| 14 | ATHENS | |
| 17/18 | TEL AVIV | |
| 22 | BANGKOK | |
| 24 | HONG KONG | |
| 28 | TOKYO | |
| 30 | OSAKA | |

**JUNE**

| | | |
|---|---|---|
| 13 | BRIGHTON | Top Rank |
| 14 | BRISTOL | Locarno |
| 15 | SWANSEA | Top Rank |
| 16 | SOUTHAMPTON | Gaumont |
| 18 | DERBY | Assembly Hall |
| 19 | HANLEY | Victoria Hall |
| 20 | SHEFFIELD | Top Rank |
| 21 | LEICESTER | De Montfort Hall |
| 22 | LIVERPOOL | Royal Court Theatre |
| 23 | MANCHESTER | Apollo |
| 24 | NEWCASTLE | City Hall |
| 26 | ABERDEEN | Capital Theatre |
| 27 | GLASGOW | Tiffanies |
| 29 | BRADFORD | Caesars |

**JULY**

| | | |
|---|---|---|
| 1 | HEMEL HEMPSTEAD | Pavillion |
| 2 | IPSWICH | Gaumont |
| 3 | BIRMINGHAM | Odeon |
| 4/5 | LONDON | Hammersmith Palais |

---

## S O L O projects

Danny has recorded four tracks with Glenn Campling as "Tones on Tail" which has just been released on Situation 2. This is their third single. Tracks are "Burning Skies" and "OK, This Is The Pops" on the 7 inch with "You, The Night And The Music" and "When You're Smiling" as extra tracks on the 12 inch. This time Tones on Tail also features Kevin who co-wrote "OK, This Is The Pops" with Danny and Glenn. Catalogue numbers are SIT 21 for the 7 inch and SIT 21T for the 12 inch. A Tones On Tail album is planned and there will shortly be another single out which is as yet untitled. Glenn reckons that they will be doing some live dates at some point but can

we believe him???

Dave has also been working on various solo projects. He will be releasing an album, also on Situation 2, called "Etiquette Of Violence" shortly. Tracks are "I Hear Only Silence", "No-one's Sending Roses", "The Fugitive", "Say Uncle", "The Betrayal", "Disease", "With The Indians Permanent", "Roulette (Melt Down With Love)", "St. Jacques" and "Jo Orton's Wedding". He is also releasing a single in July that he has recorded with the enigmatic Kurt Vile. Tracks are "Old Gangsters Never Die" and "Sinister Ducks" the latter being complete with quacking!!

**SHE'S IN PARTIES**

Learning lines in the rain
Special effects by loonatik and drinks
The graveyard scene
The golden years
She's in parties, it's in the can
She's in parties, it's in the can

Freeze frame screen kiss
Hot heads under silent wigs
Fall guys tumble on the cutting room floor
Lookalikes fall on the cutting room floor
She's in parties, it's in the can
She's in parties, it's in the can

Learning lines in the rain
Special effects by loonatik and drinks
Freeze frame screen kiss, hot head lights
And powder it's patently obvious
She's in parties, it's in the can
She's in parties, it's in the can

Hot lines under a rain of drums
Cigarette props in action
Dialogue dub
Now here's the rub
She's acting her reaction
She's in parties, it's in the can
She's in parties, it's in the can

Learning lines in the rain
Special effects by loonatik and drinks
Freeze frame screen kiss, hot head lights
And powder it's patently obvious
She's in parties, it's in the can
She's in parties, it's in the can

**LAGARTIJA NICK**

Move his way nice and slow
Paint it all black
Let the humerous glow
He feels like sacher-masoch
And the fire below
Is licking at his lips
Crack the whip
Come and crack the whip
Come and crack the whip
Oh! Whip.
Ooh! Whip.

Swallowing Flames
Sinking in the snow
He enjoys feeling pain
He enjoys peeling slow
Lagartija Nick
It's no dumb show
Your names on his whip
Crack the whip
Crack the whip
Oooh! Come and crack

A code of play
A nocturn rite
In the cruel garden of dark delights
Sixteen capes crawl in line
Desire is a heady wine
Come and crack
Come and crack
Crack the whip
Oh! Ooh! Ooh! Wah!........

WORDS & MUSIC; BAUHAUS
PUBLISHER; BEGGARS BANQUET MUSIC LIMITED

**THIRD UNCLE**        (Brian Eno)

There were tins
There was leys
There are leys
There are sharks
There was John
There are cliffs
There was mother
There's a poker
There was you
Then there was you

There are scenes
There are blues
There are boots
There are shoes
There are Turks
There are fools
They're in lockers
They're in schools
They're in you
Then there was you

Burn my fingers
Burn my toes
Burn my Uncle
Burn his books
Burn his shoes
Cook the leather
Put it on me
Does it fit me
Or you
It looks tight on you.

(c) 1984 E.G. Music Limited
reproduced by permission

---

Dear inquisitor,

Thank you for writing, it is always encouraging when
interest of this nature is shown. We hope that the notes
enclosed answer your questions.
Bela Lugosi is dead, BAUHAUS on the other hand...

love
and
dark
thoughts
BAUHAUS

---

the man of shadow thinks in clay! He dreamed trapped thoughts of suffocation clay. Seen in iron environments, with plastic sweat, out of chiseled slits for love eyes. You'll catch up you later, Rap trapped cubist vowels. Howls from a Dummy head expression. To hide his metamorphous of this time The tusk, hence his need for anonimity, seeking refuge hence the mask. — The SHADOW IS CAST FROM THE GROWTH UNDERNEATH THE CLOSED MOUTH

Take off your mask and see whats underneath!
P. Murph

---

She had painted arms,
That were hers to keep
They were also her actual arms,
Creating the presence of divinity
and her need for real life,
Compassion and Society, was her
fear.
A Myth is a sacred story of profain
eyes and ears.
The real passion of lovein is for
death! Said she — the pyramid is
wois, and the primeval hill too
even heresy became an orthodoxy
and Sanctuary possessed its
original Holyness.    (Boo) Prthingg feelaswalls.

Arriving at Milan airport at the start of our first tour of Italy.

# KEVIN

**FOR TOWER RECORDS DESERT ISLAND DISCS:**

**IF YOU WERE STRANDED ON A DESERT ISLAND
AND YOU COULD TAKE 10 RECORDS WITH YOU (AND ONLY TEN),
WHICH RECORDS WOULD YOU CHOOSE?**

1. SCREAMADELICA — PRIMAL SCREAM
2. DUB NO BASS WITH MY HEADMAN — UNDERWORLD
3. REVOLVER — THE BEATLES
4. HUNKY DORY — DAVID BOWIE
5. BEFORE AND AFTER SCIENCE — BRIAN ENO
6. THE STORY OF THE CLASH  THE CLASH
7. DEBUT — BJORK
8. THE ORIGINAL MODERN LOVERS — JONITHAN RICHMAN
9. PORTRAIT IN MUSIC — BURT BACARACH
10. THE SOUNDTRACK OF SOUTH PACIFIC

KEVIN HASKINS

# DANIEL ASH.

FOR TOWER RECORDS DESERT ISLAND DISCS:

IF YOU WERE STRANDED ON A DESERT ISLAND
AND YOU COULD TAKE 10 RECORDS WITH YOU (AND ONLY TEN),
WHICH RECORDS WOULD YOU CHOOSE?

1. HERE COME THE WARM JETS (ENO)
2. IF THE 60's WERE THE 90's (BEAUTIFUL PEOPLE.)
3. PORTISHEAD (DELUXE)
4. ~~BLACK FLYS~~ LOW (D. BOWIE)
5. (TONES ON TAIL) EVERYTHING.
6. (ROXY MUSIC) FIRST ALBUM.
7. PROPELLER HEADS (LATEST ALBUM)
8. BERLIN (LOU REED)
9. ANDY WARHOL'S VELVET UNDERGROUND. WITH NICO
10. THE IDIOT (IGGY POP)

"BUT NOT REALLY"

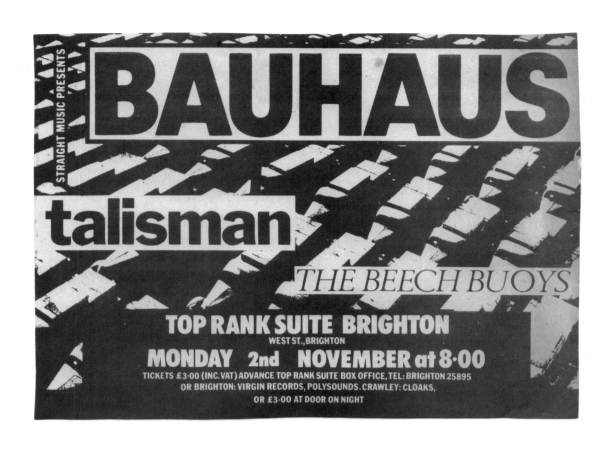

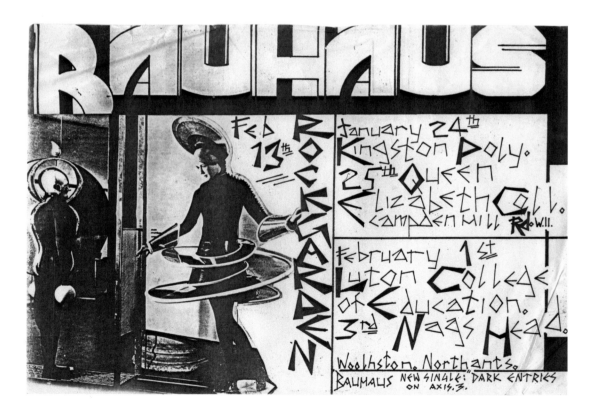

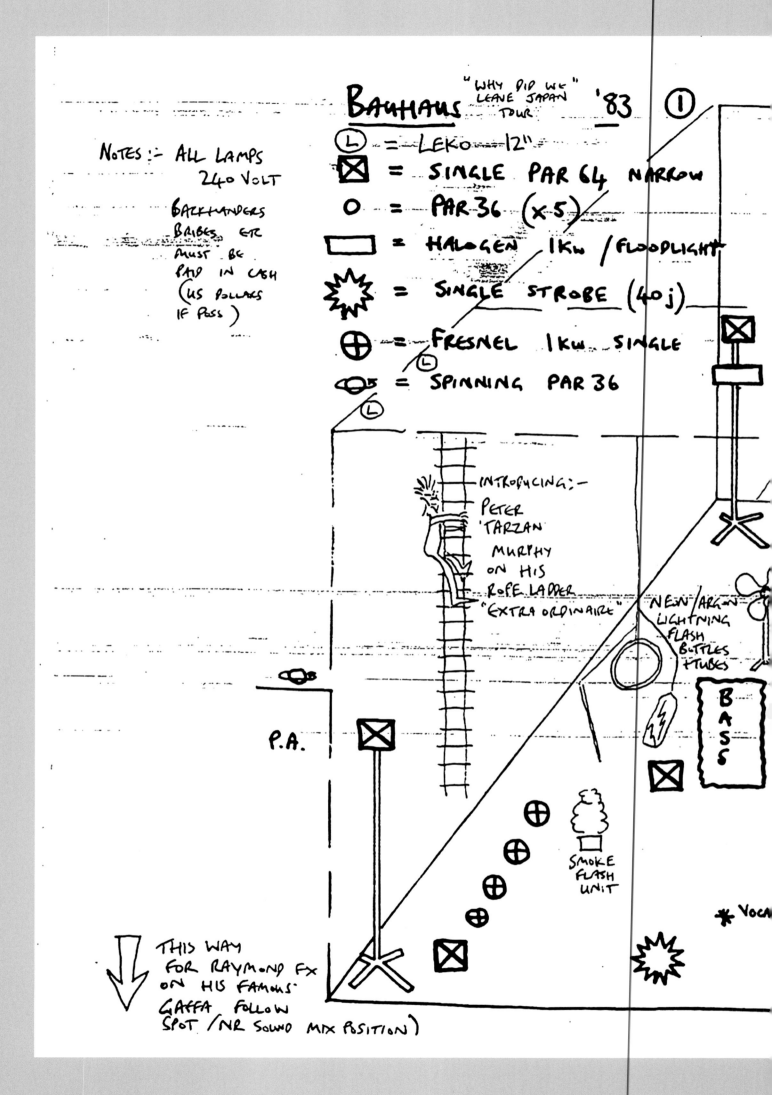

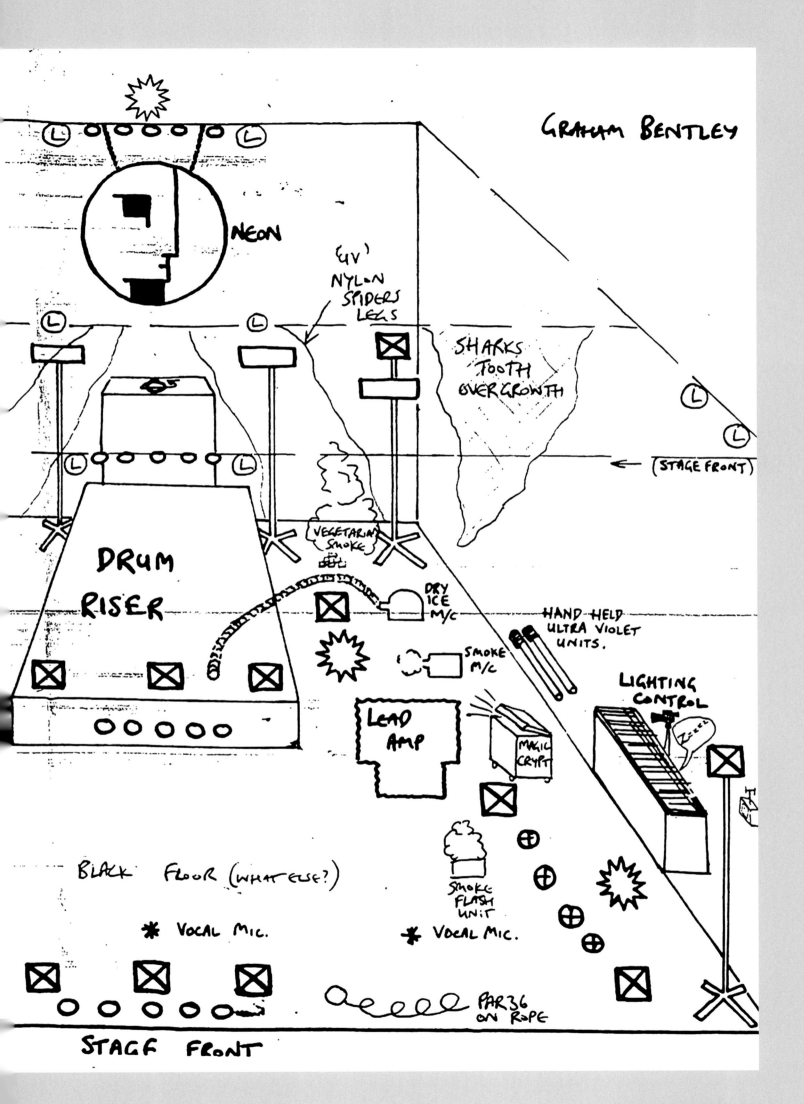

Lighting plot by Graham Bentley.

One of the original industrial lamps acquired from a local shoe factory in Northampton. In the early days Graham Bentley used several lamps such as these for our light show, simply laid on the floor. We always used white light bulbs, and from the floor, the lamps would throw long dark shadows that created a Film Noir look.

Poster: Allen Jaeger

## RESURRECTION

It all began as a rumour a couple of years before in 1996. It's unknown how these rumours start, maybe something to do with collective consciousness, but this actually made us stop and contemplate the idea. What if? It came together gradually over those 24 months. A phone call here, a mention in an interview there, and when we all inadvertently ended up on the same record label, it appeared to be written in the cards. In early 1998, following several conversations, we decided to rehearse for a couple of days to see if the magic was still there. We made a pledge that if the spirit had been left behind at our last show in 1983, then there would be no point in carrying on.

In June '98 Peter made the long flight from Istanbul, Turkey, and we all convened in Los Angeles. We began by meeting for dinner at Caioti Pizza Cafe in Laurel Canyon and afterwards repaired for a champagne toast in my neighbour Kerry's house up in the Hollywood Hills. So far so good!

We began rehearsals the next day at Swinghouse Studios in Hollywood, and thankfully the magic was still there and then some! It felt so great to be playing those songs again and it was very clear to all of us that they had really stood the test of time.

Prior to rehearsals I had the idea of incorporating a technique that I had developed in Love And Rockets. During our live shows, I would use drum pads to trigger samples taken from our recordings. These samples would include backing vocals, synth sounds, guitar overdubs, etc. It would enable us to sound more like our recordings without using the constraints and hassle of backing tapes.

Thankfully, Beggars Banquet, (our record label in the 80's) had kept the original master tapes from our early recordings. Because the tapes were so old, the coating on the magnetic tape could disintegrate when used again, so to prevent this, the tapes had to be baked in an oven at a specific temperature. They were then taken into a recording studio and our original sound engineer Peter "Plug" Edwards, ran off samples that included the backwards guitar intro to "She's In Parties", the Wasp Synthesizer intro to

"Swing The Heartache", and atmospheric wind and delayed harmonics for "Hollow Hills", among others. When I employed all this to our live set it placed the proverbial cherry on the cake!

During this time, two dates went on sale at the historic Hollywood Palladium for July 10th and 11th, which sold out in a record fifteen minutes! It appeared that there was a great deal of interest, and we realized that we were a lot more popular fifteen years after we had disbanded than we were back in the day! A third date was added and a "secret" warm up date at The Hollywood Athletic Club on July 9th.

This was it... After all the telephone calls, meetings, rehearsals, and all the huge anticipation, we were about to take the stage again almost two decades after our "final show". As the opening chords of our first song "Double Dare" rang out, I can clearly remember a great feeling of confidence and invincibility! Bauhaus were back! The passion, vitality and the energy of the band was still intact and, coupled with the fact that three of us had been performing together for the past fifteen years, we could all actually play much better! A few months later, after witnessing our performance at The Brixton Academy in London, our original tour manager from the early 80's, Harry Isles, sent us a lovely fax which included the words;

"There's not many bands can come back after fifteen years and sound as fresh and exciting as they ever did, but to come back after all that time and actually sound better, must be almost unique!"

Following the great success of these four shows an entire world tour was hastily set up before anyone changed their minds!

There were many standout moments on that tour, and we had a marvelous crew who became like family to us. One thing in particular, that was so unexpected, and that occurred at nearly every show, was to see a bunch of young kids dancing down the front and singing every word of the songs. An entirely new generation were getting into the band, and all this was something that we could never have even contemplated back in the early days.

369

Photo: Nigel Copp

## COACHELLA FESTIVAL

Founded by Gary Tovar, Goldenvoice started out as a very small operation putting on punk rock shows back in the early 80s. Through perseverance and for the love of music, it has grown into the huge promotion company it is today. The brainchild of Gary's partner, Paul Tollet, the Coachella Music Festival is the flagship event of the company. All through Bauhaus, Tones On Tail and Love And Rockets, we forged a strong relationship with Goldenvoice. It was no surprise that in the fall of 2004, Paul contacted me to see if Bauhaus would be interested in playing the main stage at the Festival. Having attended every year, I had witnessed its evolution from its first year as a small unknown gathering to attracting upwards of 80,000 attendees. Paul also informed me that he would give us a blank check to spend on production as he wanted our performance to be the stand out set of the weekend. This was a very attractive proposition so we duly agreed. Having always had a leaning towards the theatrical, we set about brainstorming our grand entrance. One of the first ideas we had, was to release thousands of bats from the stage! On inquiring as to where to obtain said bats, we learned that it would actually be illegal to release them at the time when we would be on stage. A little dismayed we set about brainstorming again. Eventually Peter came up with the brilliant idea of the inverted hanging man, based on the Greek archetype Hermes in connection to alchemy. Peter would be the hanging man or vampire bat as it was also naturally interpreted.

We consulted with a special effects technician in Los Angeles to build the special mechanical rigging that allows one to fly an actor or performer. During rehearsals we set up a rig to enable Peter to hang upside down whilst rehearsing "Bela Lugosi's Dead". This was no mean feat as it takes some physical stamina and ability to hang upside down for ten minutes, let alone to sing in the process. Peter took it in his stride.

It felt good to be back together again and rehearsals went really well. During breaks we took meetings with Martin Phillips our lighting and production designer. We asked him to construct a large Bauhaus face logo incorporated into a light box and a tower that Peter could ascend from, with a follow spot mounted on top. We also incorporated lasers for the first time. Like most festivals, Coachella has two large jumbotron screens on either side of the stage. In keeping with our German expressionist aesthetic, we chose to have the film of our performance displayed purely in black and white.

What was peculiar about this show was that it was a one off, and a very big event. We hadn't played to an audience anything near to as large as this ever

before. There was also a great deal of anticipation and expectation attached to our performance, as well as the unthinkable possibility that the bat stunt could go horribly wrong and end up in a type of Spinal Tap fiasco! Consequently, my usual pre-tour anxiety dreams reached a new plateau. They ranged from being backstage with everyone I know present, and suddenly realizing that I'm naked from the waist down, to coming on stage and my drum kit being made up entirely of cigarette packets. Strangely, I didn't ask our crew to replace them with my real drum set. Instead, I quickly and anxiously tried to arrange them into something that I could play! Quite funny really, but what would really transpire, was not funny and a little terrifying.

Our opening number was "Bela Lugosi's Dead" in which I play a two bar pattern, in a repetitive loop, for approximately ten minutes. This is not that difficult, however, it's very exposed within the minimal nature of the song (first dream?!) and as such, any slight error is greatly magnified. I always begin the song and Daniel and David gradually join in with me. Approximately three minutes in everything was going well; no one had messed up and Peter hadn't plummeted to the floor! Then, completely out of the blue, and this has never ever happened to me in twenty five years of drumming, my left leg began to shake uncontrollably! Damn! Oh no! I looked out into the audience of 60,000 people, to see if anyone had noticed, and quickly reminded myself not to do that again. I was literally terrified! I thought to myself, "of all the times, of all the shows, Why was it this one?"

The left leg controls the hi hat which consists of two cymbals, mounted on a stand, one on top of the other, and a pedal which can cause the cymbals to be apart, or held together. In one respect it wasn't actually all bad; had it been my right leg which controls the kick drum, then I would have been in serious trouble! I pressed down on the pedal as hard as I could so that the shaking leg wouldn't effect anything. This worked fine, but my mind was racing...."would my right leg begin shaking? What if? What if?" After approximately two minutes, the shaking stopped. I cannot express the relief that I felt. Ok, so we were now about five minutes into the song, and I was so grateful that the weird psychological anomaly was out of the way! After all the work, drama and anticipation, I could now begin to relax and enjoy playing the main stage of Coachella. But alas, that was not to be....around the seven minute mark the annoying aberration returned! "Really?" I thought to myself. Thankfully it only stuck around for about one more terrifying minute and then left for good. Maybe it had other people to go terrify? From that point on, everything flowed beautifully and we all put in a great performance. As we left the stage, Peter exclaimed, "Now you can say that you were there!"

BAUHAUS - SOLD OUT
DECEMBER 01, 2019 7PM

bauhaus

PETER MURPHY    DANIEL ASH

KEVIN HASKINS · DAVID J

Hollywood

PALLADIUM

NOVEMBER 3, 2019 SOLD OUT
NOVEMBER 4, 2019 SOLD OUT
DECEMBER 1, 2019 SOLD OUT

LOS ANGELES CALIFORNIA

Show poster credit: Delano Garcia

Photos: Nigel Copp

Photo: Ekaterina Gorbacheva and Paul Rae

Photo: Howard Rosenberg

Hope


Your mornings will be brighter

Break the line

Tear up rules

Make the most of a million times no

Undead.

# ACKNOWLEDGMENTS

Literally everybody that has worked with me and contributed to this book have a deep love and appreciation of the band and that has made it a very fulfilling and enjoyable process.

First of all, I'd like to give thanks to my comrades in arms, Daniel, Peter and David for without them, there would be no band and consequently no book. When we embarked on our amazing journey we had no idea what a remarkable ride lay ahead of us. This book is a celebration of the band and for all those people who worked with us and followed us.

To our hard working management, agents, promoters, record companies, publicists, recording engineers, video directors, lawyers, road crew and technicians, for their professionalism and creativity:

Graham Bentley, Harry Isles, Peter "Plug" Edwards, Tony Zurakowski, Glenn Campling, Ian Sterling, "Reasonable" Ray Kinsey, Richard Peach, Mark Price, Umberto, Kenny Rich, Melvyn McCulloch, Paul Tollet, Marc Geiger, Steve Valentine, Charlie Hewitt, Mary Jo Kaczka, Chris Raughley, John Van Eaton, Brian Lowe, John DeSalvo, Christopher The Minister, Peter Hosier, Phil Jaurigui, Nigel Phelps, Ian Robertson, Elizabeth Dameron, Maureen Burke-Hewitt, Samantha Wallace, Greg Dean, Aaron Chawala, Peter Hosier, Peter Franco, Shaun Sebastian, Troy Stewert, Martin Phillips, Leigh Fordham, Andy Figueroa Jr., Tim Van Ness, Jill Heath, Vikki Warren, Derrick Hoeckel, Brian Haught, Peter Magdaleno, Scott Simons, Amery Smith, Carlos Donohue, Brandi Lynn, Jerome Crooks, Nicolai Sabbottka, Andrew Buscher, Owen Thomas, Carlos Bath, Richard Wold, Harrison Reynolds, Mark Kaplan, Steve Ferguson, Susan Richman, Briana Wexler, Emma Banks, Joady Harper, SiouxZ, Susan Crane, Pete Stennett, Ivo Watts-Russell, Peter Kent, Martin Mills, Steve Webbon, Alex Greenburg, Derek Tompkins, Bob Ezrin, Mike Hedges, Mike Robinson, Tony Cook, Kenny Jones, John Etchells, Hugh Jones, Ted Sharp, Jeff Evens, Ken Eros, Joseph Bishara, Howard Guard, Don Letts, Mick Calvert, Ken Lawrence and Christopher Robin.

To my good friend, Matt Green who's original idea it was that I put all of my collection to very good use in a coffee table book.

To Jeff Anderson, who's remarkable enthusiasm, impeccable style, knowledge and guidance in producing this book has been priceless.

To my design team and archivists, Donny Phillips, Kaylee Carrington and Fendi Nugroho for being three of the nicest people I've ever met and who's talent and work ethic go way and beyond.

To all the poster artists: Rich Black, Emek, Alan Forbes, Allen Jaeger, Jason Walker, Jermaine Rogers, Shepard Fairey, Mayra Fersner, Lindsey Kuhn.

To the photographers; Tony Mottram, Paul Rae, Ekaterina Gorbacheva,  Mitch Jenkins, Judy Lyon, Phillip Graybill, Jean Ramsey, Nigel Copp, The Shend, Graham Trott, Fin Costello, Stella Watts, Howard Rosenberg, Eugene Merinov, Andy Marlow, Mark Atkinson, Suezan Skelton, Jackie Hardt, Joseph Brookes and Henry Peck. For those of you that I made every effort to track down but to no avail, I respectfully thank you.

To my editors and proof readers; Kaylee Carrington, Diva Dompe, Talulah Brown, and Andrew Brooksbank.

For their help and special contributions: Lynn Dompe, Christopher The Minister, Steve Webbon, Chris Salewicz, Elizabeth Dameron, Jackie Hardt, Carl Burgess, Mark Ginns, Suezan Skelton, Matt Howarth, Jason Keehn, Danny Canon, Paul James, Joseph Brookes, Paul James, Howard Guard, Sue Loder, Ian Corbridge, Chris Saleswicz, Neil Meads, The Shend, Paul James, Stacy Copp, Paul Rae, Mark Atkinson, Lilo Unger, Daniel Fuentes, Nanette, Uli and Gabor, James William Davis.

Extra special gratitude to Andrew Brooksbank, Vincent Forrest and Graham Bentley. These fine gentlemen very generously shared their extensive collections of Bauhaus memerobelia. Andrew also allowed access to his comprehensive timeline which I constantly referred to and also allowed me to draw from some of his unused sleeve notes. When I was missing some obscure piece of ephemera they would magically come forth with it and would also submit pieces that I had absolutely no recollection of existing! Their hours and hours of work, passion and tenacity is beyond compare and for that I'm truly grateful.

An extra special thank you to Pamela Dompe for her insightful guidance, intense research, informed business planning, smart decision making and strong support, and also to my pre sale research, social media and tech support team, Diva Dompe, Lola Dompe, Byron Blume, Jacquie Sylvester and Matthew McQueen for their endless commitment and hard work.

Last but not least to my Mum and Dad for taking me to drum lessons and fending off angry neighbors when I was practicing!

If I have omitted anyone that deserves a credit I am truly sorry. Every effort went in to tracing names that related to the images and stories within.